MAINSTREAMS OF *MUSIC*

by David Ewen

Opera

Orchestral Music

Solo Instrumental and Chamber Music

Vocal Music

MAINSTREAMS OF

MUSIC

Volume Three

1974

Solo Instrumental and Chamber Music

Its Story Told Through the Lives and Works of its Foremost Composers

by David Ewen

Franklin Watts, Inc. 730 Fifth Avenue · New York, New York 10019

Illustration Credits

The Mansell Collection: pages 8B, 14, 115, 130B, 155, 188, 220
The Metropolitan Museum of Art: page 9
Photographie Giraudon: pages 39, 40A, 71, 114, 151, 152, 153,
    156, 186, 222
Staatsbibliothek, Berlin: pages 40B, 111A & B, 113, 130A, 154,
    183, 185
The Bettmann Archive: pages 69, 131A & B, 132B, 187, 219,
    221, 223, 249
The Pierpont Morgan Library, Mary Flagler Cary Music Collec-
    tion: pages 70B, 112, 184
Culver Pictures, Inc.: pages 132A, 265
RCA Victor: page 133A
Don Hunstein, courtesy Columbia Records: pages 133B, 134A &
    B, 135A & B, 250, 251
Library of Congress: page 252

Jacket photo by Don Hunstein, courtesy of The Guarneri Quartet
Photo research by Wesley Day

Library of Congress Cataloging in Publication Data

Ewen, David, 1907–
    Solo instrumental and chamber music.

    (His Mainstreams of music, v. 3)
      1. Instrumental music—History and criticism.
2. Chamber music—History and criticism.
3. Composers.   I. Title.
ML460.E9   780   73-17143
ISBN 0-531-02685-X

Some Other Books by David Ewen

Dictators of the Baton

Music Comes to America

Music for the Millions

The World of Great Composers

The New Encyclopedia of the Opera

The New Book of Modern Composers

The Home Book of Musical Knowledge

The Encyclopedia of Concert Music

David Ewen Introduces Modern Music

The Complete Book of Classical Music

The World of Twentieth-Century Music

Leonard Bernstein

The Milton Cross New Encyclopedia of Great Composers
(WITH MILTON CROSS)

George Gershwin: His Journey to Greatness

Composers of Tomorrow's Music

New Complete Book of the American Musical Theater

Great Composers: 1300–1900

Composers Since 1900

Contents

Introduction

The human voice preceded the musical instrument. It is logical, then, that the first significant era in music as we know it today—a period spanning the fourteenth through the seventeenth century—should have concentrated primarily on music for voices, and only incidentally on music for instruments. This was the age of polyphony (or counterpoint), in which choral compositions consisted of different melodies of equal importance sung simultaneously. Most of this music was intended for the church. A good deal of it was unaccompanied by instruments.

Though the early composers focused their main activity on church choral music, some instrumental music *did* manage to get written, and some forms of instrumental music became crystallized. Since the organ was so basic to church services, this was one of the first instruments to which the composers of the time turned when they began to write for instruments.

Anybody who has seen or heard a modern organ would have no difficulty recognizing one of the sixteenth century, so similar is the organ of years ago to today's in appearance, equipment, and sounds produced (though, to be sure, the sixteenth-century organ was simple in each of these aspects compared to the modern instrument). In the sixteenth century, as now, the organ was the most mechanically complicated instrument performed on by a single musician. It is the only one capable of simulating the sounds of different instruments. These sounds come from holes in rows of pipes of graduated sizes (the smallest in the center, the largest on the extreme ends). Each row of pipes creates a different color tone, each pipe within the same row creates a different pitch. Different rows of pipes may be played simultaneously to produce a variety of color. On large instruments several keyboards (called manuals) control the pitch of different sections of pipes; and an extended pedal keyboard, worked by the feet, produces the low tones. Numerous valves and knobs (called stops) enable the performer to change the color, quality, and texture of the sound. Wind is needed to generate the sound blown through the pipe holes. Up through the nineteenth century wind was produced by bellows operated by hands or foot; today this is done by an electric blower.

The first form of music devised for the organ—and by the same token, the first significant instrumental music actually written down—was the canzona. This type of piece was often written in strict "imitation." "Imitation" is a contrapuntal (or counterpoint) method in which a single theme is sung or played by several "voices." (We use the term "voice" for each of the parts even in instrumental music.) Each voice enters with the theme a few measures after the preceding one. This type of musical development is also called fugal. When a full melody is used, the composition is called a "round." Everyone is surely familiar with such popular rounds as "Three Blind Mice" and "Frère Jacques," both of which use the device of imitation.

Two of the first composers for the organ were Venetians: Andrea Gabrieli (1520–86) and his nephew, Giovanni Gabrieli (1557–1612). They were responsible for developing such organ forms (later expropriated for other instruments) as the canzona, ricercar, fantasia, and toccata. The ricercar is a solemn piece of polyphonic music in which one or more themes are developed in a separate section, frequently in a fugal manner. The fantasia has a fluid form, allowing a melody to be presented and developed freely. A toccata emphasizes virtuosity, with rapid and elaborate passage work, and gives the impression of an improvisation, that is, a piece composed as it is being played.

Girolamo Frescobaldi (1583–1643) was the first organ composer striving for an instrumental style emphasizing dynamics, color, and rhythm. (In writing for the organ or other instruments the Gabrielis generally imitated the character and technique of choral music.) Frescobaldi, an Italian, was one of the leading organists of his time. He published numerous organ pieces, including fantasias, toccatas, capriccios (really fantasias under a different name), partitas (suites), and fugues (a carry-over from choral music). Frescobaldi's masterpiece was *Fiori musicali* (*Musical Flowers;* 1635), his last publication. This is a volume of toccatas, canzone, capriccios, and other items. He was frequently best in his toccatas, where he revealed a technical skill and a breadth of design not encountered in the toccatas of the Gabrielis. One of Frescobaldi's toccatas from *Fiori musicali:* has noble feeling: "The Toccata of the Elevation." Thus Frescobaldi was not only responsible for extending the technique of organ writing but one of the first to bring to organ music human feelings.

Frescobaldi's influence led to a flowering of organ music in and outside Italy. Jan Sweelinck (1562–1621) was a Netherlands composer who spent most of his life in Amsterdam, where he played the organ in a church and taught students from many parts of Europe. He was one of the earliest composers to write chorale preludes: a short organ piece for church service preceding the vocal chorale, or hymn, on which it was based. He was also one of the first to introduce to organ music the structure of variations, which, as we shall soon see, originated in England for another keyboard instrument. He also amplified the structures of the fantasia and the toccata and was one of the principal predecessors of Johann Sebastian Bach in writing organ fugues.

Samuel Scheidt (1587–1654) was one of Sweelinck's pupils. He and Johann Froberger (1616–67) became Germany's first notable composers for the organ. They and their contemporaries and immediate successors set the stage for the appearance of the foremost composer of organ music before Bach: Dietrich Buxtehude.

The virginal, popular in England, was an ancestor of the piano. Rectangular in shape, it had to be placed on a table or stand, since it had no legs. Like the later piano, it had a keyboard. When keys were depressed, quills were set in motion, plucking at strings and thus producing thin, tinny tones that could not be sustained. It is probable that the word *virginal* was concocted for this primitive keyboard instrument because it was most often performed upon by genteel young ladies.

William Byrd (1543–1623), an Englishman, was the father of music for the virginal. With no precedent to guide him, led solely by his imagination and instincts, Byrd evolved styles, traditions, and structures in which keyboard music can be said to have first come to life. Byrd wrote about 140 pieces for the virginal. Some are found in the first collection of virginal music ever published: the *Parthenia* (1612). Others were used in the *Fitzwilliam Virginal Book* and one or two other collections, all published in the early seventeenth century. Byrd's pieces include preludes, airs, rounds, variations, and popular dances. Byrd was one of the first still-remembered composers to write variations, the best of which is his "Wolsey's Wilde." "The Earl of Salisbury," from *Parthenia,* is another fine Byrd piece, this one made up of two popular dances of Byrd's time, the pavane and the galliard.

Byrd evolved a basic technique of performance on the virginal and of writing music for it. His contemporaries and immediate successors were all given direction in their own music for the virginal by him. The most famous of these composers were Orlando Gibbons (1583–1625), Thomas Morley (1557–1602), and John Bull (1562–1628).

In sixteenth-century England, the virginal was displaced by the harpsichord. The harpsichord, and its companion, the clavichord, gained prominence throughout Europe by the early seventeenth century. (For a time, in Germany, the word *Clavier* was applied to all keyboard stringed instruments, and not limited to any specific one.) Both the harpsichord and the clavichord were larger than the English virginal, boasted a richer tone, greater beauty of sound, and more varied colors and dynamics. The harpsichord (in French, *clavecin,* and in Germany and Italy, *cembalo*) was wing-shaped (similar to the later piano though smaller in size) and stood on legs. Its strings were plucked by quills. The clavichord was an oblong box resting on a stand or a table. Its tone was softer but more responsive to the touch than that of the harpsichord because its strings were not plucked but struck by brass wedges.

Jacques Champion de Chambonnières (1602–72) is one of the founders of the French school of harpsichord (*clavecin*) composers. Chambonnières published two volumes of harpsichord pieces in a polyphonic style, the melodic line enriched with ornamentations, and the harmonies pleasant. He employed the suite form, a composition of several movements most of which were such old dances as the pavane, sarabande, and gigue, although the parts were not unified. Johann Froberger (already mentioned as a composer for the organ) developed the suite form with a unified musical style. He worked in Germany, where he became a pioneer in the writing of harpsichord music. Where in his organ

4   works Froberger had imitated Frescobaldi to a fault, in his harpsichord

compositions he was speaking with his own voice by introducing bold harmonies (sometimes even discords) to enhance expressiveness.

Some of the best harpsichord music in the second half of the seventeenth century was written by England's foremost composer of that age, Henry Purcell (1659–95). Though he is now most often remembered for his opera, *Dido and Aeneas,* Purcell also wrote many harpsichord pieces and suites. All are to be treasured for their polyphonic invention and their lordly melodies. This is music that today can still afford considerable listening pleasure, whether played on a harpsichord or a piano.

During the polyphonic era, string instruments without a keyboard began to develop. The first of these was the lute. It somewhat resembled a modern mandolin, since its round body was shaped like half a pear, across whose flat side were extended strings over a fretted fingerboard. The sixteenth-century lute had eleven strings. The pegbox at the top was bent at an angle. A performer used his left hand for fingering the fretted board in order to change pitch; with his right hand he plucked the strings. Troubadours or minstrels used the lute to accompany themselves in singing secular songs, that is, songs not religious in nature. Lutes were also used in combination with other instruments, and in the first operas ever written they were used to accompany the singers. But a good deal of music was written for solo lute, including dances, fantasias, variations, and arrangements of choral music. The heyday of the lute was the sixteenth century, after which it slowly passed from general use.

All over Europe, between the fifteenth and seventeenth centuries, there existed a number of stringed instruments called viols, ranging in pitch from treble to bass depending upon the size of the instrument. The viol was held on the knee; its strings were not plucked but played upon with a bow. A grouping of different-sized (or pitched) viols was known as a consort. When other instruments, such as lutes or recorders, were combined with viols, the group was referred to as a broken consort. Some excellent music was written for both groupings, including Thomas Morley's *First Book of Consort Lessons* (1599) and *The Little Consort of Three Parts* (1656) by Matthew Locke (1630–77). Among the most significant music written for a consort of viols were Henry Purcell's fantasias, which we will discuss in Chapter 1.

The word *violin* means "little viol." This word indicates that the violin is derived from the old-time instrument (specifically, the treble viol), but with modifications. The violin is smaller in size than its predecessor;

it has four strings, whereas the treble viol had six; it is shaped with a convex instead of flat back and with round instead of sloping shoulders. Other important differences separate the violin from the viol. The violin's sound is much more brilliant than that of the viol. It boasts a wider gamut of colors and a greater range of effects. And to play the instrument, it is held under the chin and not rested on the knees.

We do not know who was the genius instrument-maker who first transformed the treble viol into a violin. We do know, however, that this happened in the sixteenth century and that one of the earliest of these masters was Andrea Amati (1530–1611), and his two sons, Antonio (1550–1638) and Girolamo (1556–1630). We also have good reason to believe that one of the first pieces for the violin, as opposed to the viol, was the "Capriccio stravagante" (1627) for unaccompanied violin by Carlo Farina (c. 1600–c. 1640), where such new techniques as trills and double stops were introduced. Just three years earlier, in 1624, Claudio Monteverdi had devised such effects as pizzicato (plucked strings) and tremolos in writing for the violins in his opera *Il Combattimento di Tancredi e Clorinda.*

A good deal of competition existed between musicians favoring the treble viol and those sponsoring the newly created violin. In 1556 one writer insisted that viols were intended for "people of taste," whereas the violin was an instrument fit only for dance music and music for the wedding ceremonies of the rabble. But beginning in the late sixteenth century, the opposition to the violin collapsed because several extraordinary instrument-makers fashioned the greatest violins ever made. This work took place in the city of Cremona. Nicolò Amati (1596–1684), the son of Girolamo, was the first of these superb craftsman to design and build the modern violin. It is to his instruments that we refer whenever we speak of an "Amati." In Nicolò Amati's shop, Antonio Stradivari (1644–1737)—the greatest violin-maker of all—had his apprenticeship. Another genius of this Cremona school of violin-makers was Giuseppe Bartolomeo Guarneri (1698–1744). The beauty of construction and tone, the exquisite finish, the delicacy of structural lines achieved by these early craftsmen have never been equaled; their secret is unknown to us. Today the best of these instruments command fabulous prices. In 1971 a Stradivarius sold in England at auction for $200,000.

Not until the first of the Amatis began building their violins did composers realize the artistic possibilities of this remarkable instrument. The first composer to elevate the violin to a status of first importance was Arcangelo Corelli, of whom we shall speak in greater detail in Chapter 1.

He was music's first great violinist and music history's first distinguished violin composer. But, as we shall soon point out, Corelli was preceded by other violin composers whose development of violin technique and the sonata form made Corelli's achievements possible.

Of the three other important string instruments played with a bow, only the violoncello has drawn composers to write distinguished solo music for it. The first violoncellos (or cellos, for short)—an outgrowth of the old viola da gamba, or bass viol—were created by Andrea Amati in the late sixteenth century. In or about 1700 this new instrument received the name by which it would henceforth be identified: violoncello, meaning "little big violin"—"little" because it was smaller than the predecessor of the double bass, the violone, and "big" because it was larger than the violin. For most of the seventeenth century the cello served almost exclusively as a partner to other instruments, or as an accompanying instrument. In the eighteenth century, composers began seriously to turn their creativity to this instrument. Chamber concertos, called *concerti per camera* for three or four "voices" with cello obbligato and a sonata for violin and cello, were written by Giuseppe M. Jacchini in 1701. After that, numerous composers wrote cello concertos, as well as compositions for solo cello or for cello and keyboard accompaniment. Among these composers were Antonio Vivaldi (1678–1741), Giovanni Battista Bononcini (1670–1747), and the great Johann Sebastian Bach.

The viola (evolved from the viola da braccio or tenor viol) has inspired little solo literature. The instrument's prime importance lies in chamber and orchestral music.

The sonata is the most significant form of music for solo violin, violin and piano, solo cello, cello and piano, solo piano, two pianos, and sometimes for several stringed instruments with or without accompaniment.

The word *sonata* existed for many years before it was used in its present sense. In its original meaning, a sonata was a piece of music to be "sounded" or "played" (distinguishing it from a cantata, a form of choral or vocal music, which is a composition to be "sung"). Consequently, at first the name sonata represented an instrumental composition; it was an alternate name for the canzona. Andrea Gabrieli wrote a sonata for five wind instruments in the year of his death (1586). After his death his nephew Giovanni published a volume of his and his uncle's instrumental music bearing the title *Canzone e sonate* (1615). One would be hard put to try to find the precise difference in style and method between the can-

Historical musical instruments

Left, a cembalo.
Below, an instrument maker.

Woodwinds

Bass viols

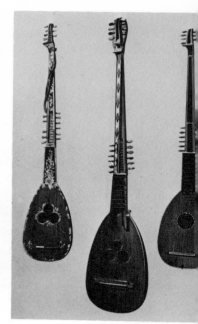

Lutes.

A harpsichord

zone and the sonatas in this volume. In the seventeenth century the term *canzona* was discarded and replaced by that of *sonata*.

For some years in the seventeenth century, composers called any kind of short instrumental composition a sonata. Gradually (though we do not know exactly when or with whom) the sonata acquired a distinct identity of its own. It developed into an extended composition in several sections in which fast and slow movements were alternated. These came to be known as "trio sonatas," not because they were written for three instruments (actually they called for four instruments) but because they combined three ranges or parts: the upper range or part was played by two viols (in earlier years) or two violins (later on); the lower part was for a viola da gamba (earlier) or a cello (later); the third part consisted of an accompaniment by a harpsichord or organ. This accompaniment was called "continuo" or "figured bass"—a kind of musical shorthand used extensively in the early history of sonata music. Numbers were placed under the bass notes of the accompanying keyboard music to indicate how the harmony for each note was to be filled out.

Toward the closing decades of the seventeenth century two distinct types of sonatas developed, both finally standardized by Arcangelo Corelli in four volumes of trio sonatas, op. 1–4 (1681–94). One was the *sonata da chiesa* ("church sonata"), originally an organ composition for church services, but soon used for other instruments as well. This form opened with a slow and stately introduction followed by a brisk episode in fugal style. A short largo then led into another fugal section. As first conceived, the sonata da chiesa was a single integrated piece, the four parts blending into an uninterrupted composition. Later composers preferred to divide the sonata into separate sections. Thus the sonata da chiesa is the forerunner of the three- or four-movement sonata of a later period.

The second type of sonata was the *sonata da camera* ("chamber sonata"). This type was originally played in a secular setting while its chiesa counterpart was played in churches. The sonata da camera comprised an introduction and three or four dance forms, and as such it anticipated the later baroque suite.

But another kind of sonata was being written even while the chiesa and camera types were being formulated and developed. Among the earliest examples of sonatas for violin and piano are the six works for violin and figured bass published in 1681 by a Bohemian composer, Heinrich Biber (1644–1704). The Sonata in C minor in this collection is representative. It has four movements in both slow and fast tempi, beginning with a contrapuntal largo. Its second movement is a passacaglia, elementary variations on a terse theme. The third movement develops into a gavotte, and the last movement is an allegro.

In 1692, Johann Kuhnau (1660–1722), a German, applied the sonata for the first time to harpsichord music. He did this in the collection *Neue Clavierübung* (*New Clavier Works*), in which is found a single sonata, in the key of B-flat. In the preface to this volume Kuhnau inquired: "Why should not such things [sonatas] be attempted on the clavier as on other instruments?" He provided his own answer with the Sonata in B-flat, following it with several more harpsichord sonatas in later publications: seven in *Frische Clavier-Früchte* (*New Clavier Fruits*) in 1696; six in *Biblische Historien nebst Auslegung* (*Musical Representations of Some Stories in the Bible*) in 1700. Kuhnau's harpsichord sonatas were in four, five, or six movements. Contrasts of mood were established between the slow and the fast movements. His structures were neatly devised; his style, elegantly formed. He was best when he told a story in his music, as he demonstrated in his six biblical sonatas, the best known of which is *The Combat between David and Goliath*. The titles of the eight movements reveal the composer's programmatic intentions: "The Bravado of Goliath," "The Terror of the Israelites and Their Prayer to God," "David's Courage Before the Terrible Enemy," "The Dispute and the Slinging of the Stone by David," "The Flight of the Philistines," "Paeans of Victory by the Israelites," "Concert of Women to the Glory of David," and "General Rejoicing." Sometimes Kuhnau's musical equivalent of nonmusical episodes approaches the naïve in its literalness: the way, for example, in which scale passages, changes in dynamics, and chord sequences realistically portray David hurling the stone from his sling at Goliath, followed by Goliath's death. But the best pages reveal a creative imagination of a high order for this period.

The most powerful influence in directing composers to the writing of instrumental music early in the seventeenth century was the emergence of a new musical style first supplementing, then predominating over polyphony. This new style was homophony, in which a single melody is prominent, supported by a harmonic accompaniment. Homophony came about in Florence as the sixteenth century was ending because a group of intellectuals there (in the spirit of the then flourishing Renaissance) sought to revive Greek drama. They discovered that in Greek drama the lines were often sung rather than spoken. Entering into the spirit of ancient Greece, these Florentines, among whom were composers and librettists, set out to write dramas with music. This is how opera first came into the world. Polyphony was an unsuitable style for the purposes of drama, since the interweaving of the voices made it impossible to hear the words and was incapable of individualizing principal characters. These musicians therefore had to conceive a new kind of music better suited to the stage. The music they evolved was homophony.

Once homophony established its importance as music for the theater, composers soon arrived at the conclusion that a single melody with accompaniment was far better than polyphony for a solo instrument or more than one solo instrument. The homophonic style, consequently, was a powerful force in the early development of instrumental music. Polyphony was not discarded; established traditions are not easily destroyed. But as time passed, composers became so increasingly partial to homophony that by the middle of the eighteenth century it far outweighed polyphony as an important style for instrumental writing. Contrapuntal techniques were reduced to subsidiary importance; but they were never totally rejected.

The first distinguished composers of instrumental music, and the first compositions that have found a permanent place in the living repertory, appeared during an epoch in music now identified as Baroque. It began in the late sixteenth century and ended in the mid-eighteenth century with Johann Sebastian Bach and Handel. *Baroque* is an art term denoting elaborate ornamentation and grandiose edifices (churches and palaces) extravagantly embellished with detailed designs. Giant musical structures were built for choral music by such masters as Vivaldi, Bach, and Handel, and for the musical stage by Monteverdi and his successors in Venice, Naples, Vienna, and Paris. "Baroque" is a fitting identification for this era, because the excessive ornamentation found on the buildings of these years was emulated in instrumental music in decorations of the melodic line with all kinds of ornaments, such as trills, grace notes, and mordents.

The chapters that follow detail the changes and developments in solo instrumental and chamber music as effected by the world's greatest composers, beginning with Buxtehude.

Solo instrumental music covers compositions for a single instrument (the organ; the piano and its predecessors; the violin and cello with or without accompaniment; occasionally other solo instruments and piano). Compositions for small combinations of instruments belong to the realm of chamber music. Chamber music is an intimate form best heard in a small auditorium. In this form each instrument plays its own music. When there are more instruments than there are musical parts, a small group becomes a chamber orchestra, and a larger one, an orchestra.

Chamber music reaches back historically to the canzone and sonatas by the Gabrielis and their immediate successors; to the trio sonatas, and the sonatas da camera and da chiesa for more than two instruments; to the music for consorts of viols or broken consorts.

The most significant form of chamber music is the string quartet, most of which are written in sonata-form structure. The group that plays this music is also called a string quartet. The makeup of the string quartet group as we have come to know it is two violins, a viola, and a cello. One of the first composers to write a work for this combination of instruments was Alessandro Scarlatti (1660–1725), a distinguished composer of Neapolitan operas.

Post-Baroque chamber music covers other types of quartet music as well: for example, piano quartets, oboe quartets, and flute quartets, in which one violin and the viola and cello are supplemented by a piano, an oboe, or a flute. Later in the book, these forms will be described, as will all the other forms of chamber music, including trios, quintets, sextets, septets, octets, and nonets, for three, five, six, seven, eight, and nine instruments respectively.

I

Significant Beginnings

Dietrich Buxtehude, Arcangelo Corelli,
François Couperin-le-grand

Johann Sebastian Bach, whom we will discuss at length in the next chapter, was twenty years old when he took a month's leave of absence from his post as organist in Arnstadt, Germany, to travel two hundred miles to Lübeck to hear Dietrich Buxtehude play the organ. By that time (1705) Buxtehude's fame had penetrated throughout Germany. He was esteemed not only as the foremost organist of his time but also as a leading composer of organ music. What Bach heard in Lübeck stirred him to the roots of his being and brought about in him a dramatic change both as a performer on the organ and as a composer for that instrument.

It is possible that, being a genius, Johann Sebastian Bach might have made his monumental leap from the type of organ music Frescobaldi and his contemporaries had been producing to that of his own making. But that leap was surely made easier because the gap between Frescobaldi and Bach had been narrowed by Buxtehude's accomplishments. This is what A. Eaglefield Hull, an English organist and writer on music, meant when he wrote: "As John the Baptist was to Christ, so was . . . Buxtehude to Bach." This is the reason why another English musicologist, C. Hubert Parry, said: "It is not too much to say that unless

Dietrich Buxtehude had gone before, the world would have had to do without some of the most lovable and interesting traits in the divinest and most exquisitely human of all composers [Bach]." There was, then, no more crucial a turning point in the history of organ music than when Bach listened to Buxtehude in Lübeck.

Though his name and music are certainly far less well known and admired than those of Bach, Buxtehude possessed much of the creative flame that fired Bach's imagination. The half century separating the middle of the seventeenth and the early part of the eighteenth is the great age of organ music, whose splendor has not since been rivaled. That age ends with Bach, but its true beginnings reach backward to Buxtehude.

Unfortunately, too few documents exist about the first thirty years of Buxtehude's life. He was born in Oldesloe, in the district of Holstein, which in those days was ruled by Denmark but which now is a part of Germany. The year was probably 1637. His father, a church organist, was the boy's only teacher. When Dietrich's training was completed he became a church organist in Helsingborg; he was then twenty. In 1660 he moved to a similar position in Helsingör (Elsinore).

In 1667 Buxtehude applied for the all-important post of organist and *Werkmeister* ("workmaster") at St. Mary's Church in Lübeck, Germany. By then Buxtehude was thoroughly capable of taking over the taxing assignment of organist, for he had become a consummate performer. The tasks of *Werkmeister* were far different from and far more prosaic than those of an organist. The post called for the combined talents of a bookkeeper, housekeeper, and statistician. A *Werkmeister* had to keep the records of baptisms, marriages, births, deaths, and burials of the church members. He had to maintain an accounting of all funds received and spent by the church. He had to serve as inspector of the building and recommend necessary repairs. He had to look after the church wine and linen.

There was one highly necessary requirement for a candidate to get the post at St. Mary's. He had to marry his predecessor's daughter. This was the stumbling block that later on kept both Johann Sebastian Bach and George Frideric Handel from taking on the assignment. Buxtehude was a practical man. After expressing his willingness to fulfill this marital obligation, he was installed at St. Mary's on April 11, 1668. Less than four months later—on August 3—he married Anna Margareta, daughter of his predecessor, Franz Tunder.

Buxtehude dominated the musical life of Lübeck for the next forty years. He played the organ with such skill and art that he aroused the wonder of all those who heard him. We have already mentioned Bach's visit to Lübeck just to hear Buxtehude. George Frideric Handel came to Lübeck in 1703 for the same reason.

For his church performances, Buxtehude produced a large, varied repertory of organ music, second in importance only to that of the great Bach himself: fantasias, fugues, chorale preludes, and toccatas, as well as chaconnes and passacaglias. The last two forms were fully crystallized for the first time by Buxtehude. Alfred Einstein, a distinguished German musicologist, maintains that had not Buxtehude done so, Bach probably would have never written his monumental Passacaglia and Fugue in C minor for organ and his grandiose Chaconne for solo violin.

Actually there is not much of a difference between a chaconne and a passacaglia. Both represent variations on a slow, short bass pattern, or sometimes on just a succession of chords. In a passacaglia this theme recurs throughout the composition in the bass. Buxtehude's Passacaglia in D minor and Chaconne in E minor are both characteristic of his gift of amplifying a simple statement with embellishments and transformations.

Buxtehude extended two other organ forms that were carried by Bach to their ultimate fulfillment: the chorale prelude and the fugue. The chorale prelude is a comparatively elaborate form in which a single subject based on a hymn melody is treated in a contrapuntal style. Buxtehude elevated the chorale prelude, says British critic Cecil Gray, "to an unexemplified pitch of elaboration and enriched it with every conceivable device of contrapuntal and decorative resource at his disposal."

Though the fugue had long been in use in both choral and organ music before Buxtehude's time, in his hands its complex structure became filled with human or dramatic values. A fugue has a rigid pattern that must be followed methodically. It is made up of a subject treated by three, four, or more contrapuntal parts (known as "voices"). First we hear the subject presented by the opening voice. As this proceeds with the subject, a second voice enters with the same subject pitched a fifth higher or a fourth lower, with the first voice presenting the countersubject. When the third voice enters, the subject is heard an octave higher or lower than originally stated, a procedure emulated by any other voices that may follow. This entire section—the presentation of the subject and countersubject by the various voices—is known as the exposition. Now there comes a free development in which the subject is amplified, changed, repeated; when the subject is repeated, the voices enter in a different order from that in which they first appeared. Most fugues end either with a single tone sustained by the bass (pedal point) behind the

17

voices or in a method known as *stretto,* in which the voices come so quickly one after another that they overlap.

Of all the composers who preceded Bach, none comes closer to the grandeur of his magnificent fugues than does Buxtehude.

Above and beyond his organ playing and his organ music, Buxtehude made another monumental contribution to instrumental music. He organized some of the earliest public concerts heard in Europe when, in 1673, he inaugurated a series of "evenings of music" (*Abendmusiken*). These concerts, held on five consecutive Sunday evenings before Christmas, featured not only organ music but other kinds of compositions as well. For these events Buxtehude supplemented his own organ works with his sonatas for strings, early examples of chamber-music writing in Germany, as well as choral compositions.

Dietrich Buxtehude died in Lübeck on May 9, 1707. A successor to Buxtehude as the foremost organ composer of his time was not long in coming: the first of Bach's masterworks for the organ, as we will see later, appeared just one year after Buxtehude's death.

The history of violin music begins officially with Arcangelo Corelli. He was the first to convince the musicians of his age how valuable the violin was for both the performer and the composer.

His contemporaries have left accounts of their admiration for his violin playing, and also of the effect his playing had on his physical appearance. They said that during a performance Corelli's countenance became "distorted," his eyes burned "red as fire," and his eyeballs "rolled with agony." They insisted he had superhuman powers. "Superhuman" may be excessive praise, but his powers with the violin were uncommon for his day. Before Corelli, violinists were amateurs, hack musicians, or plain mediocrities. Corelli was a virtuoso, the first such to play the violin. He devised his own method of bowing (which his rivals soon adopted). His fingers were agile in performing double stops, trills, embellishments, arpeggios, and rapid scale passages. He had a beauty of tone and an elegance of style none could emulate. "He is the prince of all musicians," is the way one of his rivals described him. Another called him "the virtuoso of virtuosos of the violin, a veritable Orpheus of our time." These and similar tributes were thoroughly justified.

Corelli remained an artist of first rank when he changed over from performer to composer. He was the first to develop a style of writing admirably suited to the capabilities of his instrument. He was one of the first composers to carry over the sonata to violin literature. He was one of the first to master the then new homophonic style, especially in many of his beautiful slow movements. He was the first composer for violin whose works include some that are still a joy to listen to. In addition to all this, he was an important pioneer in the development of the sonata da chiesa and the sonata da camera, of chamber music, and of the orchestral concerto grosso. In this last form of concerto a group of instruments rather than a single solo instrument is opposed to the main orchestral group.

Corelli's birth took place on February 17, 1653, in Fusignano, Italy. He began his musical education in childhood. When he was thirteen he went to the large, cultured city of Bologna where he began to study the violin with Benvenuti, then continued it with Bragnoli; he also received lessons in counterpoint from Simonelli. Four years after he had taken his first violin lesson, Corelli had already achieved recognition in Bologna by being elected to the renowned Accademia Filarmonica. One year later he left for Rome, where (except for occasional trips) he stayed for the rest of his life. For a time he played the violin in a church orchestra, and later on he directed the orchestra of one of Rome's opera houses. But even before he had assumed either of these posts his fame as a violinist began to spread around Rome. He became the pet of the Roman social and political elite. One of them was the powerful Cardinal Pietro Ottoboni, a patron of the arts. So taken was the cardinal with Corelli's talent that he had Corelli live in his palace, treated him almost like an adopted son, and continually showered on him gifts and luxuries. Corelli remained a resident in the palace as long as he lived, serving the cardinal as his maestro di cappella. Every Monday evening at his employer's palace Corelli conducted concerts that became famous in Rome.

Corelli's first four publications, op. 1–4 (1681–94) were each a set of twelve trio sonatas for two violins, a bowed bass instrument, and continuo. Here Italian chamber music makes important advances because of the manner in which Corelli used the forms of both the sonata da chiesa and the sonata da camera for three string instruments and accompaniment, and the skill with which he combined those strings into a unified texture.

In 1700 Corelli produced a volume of music for a single violin and cembalo (op. 5)—twelve sonatas that form the cornerstone upon which the edifice of solo violin music rests. Many Italians had written sonatas da chiesa and da camera before 1700—but none with the clarity, logic, and imagination of Corelli in his op. 5. Corelli was no innovator. He did not change forms, he developed them. He did not invent new effects for *19* the violin, but he wrote with far more understanding of the instrument than his predecessors had done. When he wrote allemandes, sarabandes, gavottes, and gigues within the sonata da chiesa form he poured new wine into old bottles. The forms remained static, but the thematic material became fresh and invigorating. Some of Corelli's best music was in the sonata da chiesa structure. Much of it is in a polyphonic style, but much, too, is unmistakably homophonic in the way it taps a rich melodic vein. Since some of these sonatas feature two themes, each in a different key, Corelli may be considered a pioneer in suggesting a binary (two-theme) method, used in the later classical sonata.

Still much in favor with violinists and audiences is his Sonata no. 12 in D minor for violin and cembalo from op. 5, which bears the title of *La Folia.* A "folia" is a tune probably originating in Portugal that gained popularity in Italy in the sixteenth century. Many composers of that period quoted it. This lovely tune is heard in the opening of the Corelli sonata. Twenty-three simple variations follow. This work, though called a "sonata" by its composer, is neither a sonata da camera nor a sonata da chiesa, but a theme and variations—which is also true of several other sonatas in op. 5.

Corelli published only one more volume after that. This was his op. 6, a series of twelve concerti grossi for orchestra that created the concerto grosso form.

Since Corelli's music was distributed all over Europe, his fame spread far and wide. Many musical pilgrims came to Rome, some to hear him play the violin, others to study under him. His success brought him great wealth, in spite of which he was parsimonious to a fault. His only self-indulgence was to buy great paintings (a passion for painting having been instilled in him by some of Rome's greatest artists, with whom he continually came into contact at the cardinal's palace). In time Corelli possessed a remarkable and valuable art collection. But it was painful for him to part with even a paltry coin. Though he continually moved among the famous and the highborn, he never bothered about his appearance, favoring a drab and inexpensive outfit long after it had outlived its usefulness. He gave the impression of being an impoverished workingman; when he stepped out of the opulence of the cardinal's palace, he lived like a poor man. Even when he had to travel substantial distances he refused to pay the price of a hired carriage, insisting on making the journey on foot. Despite his fascination with art, he never went to a gallery when a price of admission was charged, preferring to wait for those days when he could enter free.

Between 1689 and 1690 he officiated musically at the court of Modena. Sometime between 1702 and 1708 he visited Naples, where he met and performed for its most famous opera composer, Alessandro Scarlatti. Back in Rome, after this excursion to Naples, Corelli discovered that a new and younger violinist Valentini, had become a favorite of Roman music lovers. Corelli was incapable of accepting rivalry gracefully. One evening, attending a concert by an oboist who was given an ovation, he became so jealous that he swore he would never again appear in public.

In his last years he was a man broken in health as well as spirit. He died in Rome on January 8, 1713, and was buried in the Pantheon, his magnificent marble monument paid for by Cardinal Ottoboni. For some years the anniversary of Corelli's death was commemorated at his tomb with a service and performance of his music. After his death, as during most of his life, his high station in music was respected—particularly by his pupils, who had come from all parts of Europe to learn the art of violin playing. These Corelli students helped to bring into existence a "school" of violin playing and composition (the first such in the history of violin music). Through their own works they enriched the literature for the violin that Corelli had helped to initiate so fruitfully.

One such pupil was Pietro Locatelli (1695–1764), an outstanding performer who wrote violin concertos and chamber music caprices gathered in *L'arte del violono* (*The Art of the Violin*) in 1733, a volume of concerti grossi for orchestra in 1735, and in 1737 a group of trio sonatas and chamber music works including trios (two violins and bass). Another of Corelli's famous pupils was Francesco Geminiani (1687–1762), the composer of twenty-four sonatas for violin and continuo and a number of violin concertos (as well as trios and concerti grossi), and the author of the first instruction book on violin playing. This was published anonymously in 1730 in the English language and only years later issued with Geminiani identified as its creator.

Even those who had not studied with Corelli received from his works important direction in writing for and playing the violin. Antonio Vivaldi (1678–1741)—now most famous for his concerti grossi and his concertos for solo instruments and orchestra—published a volume of twelve sonatas da camera for two violins and continuo, op. 1 (1705) and eighteen sonatas for solo violin and continuo, op. 2 and 5 (1709). Here he modeled his writing after Corelli. He also wrote numerous trio sonatas. Occasionally we get to hear one of the works from op. 2—such as the Sonata in A major, though this is most frequently given in various rewritten editions (including the well-known version by Ferdinand David), and also in transcriptions for the viola, cello, and so forth.

Other Italians, after absorbing all that Corelli had to teach them, went on to develop the technique of violin playing and the style of writing for the instrument. Francesco Veracini (1690–1750) produced two sets of twelve sonatas each for solo violin and continuo, op. 1 and 2 (1721, 1744), which were original for that time in harmony, in modulations, and in working out of thematic material. Tommaso Vitali (c. 1655–date of death unknown) composed the most famous chaconne for violin, second only to that of Bach. He was the son of Giovanni Battista Vitali (1644–92), who himself, in 1667 and 1669, published two volumes of important sonatas for solo violin and continuo, all in the sonata da chiesa form.

Perhaps the most significant of all the immediate successors of Corelli in Italy was Giuseppe Tartini (1692–1770). His vast output for the violin includes some one hundred sonatas, the masterpiece of which is the one in G minor that carries the strange title of *Devil's Trill*. Tartini himself revealed how he came to write this work. "One night . . . I dreamed that I had made a compact with the devil, who promised to be at my services on all occasions. . . . At last I thought I would offer my violin to the devil in order to discover what kind of musician he was, when to my great astonishment I heard him play a solo so singularly beautiful and with such superior taste and precision that it surpassed all the music I had ever heard or conceived in the whole course of my life. . . . The violence of the sensation awoke me. Instantly, I seized my violin. . . . The work which this dream suggested is doubtless the best of my compositions. I call it *Il Trillo del diavolo*." The sonata is in six movements, alternating long and short, with the fourth embellished with the trills that gave this fine composition its name.

In writing violin sonatas, Tartini's technique was more advanced than Corelli's, and so was his expressiveness. When he wrote his sonatas, Tartini habitually kept in mind some lines, or even phrases, from the works of the great fourteenth-century Italian poet Petrarch, which may very well be the reason why there is such a variety of expression in his melodies. Often Tartini used a secret code (which he never revealed), placed at the top of a composition to identify the Petrarch lines or phrases that had inspired his music.

Tartini—as did many of the other Italians commented on in the preceding paragraphs—also wrote chamber music (mostly trios), but today these compositions are virtually ignored in favor of their best violin works.

The influence of Corelli was not confined to Italy. It permeated the rest of Europe. In England, Henry Purcell (1659–95) made his first excursion into chamber music by writing fantasias for viols, without continuo, a form he had inherited from his English predecessors and to which he brought considerable advancement both in technical skill and imaginative materials. He published two such volumes in 1680, one comprising three fantasias in three parts, and the other nine fantasias in four parts. His most celebrated fantasia, written about this time, is in five parts. It is the F major, published independently. What is particularly unusual about this composition is that the note C is sustained throughout while the other four viols weave melodic figures around it. In 1683 Purcell published twelve sonatas in three parts for two violins and bass, and in 1697 ten such sonatas were published posthumously. In the latter volume we come upon two of Purcell's most celebrated chamber music works. One of them is the *Golden* Sonata in F major. We do not know why it has become known as "Golden," unless it is because the second of its four movements is pure shining gold throughout. This movement is made up of a Largo and a Canzona. It is preceded by an Allegro and followed by a sober Grave and a brisk Allegro. The other distinguished composition in this set is not a sonata at all, but a Chaconne in G minor, which has a five-measure ground bass that is repeated forty-four times with fanciful trimmings to cover a remarkably wide emotional gamut.

In his autobiography, Georg Telemann (1681–1767), a highly respected German composer of his time, conceded that Corelli had been his guide in writing instrumental music, and most especially chamber music and sonatas for violin and continuo.

In France, François Couperin-le-grand freely admitted that he first became interested in writing sonatas "in the Italian manner" because of Corelli. In the preface to his first set of four sonatas for two violins and continuo issued in 1692, Couperin wrote: "The first sonata in this collection was also the first which I composed, and which anyone composed in France. . . . Charmed by those works by Corelli whose compositions I have loved as long as I lived . . . I attempted to compose one."

He is called François Couperin-le-grand ("the great one") to distinguish him from his uncle, a composer also named François. "Great one" is a description that fits the younger François Couperin well.

For four centuries the Couperins had produced professional musicians before this particular François Couperin came along to surpass his predecessors. As the first composer to write a sonata in France, and as one of the earliest to create important chamber music and compositions for the harpsichord, Couperin holds a high rank among the great composers before Bach.

He was born in Paris on November 10, 1668. In his early childhood he received music instruction from his father, the organist of St. Gervais Church. When the father died in 1679, Couperin found another remarkable teacher in Jacques-Denis Thomelin, the organist of the Chapel Royal at the Palace of Versailles. By the time he was eighteen, Couperin had inherited his father's post at St. Gervais, holding it for the remainder of his own life. On April 26, 1689, Couperin married Marie-Anne Ansault; they had two daughters.

When Thomelin died in 1693, the king announced that Thomelin's successor would be chosen in a competition, which François Couperin had little trouble in winning. Couperin henceforth combined his duties at St. Gervais in Paris with playing the organ at the Chapel Royal, serving as the official harpsichordist for Louis XIV, teaching music to the royal family, and directing Sunday evening concerts at Versailles for which he wrote instrumental compositions.

He assumed his post at Versailles on December 26, 1693. By that time he had already placed one foot solidly in music history by having become the first composer to introduce the sonata da chiesa form into France (in 1692). Later on, as an employee at the royal palace, he wrote an important sonata for two violins, two cellos, and continuo called *La Sultane,* or *The Sultana* (1695), a six-movement composition. His masterpiece in the sonata form, and in chamber music, appeared in 1725: a work for two violins and continuo, *Apothéose de Lulli* (*The Deification of Lully*). This composition has a far more complicated programmatic story to tell than you might expect in a chamber music work. It is a tribute to the great Italian-born but French-oriented opera composer Jean Baptiste Lully (1632–87). The opening movement, an overture, describes Lully wandering in the Elysian fields. In subsequent movements there unfold the intrigues instigated by Lully's enemies in Paris, and the raising of Lully to Parnassus, where he is greeted by Corelli and the Italian muses. Apollo now argues with Lully and Corelli that the union of the Italian and French styles of music would make possible the creation of a superior musical art. Couperin's sonata ends with a sonata da chiesa (supposedly performed by Lully and Corelli) in which the Italian tradition of sonata writing achieves a Gallic personality.

As the favorite musician of Louis XIV, Couperin continued to shape musical history by producing for his Sunday evening court concerts other outstanding chamber music works. Collectively these works were called *Concerts royaux* (*Royal Concerts*). They comprise four dance suites for undesignated instruments and harpsichord, published in 1722. Couperin wrote them, he said, to "soften and lighten the king's melancholy." This purpose makes each of these compositions pleasant and easy to listen to. They became so popular at court that Couperin was impelled to write ten more such suites. They were called *Les Goûts-réunis* (*Reunited Tastes*), and were published in 1724.

With all these varied and unusual compositions we have the significant beginnings of French chamber music. However, their significance is surpassed by Couperin's monumental contribution to harpsichord (clavecin) music: four volumes of over two hundred pieces gathered into twenty-seven suites. The first of these volumes appeared in 1713, the last in 1730. What is so exceptional about this cornucopia of harpsichord music riches is not only the development of the techniques of writing for the keyboard, and the high caliber and great variety of its musical content, but their fascinating programmatic intent. Most of these pieces are descriptive ones, covering practically every phase of French society in Couperin's time.

Couperin, of course, was not the first French composer to write important music for the harpsichord. We have already seen in the Introduction that he had been preceded by Chambonnières. Another significant predecessor was Jean Philippe Rameau (1683–1764), who is best remembered for his operas, and for the new operatic ideals and methods he promoted, but who occasionally wrote music for instruments. Rameau's first published volume of harpsichord music came in 1706, preceding Couperin's own first volume by seven years. It was made up of ten movements, including a prelude and a number of dances. Rameau later issued two more large sets of harpsichord pieces, the second embracing twenty-four numbers (1724), and the third, sixteen (year of publication not known). The first set served to stimulate, influence, and guide Couperin in the writing of pieces for the harpsichord. After that, Couperin, the man who had been influenced, became an influence on Rameau. There is no doubt that Rameau's more sophisticated style and techniques—together with the way in which he began favoring programmatic rather than absolute music and using picturesque titles—was the immediate result of his having come into contact with Couperin's little masterpieces. Rameau's own contribution to harpsichord music was a valuable one. Several of his items have still not been forgotten. In fact one of the most popular pieces of instrumental music Rameau ever wrote is the "Tambourin" from the second set. Distinguished, too, are such pieces as the Allemande in A minor, *Le Rappel des oiseaux* (*The Recall of the Birds*) and *Les Tendres plaintes* (*Tender Complaints*).

Before we leave Rameau we should add that in 1741 he published five major chamber music compositions. He called them *Pièces de clavecin en concert* (*Pieces for the harpsichord in concert*) for harpsichord, violin (or old-time flute), and viol (or second violin). Each work he called a "concert." Three are in three movements (the first, fourth, and fifth); the two other have five movements. Sometimes he uses dance forms for some of the movements. Sometimes the movements are intended as portraits of famous French musicians of his time. One movement pays tribute to Rameau's patron, La Popelinière, while another is a self-portrait. Sometimes movements bear such descriptive titles as "irritating" or "the timid one" or "the babbler."

Between the publication of Rameau's first and second harpsichord series there appeared Couperin's initial volume. With it a bright new day dawned for French harpsichord music—one so bright that it threw a good deal of previous harpsichord music into a comparative shade.

Among the more than two hundred items in Couperin's four volumes are pictorial, satirical, realistic, atmospheric, and emotional pieces. So wide a span of subject matter, feeling, and musical style has no parallels in the harpsichord music produced up to that time, and few in the piano music of a later generation. In Couperin there stretches before us the panorama of life during the age of Louis XIV: the dress, customs, daily routines, street scenes, court activity, and so forth. Some pieces that do not reflect the era offer instead a variety of other picturesque subjects and people: a prude, a seductress, a hurdy-gurdy player, jugglers, fortune-tellers, the heat of summer, windmills, tolling bells, the tragic and comic facets of a harlequin, insects, flowers. "I have always had the object in composing all these pieces to describe various events," Couperin explained. "The titles correspond to the ideas I had in mind." Couperin thus became the first French composer of harpsichord music to use programmatic titles on such a vast scale.

In all four volumes, Couperin collated a number of pieces into
suites, for which he preferred to provide the term *ordre* ("order"). The

first book has five *ordres;* the second, seven; the third, seven; and the
fourth, eight. The individual pieces in these *ordres* are in such forms as
chaconne, passacaglia, theme and variations, allemande, rondeau, mu-
sette, and sarabande. Stylistically these pieces are highly individual for
their time because Couperin introduced new ways of fingering, new
kinds of phrasing, new varieties of embellishments with which the gamut
of color and effects of the harpsichord were immensely extended.

Couperin could be picturesque and witty; he was also capable of
being musically profound. *La Favorite* (*The Favorite One*), a Chaconne
in C minor in the third *ordre* of the first volume, is stately music suggesting the grandeur of court life in Versailles. The Passacaglia in the eighth
ordre, second volume, has no programmatic intent, and *La Mistérieuse*
(*The Mysterious One*) the sixth *ordre,* fourth volume, evokes an atmosphere of mystery; each is a treasured item in early-eighteenth-century
harpsichord music.

When Louis XIV died in 1715, Couperin decided to curtail most of
his court activities. From then on he served only occasionally at Versailles, while spending most of his time in Paris, where he continued to
play the organ at St. Gervais and where he arranged concerts in his own
apartment. In 1716 he published one of the most important theoretical
treatises on harpsichord playing ever written, *L'Art de toucher le clavecin* (*The Art of Playing the Harpsichord*). This book was studied by
harpsichordists and clavichordists of the early eighteenth century, Johann Sebastian Bach included. By 1730, when the last of Couperin's
four volumes of harpsichord pieces was published, the composer went
into complete retirement. Couperin's daughters were faithful to the
long-standing tradition that Couperins were professional musicians.
They held important musical posts, one as a church organist, and the
other as her father's successor as harpsichordist for the king of France,
both unusual accomplishments for women in those days. Couperin himself, after his retirement, lived in virtual seclusion in Paris up to the time
of his death there on September 12, 1733.

While Couperin was still alive, George Frideric Handel
(1685–1759)—the German-born master who lived his mature years in
England—was also writing a good deal of music for the harpsichord, his
first such being a suite of eight "lessons" written in or about 1720. From
then on, until about the year of Couperin's death, Handel completed
other suites, as well as fugues, sonatas, and numerous short pieces. The
bulk of his harpsichord works are not representative of the genius who
wrote the *Messiah* and other towering choral masterpieces. They are not

often played, with the exception of two movements from two of his suites for harpsichord. One is a beautifully contrived and deservedly famous Passacaglia from the Suite no. 7 in G minor, which has been arranged for violin and viola, and for solo harp. The other, more familiar still, bears the name of "The Harmonious Blacksmith"—an air and variations from the Suite no. 5 in E major. For a long time people believed that this composition was first suggested to Handel during a storm when, seeking refuge in a blacksmith's shop, he heard the rhythm of a striking anvil, which suggested a melody to him. This is a myth. The title "Harmonious Blacksmith" was the invention of an English publisher who thought it up because he repeatedly heard a local blacksmith humming Handel's charming eight-measure melody. In issuing the composition, the publisher felt it would have far greater salability if it had a descriptive title. He used "The Harmonious Blacksmith" even though there is nothing in the music to suggest a blacksmith or striking anvils. And it is by this title that this movement from the E major Suite is invariably identified.

Handel visited Rome in or about 1706. There he, too, became acquainted with Corelli's works. This discovery led Handel eventually to write his first series of concerti grossi, op. 3, in emulation of Corelli. Subsequently, in or about 1732, Handel wrote six sonatas for violin and continuo collected in his op. 1, and several trio sonatas in op. 2 and 5. Some of Handel's violin sonatas, though hardly of the exalted station of his oratorios and the best pages of his operas, contain music that still engages the interest of performers and music lovers, such as the Sonatas in D major, A major, and E major, in op. 1. Also in op. 1 is a delightful sonata for the old-type German flute and continuo (B minor), which is remembered for an eloquent Andante movement that has been transcribed for violin and piano, for cello and piano, and for string quartet.

The Summit of the Baroque Era

Johann Sebastian Bach

Almost all musical roads lead to Johann Sebastian Bach. Much of what had happened to music up to Bach's time was a prelude to his own unparalleled achievements. Few phases, styles, and structures were not wondrously transformed by him. The advances he made in the field of solo instrumental music are by no means any less prodigious than those in choral or orchestral music. For Bach is the summit of the Baroque era, higher than which the music of this age could not climb. Bach had fully exhausted all the technical and artistic possibilities of the polyphonic style. The next generation was compelled to find a mountain of its own to scale (it would find it in Classicism). At the same time, while elevating the musical art he had inherited from his predecessors to unprecedented levels, Bach also had a vision of music's future. Time and again he opened new horizons toward which his successors reached. Those new vistas are found abundantly in his solo instrumental masterworks.

As with the Couperins in France, so with the Bachs in Germany. For generations they produced professional musicians. The one destined to make the name of Bach an immortal of immortals—Johann

Sebastian—was born in Eisenach, Germany, on March 21, 1685. He was the youngest son of a professional violinist. Both of Johann's parents died when the boy was about ten. Johann was compelled to make his home with a stern older brother who treated him harshly and who seemed to envy the boy's obvious talent. When one day the brother discovered how his own collection of music fascinated the boy, he locked it up. Johann managed to gain access to this library with a duplicate key. He spent night after night for months copying the music painstakingly so that he, too, might be in possession of this priceless treasure. He almost ruined his eyesight because he worked under the dim light of the moon. When his brother finally learned what Johann had been up to, he ruthlessly confiscated the fruits of Johann's hard labors.

The misery Johann Sebastian suffered at his brother's house ended after five years. During that time, the boy continued studying the clavier with his brother having previously been given violin and viola lessons by his father. Then in 1700 Johann Sebastian left his brother's house to become a chorister in a church in Lüneburg. This was a time of intense preoccupation with music. Bach mastered the organ, the clavichord, and the violin, besides learning the rules of composition.

Bach assumed his first organ post in 1703 in the city of Arnstadt. In 1705 he took a month's leave of absence to make the trip to Lübeck to hear Buxtehude play the organ and to become acquainted with Buxtehude's music for that instrument. So enthralled did Bach become with Buxtehude's music that a month's leave was stretched out into four before he was willing to return to Arnstadt. There he became enmeshed in difficulties with his churchgoers, who were upset each time Bach embarked upon spontaneous organ improvisations during services. They made life so hard for him that he decided at last to abandon Arnstadt in 1707 for an organ post in Mühlhausen. Despite the sparse income he earned in Mühlhausen (about forty dollars a year, supplemented by three measures of corn, two trusses of wood, and six trusses of fagots), Bach entered upon matrimony on October 17, 1707, with his cousin, Maria Barbara Bach.

In 1708 Bach found a new position, this time as chamber musician and organist (Kapellmeister) at the ducal chapel in Weimar. Though the duke treated him high-handedly, regarding him more as a menial servant than as an artist, Bach remained in Weimar nine years, possibly because the chapel boasted one of the best organs in Germany. It was here that Bach finally emerged from the shell of his apprenticeship to become so remarkable an organ virtuoso that the prince of Hesse, after hearing him play, took a precious ring off his finger and presented it to Bach. The great Reinken, a famous organist and composer, remarked following one of Bach's improvisations, "I thought that this art was dead, but I see it still lives in you." And when France's foremost organist, Marchand, was scheduled to enter into an organ-playing contest with Bach, he withdrew from the contest after hearing Bach practice.

In Weimar, between the years of 1708 and 1717, Bach wrote most of his greatest works for the organ. Nobody before him or since has equaled the grandeur of the organ literature he produced so copiously in Weimar: fantasias, passacaglias, toccatas, preludes, and fugues, together with forty-six chorale preludes gathered in the *Orgelbüchlein* (*Little Organ Book*). Not only does this music represent the ultimate in technical and architectonic perfection, but nobody has poured into these organ forms such poetic, dramatic, or religious feelings. Masterpiece follows masterpiece. One can only contemplate this majestic procession with awe. If we must single out a few of these works that have become most familiar to concertgoers, we would select the following: the giant Fantasia and Fugue in G minor (the fugue identified as "the great" to distinguish it from an earlier G minor organ fugue now known as "the little"); the awesome Passacaglia and Fugue in C minor; the dramatic Toccata and Fugue in D minor; and monumental three-part Toccata in C major. The theatrical sweep of sound in the fantasia of the Fantasia and Fugue in G minor, crowned by one of the most brilliantly conceived of Bach's fugues; the seemingly inexhaustible imagination that allowed Bach to provide such varied designs and moods to his eight-measure bass theme in his Passacaglia in C minor; the power and brilliance of the two toccatas, in D minor and C major (that in C major unusual in that the toccata and fugue are separated by an eloquent adagio)—these surely have few rivals in organ music.

The first thirty-six of the forty-six chorale preludes in the *Orgelbüchlein* were intended for the different seasons of the church calendar, beginning with Advent and ending with Whitsuntide. This is why the collection is known as "the church year in music." The concluding group of chorale preludes concentrates on aspects of the good Christian life. "The changing seasons of the year," writes E. Power Biggs, a distinguished American organist and an acknowledged authority on Bach's organ music, "are depicted in these miniatures, portraying moods of tenderness, of hearty jubilation, of deepest sorrow, of grave and solemn joy, and abounding in symbolical and even frankly pictorial suggestion."

There was a long hiatus in the writing of organ music between the time of Bach's death (1750) and the mid-nineteenth century. A revival of interest in organ music first came about with Felix Mendelssohn, who wrote six sonatas and several preludes and fugues. After Mendelssohn, various composers have added abundantly to the organ repertory. In France, for example, there were César Franck, Charles Widor (1844–1937), Alexandre Guilmant (1837–1911), Louis Vierne (1870–1937), and Olivier Messiaen (1908–   ); in Germany, Brahms, Liszt, Josef Rheinberger (1839–1901), Max Reger (1873–1916), and Paul Hindemith.

Unhappy that he was turned down for promotion to the post of Kapellmeister, and continually upset by the ill-tempered treatment he was receiving from his employer, Bach decided to leave his post in Weimar after holding it for almost a decade. Spitefully, the duke delayed giving Bach permission to seek another job as long as he could. But in 1717 Bach was finally free to leave. He became Kapellmeister in Cöthen, where his duties included directing orchestral and chamber music concerts. Because of these duties, Bach wrote many orchestral and solo instrumental compositions during the Cöthen period, which lasted six years.

The dedication and fertility he had previously given to the organ he now directed to the clavier. The word *clavier* is consistently used in conjunction with Bach's keyboard music (other than that for the organ) to point up the fact that it could be played on either the harpsichord or clavichord. To the clavier Bach once again confided personal, deeply felt emotion. Sometimes he ventured on bold experiments; sometimes he devised valuable instruction pieces for his family. Into the latter category falls the *Clavier-büchlein für Wilhelm Friedemann Bach* (*The Little Clavier Book for Wilhelm Friedemann Bach*) of 1720, Wilhelm Friedemann being one of Bach's sons who grew up to become a highly respected musician. In this volume we find some minuets, preludes, allemandes, and other slight pieces. Thirty *Inventions* were published about the same time: fifteen for two "voices," and fifteen for three. In these short compositions Bach used the contrapuntal technique of imitation with simplicity and economy. Is there a piano student anywhere who has not had these cherished miniatures as training ground for Bach's more ambitious clavier compositions? But however valuable these *Inventions* are for educational purposes, they are also, for all their elementary style, a musical

treat for the ear. Wanda Landowska, probably the greatest harpsichordist of the twentieth century, regarded these *Inventions* as a "miracle of Bach's inspiration . . . in its purest, most beautiful, most succinct form."

The two books of *The Well-Tempered Clavier* were also intended as teaching material, but with a far different purpose than that of developing clavier technique. These two books contain forty-eight preludes and fugues, the first twenty-four of which appeared in 1722, and the second set in 1742. Each prelude and fugue is in a different key of the major and minor scale, beginning with C major—and here we get a clue to what Bach was trying to accomplish in these compositions. Before Bach's time the keyboard was tuned (or "tempered") in such a way that some keys were in tune and others were not, since there was a discrepancy of pitch among the tones of the octave. A theorist, Andreas Werckmeister, proposed to divide the octave into twelve equal semitones (called "equal temperament") in order to distribute more evenly the discrepancy in pitch among the twelve tones of the octave. This innovation made it possible to modulate with greater facility from one key to another. To prove the efficacy of writing music for the "well-tuned" or "well-tempered" clavier, Bach decided to write a prelude and fugue in each of the newly tuned keys. *The Well-Tempered Clavier* helped once and for all to establish the effectiveness of using this new tuning process. What must surely be of far greater interest to present-day music lovers, however, is the fact that these two volumes are a repository of eloquent thoughts and states of emotion in the preludes, and of extraordinary skill in polyphonic writing in the fugues.

The *Chromatic* Fantasy and Fugue in D minor, from this Cöthen period, had an exclusively artistic mission without the fringe benefit of being educational. The word *chromatic* in the title springs partly from the use of accidentals in the modulations of the opening fantasy and in the subject of the fugue, and partly because of the daring modulations of the opening part. The fantasy is a powerful recitative filled with brilliant virtuoso effects and exciting chromatics. The three-part fugue opens quietly, to be built up into a stunning climax.

The Cöthen years also yielded important music for solo instruments: trio sonatas for two violins and continuo, or two flutes and continuo (Bach's rare excursion into chamber music writing for more than two instruments); sonatas for violin and clavier and for flute and clavier; sonatas and partitas for unaccompanied violin and suites for unaccompanied cello. In writing for a solo instrument—whether violin, cello, or flute

—Bach gave full play to his uncommon ingenuity in writing polyphonically and in fashioning wonderous melodies full of tenderness and pure beauty.

As exquisite a melody as Bach ever conceived is the Siciliano movement from the Sonata no. 2 in E-flat major for flute and clavier. It is important, however, to remember that up to the time of his Leipzig period, Bach did not write his flute sonatas for the modern instrument on which they are now played, but for what in Bach's time was called *Blockflöte,* or recorder. His flute sonatas, therefore, were actually sonatas for the recorder. The recorder is an instrument of the flute family that is held in a vertical rather than horizontal position and has a somewhat smoother, richer, and reedlike tone than today's flute. The recorder passed from general usage just about the time of Bach's death (to enjoy a revival of interest in the twentieth century among musical amateurs). During the Leipzig period, Bach employed in the orchestration for some of his choral works another kind of flute that more closely approximates the one we know: the transverse flute, which had a fuller and more precise tone than the *Blockflöte* and was capable of more brilliant effects.

There is surely no piece of music for unaccompanied violin more famous or more noble than the Chaconne, the fifth and concluding movement, of the Partita no. 2 in D minor. The majestic theme is heard in full chords. The thirty-one variations on this theme pass from grandeur to introspection, from strength to poignancy. "The master's spirit," remarked one of Bach's early biographers, Philip Spitta, "inspires the instrument to express the inconceivable."

Another well-known movement from the solo violin partitas is the Prelude from the Partita no. 3 in E major. This music is memorable for its exciting motor energy. The momentum initiated in the opening measures does not relax until the final breathtaking notes.

What is particularly important about the sonatas for violin and clavier is the attention Bach pays to the accompanying instrument. We have frequently noted that a solo instrument or several solo instruments were accompanied by a formalized continuo, or figured bass. At other times accompaniments consisted merely of written-down routine chords as a support for the melody. Bach knew that the clavier could serve a higher purpose than just as a functional background. He realized it could make its own contribution to project musical thought and emotion. He made this clear in the Sonata no. 6 in G major for violin and clavier by assigning the entire third movement to the clavier.

Another salient feature of the works for violin or cello is the glorious beauty of the slow movements. Homophony gains increasing importance in these pages, where the entire interest is focused on the melody. The Siciliano, the first movement of the Sonata no. 4 in C minor for violin and clavier, is one of several such examples. This sonata also boasts an Adagio of beatific radiance, which is encountered once again in the third-movement Andante of the Sonata no. 2 in A minor and the opening Adagio of the Sonata no. 3 in C major, both for unaccompanied violin.

Bach so liked the sound of the cello that in writing sonatas for it he preferred to dispense with the accompaniment. He wrote six unaccompanied cello sonatas, taking full advantage of the mellow voice of the instrument to unfold dark-colored melodies. Bach also knew how to exploit the sonorities and technical capabilities of the instrument—so much so that we can truly say that in his hands the cello became emancipated as a solo instrument. On the rare occasions that a Bach sonata for cello and piano is given, what is being performed is a transcription of one of three sonatas Bach wrote for the viola da gamba and clavier —the viola da gamba being, as we have already noted, the predecessor of the cello.

Bach's later music for the clavier and for the organ was written in Leipzig, the German city to which he went in 1723 to assume the job of cantor of the Thomasschule. In Leipzig, Bach was required to direct performances of church music and to write compositions for those services at the two churches of St. Thomas and St. Nicholas. He stayed at this post for the last twenty-seven years of his life, doing everything that was expected of him, and at the same time bringing to life music of a wonder and a glory to stagger the imagination, including the choral epics, the *Passion According to Saint Matthew* and the Mass in B minor, numerous chorales and other forms of choral music, and additional masterpieces both for the organ and for the clavier.

Between 1731 and 1742 Bach completed the *Clavier-Übung* (*Clavier Study*), four volumes of keyboard music. The third volume (1739), devoted exclusively to the organ, includes several organ chorales and the well-known Prelude and Fugue in E-flat major, the "Saint Anne." "Saint Anne" was a popular English hymn. The subject of Bach's fugue resembles the opening folklike phrase of the church melody, so that the fugue has come to be known as the *Saint Anne*.

The first, second, and fourth volumes of the *Clavier-Übung* contain some of the greatest music Bach wrote for the clavier. In the first volume (1731) will be found six partitas and in the second (1735) the *Italian*

Concerto. Since the terms "partita" and "suite" are synonymous, the six partitas in this first volume are made up principally of dance movements. Somewhat off the beaten track, however, is Partita no. 3 in A minor, two of whose movements are in a somewhat humorous vein, the "Burlesca" and a scherzo. However, what Albert Schweitzer (the world-famous humanitarian who was also a distinguished organist and Bach authority) said of Bach's suites applies as well to these partitas: "He [Bach] . . . raises the form to the plane of the highest art, while at the same time he preserves its primitive character as a collection of dance pieces."

A concerto is invariably a work for a solo instrument, or solo instruments, and orchestra. Bach's *Concerto nach Italiaenischen Gusto* (Concerto in the Italian Style or, as it is most frequently identified, the *Italian Concerto*) in F minor is unusual in that it is for solo clavier. What Bach attempted to do here is to create a work for solo clavier in the style of the traditional Italian concertos for an instrument and orchestra. The singing character of the slow movement is almost operatic in its eloquent Italian lyricism, while the strong fiber of the two outer fast movements carry echoes of the fast movements in, say, Italian concerti grossi.

One of Bach's giant clavier works appears in the fourth volume (1742)—the *Aria mit 30 Veränderungen* (*Aria with Thirty Variations*), popularly called the *Goldberg* Variations. Johann Theophilus Goldberg was a chamber musician for Count Kayserling, the ambassador from Russia in Dresden. The count suffered from insomnia. To lull his employer to sleep, Goldberg used to play the clavier for him before bedtime. Goldberg commissioned Bach to write for him some music for this purpose, specifying that it be "soft and yet a little gay." Bach fulfilled the commission so successfully that he was rewarded with a golden goblet and a hundred gold pieces.

The work opens gently, with a slow and meditative melody of two sixteen-measure phrases. The thirty ensuing variations are based frequently on this melody but sometimes, too, on the harmonies supporting the melody. Some variations are "soft," some "gay"; some are majestic and some delicate; some are romantic and some pastoral. A climax arrives in the twenty-ninth and thirtieth variations, after which the aria is repeated, ending this huge work as serenely as it had started.

On rare occasions Bach left Leipzig for brief visits elsewhere. One of these excursions took place in 1747 when he visited the court of Frederick the Great of Prussia in Potsdam, where Bach's son Carl Philipp

Emanuel Bach, was a chamber musician and clavecinist. The presence of the older Bach created quite a stir in court. Frederick was so impatient to hear Bach play that as soon as the master arrived, the king refused to allow him time to change his clothes but had him sit right down and perform on various claviers, pianos, and the organ. The king was beside himself with delight at Bach's extraordinary invention in improvisations, especially when Bach worked out a three-part fugue on a subject the king supplied to him. In gratitude for the royal manner in which he had been received, Bach, back in Leipzig, evolved an elaborate work based entirely on the same melody Frederick the Great had invented for him. This large work is *Das musikalische Opfer,* or *The Musical Offering* (1747), a group of twelve one-movement compositions and a four-movement sonata, all in polyphonic style and all in the key of C minor. This is Bach's major chamber music creation. It opens with a three-part fugue with accompaniment and five canons, continues with a trio sonata (the main body of the whole composition), proceeds with five more canons, then ends with a six-part fugue. Bach did not designate what instruments should be used for the various voices, the decision being left to the performers themselves.

Victimized by failing eyesight in his closing years, Bach had to suffer an operation that left him totally blind. For a brief period, just before his death, sight returned, but by then he had been afflicted by paralysis and had become a complete invalid. During this time of terrible physical suffering, through the darkness of pain and approaching death, he summoned all of his depleted energies to write a last work. It is more than probable that he intended his final composition, not for public performance, but rather as a demonstration of his powers in polyphonic writing. He took a simple subject in D minor, then went on to vary it by every possible polyphonic method at his disposal. He ended the composition with a section of monumental proportions consisting of sixteen fugues, two canons, two fugues for two claviers, and a final fugue. In spite of his infirmity, solely through the strength of his indomitable willpower, he managed to finish all but the last part of the closing fugue.

This composition is called *Die Kunst der Fuge (The Art of the Fugue)*; once again here Bach failed to specify what instrument or instruments he had in mind in writing this music. It has been adapted for string quartet, for string orchestra, for two pianos, for harpsichord, and for the organ. In whatever version it is heard, it emerges as the most gigantic polyphonic venture in instrumental music. Bach may have intended *The Art of the Fugue* as a theoretical exercise, but it has become accepted as one of his most ambitious and remarkable excursions into musical invention.

Bach died in Leipzig on July 28, 1750, after having put down on paper the 239th measure of the last fugue. So little esteem did Bach's employers and contemporaries have for him that they had him buried without any identification in the churchyard of St. John's Church in Leipzig. Many years later (in 1894), when excavations were made in those church grounds for the purpose of extending the building, Bach's remains were found. By that time his greatness had become universally established. With proper ceremony, then, his body was placed in a sarcophagus and reburied within the church itself.

François Couperin-le-grand.

*Right, King Louis XIV of France,
a painting by H. Rigaud
in the collection of the Louvre.*

*Opposite,
Johann Sebastian Bach.*

A page from
The Well-Tempered Clavier
*by J. S. Bach.
A facsimile of
an autograph manuscript.*

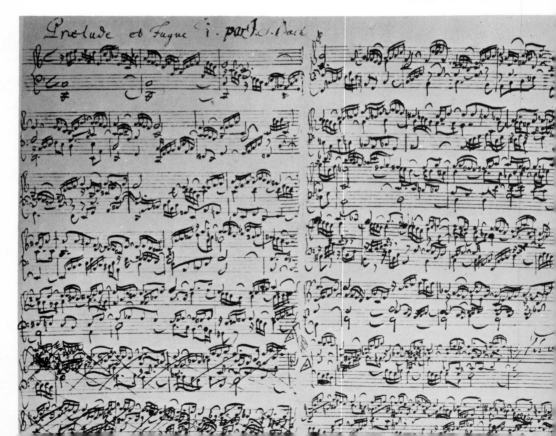

3

The Classic Piano Sonata Emerges

Domenico Scarlatti,

Carl Philipp Emanuel Bach

Despite his prodigious output for the keyboard, and though he wrote so many violin and cello sonatas, Johann Sebastian Bach never wrote a sonata for solo clavier. This gap was filled first by one of his contemporaries, Domenico Scarlatti, who, by coincidence, was born in the same year that Bach was, and then by Bach's own son Carl Philipp Emanuel.

Scarlatti was the first significant composer to write sonatas for a stringed keyboard instrument other than the organ since Johann Kuhnau. Scarlatti used the term "sonata" in the same way that Kuhnau and other early creators of instrumental music did: as a piece of "sounded" or "played" music without any specific structure. Though the forms of the sonata da chiesa and the sonata da camera had been fully developed by Scarlatti's time, he used niether one of these two forms. Scarlatti's approximately five hundred and fifty sonatas for harpsichord are miniatures, each requiring from two to six minutes for performance. Usually they are in two sections.

Actually the overall title Scarlatti used for his first important volume of sonatas is far more appropriate for these pieces than "sonata" is. He called them *Essercizi* ("Exercises"), because, more often than not, they are technical lessons in keyboard virtuosity. Sometimes a piece emphasizes scale passages, sometimes trills, sometimes arpeggios, sometimes tremolos. Some sonatas accentuate such techniques of keyboard performance as crossed hands (even when this was not essential for the proper performance of the notes); some, the spanning of intervals larger than the octave; some, hands moving in contrary motion; and so forth. Being himself a harpsichord virtuoso of extraordinary attainments, Scarlatti was continually tempted into devising new effects and feats of fingering. By doing so, he went beyond Johann Sebastian Bach in enlarging the techniques of keyboard playing. Some historians single Scarlatti out as the founding father of modern piano playing.

As exercise pieces these Scarlatti sonatas are still of immense value to piano students. But the fact that so many of the sonatas are recorded and performed so extensively is evidence that Scarlatti (like Bach before him) could rise high above the level of pedagogy into the realms of great art. His sonatas are not just a "frolic in art intended to increase confidence in the clavier," as he himself phrased it. They are musical art of high order, filled with a variety of tonal riches. His exquisitely fashioned melodies, delicately trimmed, fall gently on our ears. One can listen to an entire concert of Scarlatti sonatas without losing interest; there is always some new musical adventure to enjoy in each different work. Scarlatti holds the fascinated attention of his audience through his love of surprise in the way he develops his structure, in his changing moods, variety of expression, and in the way he combines gaiety with gravity, contemplation with extrovert feelings.

He was the famous son of a famous father: his parent was Alessandro Scarlatti, the leading figure in a group of Neapolitan composers who helped to establish the traditions of Italian opera. Born in Naples on October 26, 1685, Domenico, in early boyhood, received instruction in playing keyboard instruments, in singing, and in counterpoint from his father, his older brother Pietro, and other members of the family. Not yet sixteen, Domenico became organist at the royal chapel in Naples (where his father was also employed). He did not remain there long. Political unrest in Naples (and the irresponsibility of the king in failing to pay musicians their salaries) compelled Alessandro to abandon that city to find a more serene setting and employment that was financially more rewarding. His failure to do so brought Domenico back to Naples, while his father went on to Rome to search for better opportunities. Meanwhile, in 1702, Domenico had written the first two of his compositions still in existence—two cantatas. In Naples he completed several operas that were privately performed.

From his vantage point in Rome, Alessandro saw that conditions in Naples were still inconducive to the proper development of his son's talent and career. In 1705 he convinced Domenico to go to Venice. This city was then one of the most active centers of music in Italy. Domenico had an opportunity to hear the music of Antonio Vivaldi, who at that time was teaching the violin and having his works performed at the Ospedale della Pietà. Scarlatti also found the opportunity to study harpsichord with a distinguished performer and composer, Francesco Gasparini.

In 1709 Scarlatti left Venice for Rome, where an incident took place proving how gifted he had become as a performer on the harpsichord. Since George Frideric Handel was in Rome at that time, Cardinal Ottoboni (Corelli's highborn patron) arranged a competition between Scarlatti and Handel in the playing of both the harpsichord and the organ. Handel surpassed Scarlatti in performing on the organ, but in playing the harpsichord they were judged to be equals.

Scarlatti met and became acquainted with the music of the great Corelli at Cardinal Ottoboni's palace. The way in which Corelli was introducing a new freedom of style in his compositions made a deep impression on Scarlatti that was never erased. Years later, Scarlatti attempted to emulate this freedom in his sonata writing.

In Rome, Scarlatti found employment at the palace of Queen Maria Casimira of Poland. While in this position he wrote an oratorio and seven operas. In 1713 Scarlatti was engaged as assistant maestro di cappella at the Vatican, and when the maestro died the next year, he himself was named to the position. For the next five years he produced an abundant amount of music for the church and for the stage.

We next encounter Scarlatti in Lisbon, Portugal, where by 1721 he was functioning as the maestro di cappella at the royal chapel and as teacher of the harpsichord of Princess Maria Barbara. By 1724 he was back in Rome again, there, four years later, to marry Maria Catalina Gentili, a beautiful sixteen-year-old girl (Scarlatti was now nearly forty-three). They had five children.

When, in 1729, Scarlatti's royal pupil, Princess Maria Barbara, left for Madrid to marry the prince of Asturias, she took Scarlatti with her to be music master at her palace. It was through her influence that in 1738 Scarlatti was knighted in the Portuguese order of Santiago by order of the king of Portugal. In grateful response to this high honor, Scarlatti dedicated to the Portuguese king his first published collection of harpsichord sonatas (thirty in number), the *Essercizi,* most of which had been written as exercise pieces for Maria Barbara.

These were by no means his first compositions for the harpsichord. By this time he had written toccatas, fugues, and some early sonatas, in which he transferred to the harpsichord the stylistic mannerisms of Italian organ music. Scarlatti failed here to achieve his own identity either in his creativity or in the way he wrote for the keyboard, submitting to patterns rather than creating them, being the imitator rather than the one who was imitated. But in his first published volume of harpsichord sonatas he suddenly arrived at individuality. Fifty-three years old, he was beginning to find his own voice. From this time on he kept growing creatively until his last days, producing some of his greatest compositions in old age.

How is it that a man who had written so much music before he was fifty, all derivative, was able so late in life to find his own identity? One explanation lies in the fact that when his father, Alessandro, died in 1725, Domenico had been liberated from an influence that had stultified him, that had proved too domineering and powerful for him to assert himself either as a man or as a creator.

There is another reason why Scarlatti managed to fulfill himself as a composer: his change of residence to Spain, which remained his homeland until his death. By transferring to a foreign land and subjecting himself to all kinds of new influences and experiences, Scarlatti was able to tap a wealth of fresh subject material for his music. This material enabled him to write in a new way, his own way. Again and again, in his sonatas, Spain emerges in all its glamour and color: the Spain of royalty and the common man; the Spain of guitar and castanets; the Spain of gypsy songs and flamenco dances; the Spain of street cries and tolling church bells. Already in his first volume we find a reflection of Spain, where piece after piece suggests the sounds of small-town Spanish orchestras through keyboard sonorities and dynamics. In later sonatas he captures the style and spirit of Spanish dances. The Sonata in A major, L. 238, is a flamenco dance, while that in G major, L. 428, is a jota.

(The letter *L,* followed by a number, by which all Scarlatti sonatas are identified refers to Alessandro Longo, who edited and published an eleven-volume edition of practically all of Scarlatti's sonatas. The number following the letter *L* represents the place of the sonata in this publication.)

Even when Scarlatti made no attempt to be programmatic, we sense   *45* the feeling and the backgrounds of Spain in his music. Apparently he always kept some image or experience in mind in writing his music, even when he failed to identify that image or experience. For this reason the sonatas have strong descriptive qualities. They always seem to be portraying something extramusical. For this reason publishers and editors have often chosen to affix picturesque titles to some of Scarlatti's sonatas.

All the thirty sonatas in his first volume are fast. Only late in life would he write effectively in a slow tempo. Most are in the two-section structure. Several of these sonatas are repertory numbers: for example, the Sonatas in E major (L. 375) and D minor (L. 413), respectively named "Capriccio" and "Pastorale" by Karl Tausig in his adaptations for the modern piano. Famous, too, is the Sonata in D major (L. 461), whose sudden changes of tempo, dynamics, and melodic themes endow it with dramatic interest.

The diadems of subsequent volumes are also well studded with shining jewels. Beginning with that issued in Venice in 1749, one striking piece follows another, as Scarlatti's increasing command of the keyboard provides him with the means of giving his imagination full freedom of expression: the G major, L. 487; the C major, L. 104; the G minor, L. 338; the D major, L. 463. And the masterpieces keep on coming. "Like the final displays in an evening of fireworks," wrote his biographer, Ralph Kirkpatrick, of Scarlatti's last sonatas, "scintillating riches and ever-varying spectacles are showered on us until they disappear into blackness. Now Scarlatti is showering the largesse of his whole musical legacy on us in an ever-increasing crescendo that is interrupted only by death."

Scarlatti's first wife died in 1739. Sometime between 1740 and 1742 he married a Spanish girl from Cadiz, Anastasia Ximenes; they had four children. In his last years Scarlatti suffered disastrous financial reverses through gambling, a frailty to which he had been prone through most of his adult years and which time and again nudged him to the brink of ruin, from which he was always rescued by his royal patroness, Maria Barbara (who in 1746 had become queen of Spain). Scarlatti died in Madrid on July 23, 1757. He left his wife and children destitute, a condition that was permanently relieved through a generous yearly pension bestowed by the queen.

"For what I know," Haydn once said, "I have to thank Carl Philipp Emanuel Bach." Mozart said, "He [Carl Philipp Emanuel Bach] is the father and we his children. Those of us who know what is right have learned it from him; and those who have not confessed it are scoundrels."

Who is this Carl Philipp Emanuel Bach who was so highly esteemed by two of the world's greatest composers? What had he done to deserve such encomiums?

He was a son of Johann Sebastian Bach. Both in his lifetime and afterward he was a Bach not only in name but also in deed. In more ways than one he was a trailblazer in music.

Carl Philipp Emanuel Bach was the one most responsible for establishing the classic form of the piano sonata. He developed a writing style that was even more pianistic than that of Domenico Scarlatti. In an all-important treatise—*Versuch über die wahre Art, das Clavier zu spielen* (*Essay on the True Art of Playing the Clavier*), published in two parts in 1753–62—he not only analyzed existing keyboard practices but also suggested new methods for arriving at greater expressiveness. Haydn, Mozart, and Beethoven all profited from studying this text. (It was published in the United States in an English translation in 1949.)

This Bach began the Classical era. Though he did not altogether abandon counterpoint, he regarded polyphony disdainfully, sometimes even contemptuously. "Many more necessary things than counterpoint are essential to a good composer," he wrote. He was, of course, thinking of homophony. And though he still clung to some elements of the Baroque style, he insisted, as far as he could, on stripping music of meretricious trimmings so characteristic of the Baroque era, on writing with the lucidity, clarity, balance, and formalism that were the identifying traits of Classicism.

Carl Philipp Emanuel Bach, the second surviving son of Johann Sebastian and Maria Barbara Bach, was born in Weimar, Germany, on March 8, 1714. His godfather was Georg Philipp Telemann, one of the most eminent composers of choral and instrumental music and of operas of his time.

The only teacher Carl Philipp Emanuel ever had was his own father, who gave him a comprehensive training in composition and in the playing of the clavier. Carl was still a child when he began collaborating with his family in presenting formal concerts at home. When Carl was nine, his father removed his family from Cöthen to Leipzig. There Carl's boyhood years were crowded with music-making and listening to and learning about music. He often attended the rehearsals and performances at the Thomasschule over which his father officiated. He also rubbed elbows with some of the foremost German musicians of the period. "Although I . . . saw little of the world," he wrote, "yet no master of music passed through this place without coming to make himself known to my father and play before him."

Strange as it may sound, his father wanted him to become a lawyer rather than a musician. Could it have been that the great master did not value his son's musical capabilities? Or was the boy, in comparison with some of his brothers, no dazzling musical light? We do not know the answer, but we do know that from 1731 to 1734 Carl Philipp Emanuel attended the Thomasschule in preparation for law study, which he pursued for three years at the university at Frankfurt on the Oder. But Carl refused to abandon music; it had become too much a part of his being. He was left-handed and so concentrated on keyboard instruments instead of the violin, perfecting himself as a performer on the harpsichord. He also organized a choral society that presented some of his earlier compositions. In 1737 he gave a concert featuring some of his works, which were enthusiastically received by a distinguished audience, including Frederick William I, king of Prussia.

By 1738 Bach decided that his place in society would have to be as a professional musician and not as a lawyer. He went to Berlin, where he found a powerful patron in Crown Prince Frederick. When the crown prince ascended the Prussian throne in 1740 (later to be known as Frederick the Great) he engaged, as we have already mentioned, Carl Philipp Emanuel as a chamber musician. Frederick the Great played the flute with considerable skill and was an amateur composer. The first flute solo he performed as king was accompanied on the clavier by Carl Philipp Emanuel.

For over a quarter of a century Carl Philipp Emanuel Bach remained in the king's employ. He gave concerts on the clavier; he arranged and directed five evenings a week court concerts for which he wrote orchestral and chamber music; and he accompanied the king's flute playing at the clavier. His salary was about two hundred dollars a year, by no means a generous income even for those times, but enough to support a family. In 1744 Bach married Johanna Maria Dannemann, daughter of a wine merchant. They had three children, none of whom were practising musicians. Of the two sons one became a lawyer and the other a painter; the third child was a daughter.

During his long stay at the Prussian court, Bach published his first set of sonatas for the clavier, the *Prussian* Sonatas (1742). He wrote this music for the clavichord, since he greatly preferred its richer sonorities to the tinkling sounds of the harpsichord. These compositions are still grounded in practices and procedures of the past from which Bach had not yet freed himself. He was here simply working in the patterns established by his predecessors and contemporaries. His greatest sonatas—those in which he would develop new music for the future—were to come some years later.

Bach was not happy working for Frederick the Great, for whose conservative musical tastes and modest talent he had little respect. As time passed, Bach became restless and tried to find a place for himself elsewhere. It took more than a decade for a suitable post to become available to him. His godfather, Telemann, died in 1767, leaving vacant the office of Kapellmeister for the city of Hamburg. Bach had to humble himself by pleading with Frederick the Great to release him from his obligations in Berlin, which the king finally consented to do. Bach was to remain the Kapellmeister in Hamburg until his death from pulmonary consumption on December 14, 1788.

There is much to admire in C. P. E. Bach's choral, orchestral, and chamber compositions—particularly in his concertos, sinfonias, and his most celebrated choral work, the Magnificat in D major. His sonatas for violin and clavier, for flute and clavier, and for cello and clavier, and his trios are thoroughly charming, though not of historic importance. He also wrote many fine small pieces for the piano. Piano students are well acquainted with one of them, the "Solfegietto," which imitates the runs of a vocal exercise on the clavier; the meaning of "solfegietto" is a "little solfeggio," or a "little vocal exercise." All this notwithstanding, it is with his sonatas for the clavichord (and later for the piano) that he reserved for himself a permanent place in music history. In 1774 he published his second set of sonatas (six in number) for the clavichord, the *Württemberg* Sonatas, so called because they were dedicated to the duke of Württemberg. Here we meet his first attempts to achieve a new style—*Empfindsamer Stil* ("expressiveness"), which is a personalized and dramatized way of writing. Sudden changes in tonality and in harmony, unexpected turns of the melodic line, the use of effective accents and pauses all introduce surprise in these sonatas. Theatricalism is realized through harmonic, rhythmic, and dynamic means. His passionate passages—those torrents of sweeping music described in the history book as *"Sturm und Drang"* ("storm and stress")—were one side of the coin of his expressiveness; the other was a "melodic sigh," achieved through a descent from a strong beat to a weak one. The eminent English music historian of the eighteenth century, Charles Burney, commented thus on the impact of this "melodic sigh" by saying: "In the pathetic and slow movements, whenever he had a long note to express, he absolutely contrived to produce from his instrument a cry of sorrow and complaint such as can only be effected . . . by himself."

For the kind of sound and expressiveness he was seeking, Carl Philipp Emanuel Bach needed a new type of keyboard instrument. He found it in the piano, for which he wrote his sonata masterpieces—the six sets published between 1779 and 1787, all bearing the title of *Für Kenner und Liebhaber* (*For Connoisseurs and Amateurs*). Here are collected eighteen sonatas, together with fantasias and rondos.

The piano was developed into its final stage of evolution early in the eighteenth century by Bartolomeo Cristofori (1655–1731), who was employed by Prince Ferdinand de' Medici in Florence. Cristofori called his instrument *"gravicembalo col piano e forte,"* which can be freely translated to mean a harpsichord capable of creating gradations of soft and loud sounds. This long Italian term has since been contracted to the simple word *piano*. Cristofori was the first to solve a problem that had long harassed instrument-makers: to produce a keyboard instrument in which the strings could be struck by little padded hammers when the keys are depressed, producing a rich tone and full-sounding sonorities, but with the hammers springing back instantly into place to allow the strings to vibrate. Cristofori solved this problem with several of his pianos between 1720 and 1724. He used thick brass strings (today steel is used, which is capable of considerably more tension). He strengthened the frame of his instrument with metal braces to withstand the impact made by the hammers striking the strings, and by the tension of the strings themselves. In order that the sound of the struck strings could be immediately silenced when the key was released, dampers (oblong pieces of wood covered by felt), placed against the strings, were released once the key was struck, to fall back into place at the release of the key. One pedal allowed all the dampers to be lifted simultaneously, permitting the vibration of the strings to continue when other keys were being depressed. Another pedal smothered the volume by decreasing the impact of the hammer. (The modern piano has a middle pedal to help sustain the tone.)

The piano was capable of gradations of softness and loudness, depending upon the pressure exerted by the fingers on the keys, which neither the clavichord or the harpsichord could duplicate. In addition, the soft bell-like tinkle of the harpsichord and the sharp metallic sound of the clavichord were replaced by the sonorous resonance of the piano.

Melodies that could be stated only crisply and sharply on the older instruments could now be spun out legato into what Carl Philipp Emanuel Bach called a "cantabile" or "singing" style.

The piano, then, was an instrument ideally suited for the kind of music for which Carl Philipp Emanuel was reaching in his *Württemberg* Sonatas. That he was finally able to write the masterworks in the *For Connoisseurs and Amateurs* collections was not only due to his growth as a creative artist but also to the fact that now he had the instrument with the resources capable of projecting his "expressive" style—those storm and stress passages and those affecting melodic sighs.

It is also in these late collections that the classic sonata form becomes clearly defined and formulated for the piano. In many of his sonatas, Bach uses three movements, the first and third fast, and the middle one slow. The first movement at times is built from two themes, which are carried through three sections: an exposition, in which they are presented; a development, in which they are elaborated upon; and a recapitulation, in which the exposition is repeated. His slow movements are in a *galant* style—a refined, aristocratic kind of melody that is elegantly fashioned—and his finales sometimes suggest the rondo form (in which a principal theme recurs continually after the presentation of each new melodic subject). Thus the format of the three-movement classic sonata is at last established. It would, to be sure, be amplified and altered with subsequent composers. But the basic structure clarified by C. P. E Bach would be adhered to.

The clarity of Bach's sonata form, his *galant* style in his more sensitive pages, and his outbursts in the more emotional ones were things Haydn emulated when he began writing his own piano sonatas. Bach's expressive style was the source of the deep emotionalism and at times passion that characterize so many of Mozart's piano works, especially his fantasias. Beethoven was influenced to a marked degree by Bach's storm and stress passages, in which he hurled bolts of lightning and unleashed thunder and storms. Surely there is something eloquently symbolic in the fact that the opening of the first movement of Beethoven's first published piano sonata should so strongly resemble the opening movement of Carl Philipp Emanuel Bach's Sonata in F minor (from *For Connoisseurs and Amateurs*). It was almost as if, as he began to write mature sonatas for the piano, Beethoven was consciously paying tribute to his distinguished predecessor; as if Beethoven were announcing through his music that in writing for the piano he wished to carry on from the point where Carl Philipp Emanuel Bach had leff off.

4

Classical Grandeur

Joseph Haydn,

Wolfgang Amadeus Mozart

Carl Philipp Emanuel Bach, Haydn, Mozart and the early Beethoven are the four stalwart pillars on which rests the age of musical Classicism.

The Classical era, which replaced the Baroque, began roughly in 1750 with the death of Johann Sebastian Bach and ended during the first decade of the nineteenth century during Beethoven's middle creative period. In this Classical period instrumental music began to surpass choral music in popularity; homophony replaced polyphony as the style most favored by composers; orchestral and chamber music came into their full glory; the piano completely supplanted the harpsichord and the clavichord; and the violin and cello attained a new importance as solo instruments.

The music of the Classical era is subservient to discipline and order. It is music with aristocratic manners, conforming to rule and propriety. In it, old instrumental forms (the concerto, sonata, symphony, theme and variations, minuet, rondo) were structurally enlarged. Still older forms (the concerto grosso, sonata da camera, sonata da chiesa, passacaglia, chaconne, the most of the old dance forms) went into discard.

The sonata form became the principal structure for all instrumental music, including that for orchestra and chamber music combinations as well as solo instruments. The Classical sonata form underwent some significant transformations during this period. The two themes of the first movement became of a contrasting nature—the first being vigorous, and in the tonality of the composition; the second, more lyrical, and in a complementary key. In the second movement, the theme and variations supplemented the two- or three-part song form; a minuet (later the scherzo) became the third movement; and the finale took the sonata, theme and variations, or rondo form. Some works in sonata form, many concertos among them, have only three movements.

The Baroque composer liked to concentrate on a single melody or rhythmic pattern and embellish it throughout a movement. Composers of the Classical period worked with contrasts—in the melodies, rhythms, harmony, and tonality of each movement, and in the emotion or mood or feeling generated from one movement to the next.

The piano sonata progressed toward Classical perfection with Haydn. But it took many years for this to happen. Haydn's best piano sonatas came long after he had achieved full maturity and greatness as a composer of string quartets and symphonies.

As a young man Haydn had studied Carl Philipp Emanuel Bach's sonatas painstakingly, had committed them to memory, and was profoundly impressed by them. Their influence, however, did not filter into Haydn's piano writing for some time, and it took longer still before Haydn fully absorbed Bach's structures and methods. Only then was Haydn able to allow his own individuality full freedom of expression.

However distinguished Haydn was as a composer of piano sonatas, his importance as creator of string quartets was far greater still. In fact, it can truthfully be said that it is Haydn who first realized the full artistic capabilities of the string quartet as a medium for musical creativity. Whereas Haydn had profited in his piano sonatas from Carl Philipp Emanuel Bach, and in his symphonies from such eminent predecessors as Johann Stamitz (1717–57), he had to beat out his own path in writing string quartets. The string quartets by the Italians preceding Haydn are primitive when compared to his. The Italians did not use the sonata form; they did not comprehend the individual capacities of the viola and the cello in contributing to the overall musical texture; they had little concept of musical development; they usually concentrated on a single principal melody, which they often assigned to the first violin while the other instruments served as an accompaniment. But with Haydn the string quartet developed along the lines it would henceforth pursue. *53*

Let us single out the main events in Haydn's life to put his string quartets and his piano sonatas in proper biographical and historical perspective.

Born in the Austrian town of Rohrau, near the Hungarian border, on March 31, 1732, Joseph Haydn received his initial intensive instruction in music from a cousin of his father's, Johann Mathias Frankh, with whom he went to live at the age of five. Frankh was a hard, cruel taskmaster who made Haydn's boyhood years thoroughly miserable. But Frankh was also a good musician, and the training he gave the boy Haydn was something for which the latter was grateful in his adult years. Thus, when Haydn was eight, he was musically well equipped to become a chorister at St. Stephen's Cathedral in Vienna. For the next nine years he continued formal music study at its school, while singing in the choir. Life at St. Stephen's proved harder even than it had been at his cousin's household. To cold, hunger, and the fatigue brought on by a strict regimen was added the abuse he suffered at the hands of his teachers. The boy's musical industry and his eagerness to learn apparently passed unnoticed because he had an incorrigible weakness for mischief-making and getting into trouble that caused his teachers to resent him and frequently punish him.

His teachers, then, were not too sorry to see Haydn leave St. Stephen's when, in his seventeenth year, his voice broke. Without any financial resources, and with the clothes on his back as his only possession, he wandered Vienna's streets until a casual friend allowed him to share his roof. When Haydn was able to earn some money from teaching, he rented a garret room of his own in an apartment house called the Michaelerhaus.

During the interim between the time when he left St. Stephen's in 1749 and when he found a permanent job in 1758 as musical director and chamber composer at the palace of Count Ferdinand Maximilian von Morzin, Haydn devotedly and intensively pursued the study of music by himself. For hours at an end he practiced on the clavier, and when he was not at the keyboard he was mastering the sonatas of Carl Philipp Emanuel Bach. Yet there is very little trace of Bach in the piano sonatas Haydn completed about 1760. Their style was more Baroque than Classical; the keyboard writing was better suited to the clavichord than to the piano, the instrument Bach had already begun to favor over the harpsichord or clavichord.

54 For Baron Karl Josef von Fürnberg, who was his first patron, Haydn

wrote his early string quartets. They are a far cry from the genuine product he would later fashion. His first string quartet came in 1755; the first dozen, published as op. 1 and 2, were completed between 1755 and 1760. Structurally, these were not string quartets at all but divertimenti —suites in a light and pleasing style made up of more than four movements. Stylistically, they were more orchestral than chamber music; indeed, the op. 2 set was identified as "sinfonias." There still stretched a long road ahead for Haydn before he would reach the goal of true string quartet writing!

Two years after becoming musical director at the court of Count Morzin near Pilsen, Haydn embarked on an unfortunate marriage—with Maria Anna Keller, daughter of a wigmaker. It proved unfortunate because Haydn had been in love with her younger sister, whom he had sought as a wife. He married Maria Anna only after the one he loved decided to enter a convent. Maria Anna proved to be a shrew who had no respect for her husband's talent or profession, and whose evil tempers almost drove the gentle and kindly genius mad. After several years of bickering and quarrels, they separated, with Haydn providing for her financially until her life's end.

Haydn found a new employer in 1761: Prince Paul Anton Esterházy, at whose palace in Eisenstadt he became second Kapellmeister. A little more than a year later Prince Paul died and was succeeded by his brother Nicolaus Joseph. Later, when Prince Nicolaus had built for himself a magnificent new palace at Esterháza, Haydn was elevated to the post of first Kapellmeister. Elegantly dressed and always with a pigtailed powdered wig on his head, Haydn directed the operatic and concert performances at the palace, for which he produced a vast output of music that made him in his lifetime a world figure.

Together with symphonies, concertos, masses, and operas, Haydn also wrote his first significant piano sonatas and string quartets. At long last, in his writing for the piano, he revealed the impact of lessons learned so many years earlier from the sonatas of Carl Philipp Emanuel Bach. Between 1775 and 1780 a stress and passion began to course through Haydn's piano style, which springs from Bach's *Sturm und Drang* passages. At the same time Haydn arrives at striking contrasts through sudden excursions from sobriety to gaiety, and through unexpected key changes. Melody more than ever before so absorbs Haydn's interest that he demonstrates how one and the same theme can change its character when it is used in two different works—a curious experiment that he brings off successfully in the second movement of his Sonata in C-sharp minor, op. 30 no. 2 and in the first movement of his Sonata in G major, op. 30 no. 5 (1779–80).

Haydn is now ready to pass far beyond Carl Philipp Emanuel Bach both in the skill with which he designs his structure and in the boldness of invention with which his structures are filled. Now come the masterworks: the Sonata in C major, op. 30 no. 1 (1779–80), with its wonderful slow movement; the Sonata in D major, op. 37 no. 3 (1784); the Sonata in E-flat major, op. 66 (1790), which surprisingly ends with a minuet; and the Sonata in D major, op. 93 (1792), which has only two movements, an andante and a presto.

While thus carrying the piano sonata to the very threshold of Beethoven, Haydn was crystallizing the string quartet, which is perhaps the greatest of all his achievements, not barring his development of the symphony. By the time he completed the six works in op. 20 (1772) Haydn had written about twenty-four string quartets. He was now in full command of this new medium, a master of string quartet writing. These six compositions are entitled the *Sun* Quartets, only because an early publisher in Berlin used the picture of the sun as his trademark in releasing this set. But the word *sun* applies to these masterpieces for a far more cogent reason. These quartets are (as W. W. Cobbett, editor of the famous *Cobbett's Cyclopedic Survey of Chamber Music,* remarked) "a sunrise over the domain of the sonata style as well as quartets in particular. . . . There is perhaps no single or sextuple opus in the history of instrumental music which has achieved so much or achieved it so quietly." For the first time the four instruments become individualists, each assigned its own importance in the overall musical scheme. A new wealth of melodic invention, a new power of thematic development, a wide gamut of expression and emotion now invade the field of string quartet music.

Haydn's six quartets in op. 33 (1781) are sometimes called *Russian* (because they were dedicated to a Russian grand duke) and sometimes *Gli scherzi* (since scherzos or scherzandos replace the expected third-movement minuet). Two of these quartets have other identifying titles. The Quartet in E-flat major is known as *The Joke.* In its finale Haydn impishly included unexpected rests, so goes a familiar explanation, in order to see if anybody in the audience was talking while his music was being played. The Quartet in C major has the name of *The Bird.* In the first movement the grace notes, or ornaments, decorating the main melody sound like the chirping of birds and the trio section of the Scherzando also has a birdlike sound.

Ever more commanding becomes Haydn's technique and ever more impressive his inspiration in the six quartets of op. 50 (1787). Dedicated to the king of Prussia, these works bear the title of *Prussian*. Here Haydn developed a new thematic process (monothematic) in which the second theme, or group of themes, in a movement in the sonata form is derived from or is a variation of the first theme, or group of themes.

Haydn's last and greatest quartets are the twelve found in the *Tost* Quartets, op. 54, 55, and 64 (dedicated to Johann Tost, a violinist in the Esterházy orchestra), the six quartets in op. 71 and 74 (1793), the six *Erdödy* Quartets, op. 76 (1797) dedicated to County Erdödy, and the two quartets op. 77 (1799). Haydn has arrived at the pinnacle of his genius in writing string quartet music. In the *Tost* group we find the String Quartet in D major, *The Lark* (op. 64 no. 5), in which the soaring melody for the first violin in the opening movement has the spontaneous eloquence of a song by the bird that gives the work its name. In the *Erdödy* set are the *Quinten, Emperor,* and *Largo* Quartets. In the second of this set, in D minor, the opening subject of the initial movement is built on intervals of the fifth, hence the title of *Quinten*. The *Emperor* (C major) uses in its slow movement as the subject for variations the national anthem that Haydn had then recently written at the request of the Austrian emperor. The *Largo* (D major) boasts what may well be the most sublime slow movement Haydn ever wrote, after whose tempo marking of largo the entire work was named.

Haydn was the first composer of consequence to write piano trios for piano, violin, and cello. He wrote over two dozen of them. In the last of these, the Piano Trio in G major, op. 73 no. 2, published in or about 1795, there is a finale in the Hungarian style. In various transcriptions (the most famous of which is that for violin and orchestra or violin and piano by Fritz Kreisler) it has been popularized under the title of *Gypsy* Rondo or *Hungarian* Rondo.

The twenty-five years Haydn spent at Esterháza as Kapellmeister were lonely ones. He had few opportunities to travel, except for occasional visits to Vienna. He felt that in Esterháza he was shut off from the rest of the world. He missed terribly not having a family life. This was one of the reasons he suffered many hours of melancholy—though his natural sense of fun and bright spirit soon helped to dissipate the clouds that, from time to time, hovered so darkly over him.

When Prince Nicolaus Esterházy died in 1790, and musical activity at court was sharply curtailed, Haydn decided to leave the post he had held with such honor for so long a time. By now his fame had spread the world over. On two occasions—in 1790–91 and again in 1794—he was invited to London to conduct symphony concerts, for which he was required to write new symphonies. He came as a hero; social engagements, adulation, gifts, and tributes were heaped lavishly upon him.

Returning to Vienna from his second London trip, Haydn lived quietly and in seclusion in a house in a suburb of the city. His last major works were oratorios, *The Creation* (1798) and *The Seasons* (1801). His final appearance as conductor took place in Vienna in 1803 in a performance of his *Seven Last Words of Christ.*

In his closing years he was an invalid. When he was last seen in public (at a performance of *The Creation* in 1808) he had to be carried in and out of the auditorium in a chair. He died at his home on May 31, 1809. With his typical thoughtfulness and generosity, he forgot nobody in his will, not even those who had done him little favors a half century and more before his death.

At a memorial service for Haydn a few weeks after his death the *Requiem* by Wolfgang Amadeus Mozart was performed. How appropriate that this noble work by Mozart should have been heard as the farewell to the great Haydn! Haydn held no composer of his time in higher esteem than he did the much younger Mozart. No other of Haydn's contemporaries had proved to be such a bountiful source of inspiration to that master, no other such a force in Haydn's evolution and development, an influence that had effect even after Haydn had won world renown. No musician did Haydn love more, even though his personal meetings with Mozart were few and far between.

Mozart well deserved Haydn's admiration and respect. There was no branch of music that was not turned into pure gold by the Midas touch of Mozart's genius. Haydn was one of the few established musicians of Mozart's day to realize this. Nothing in music seemed beyond Mozart's capabilities. He had been an unparalleled musical phenomenon as a child. As a mature musician, Mozart's accomplishments were more wonderful still. In every musical area he produced masterpieces incomparable for their workmanship, loftiness of musical content, and daring imagination. Haydn was perceptive enough, and generous enough, to concede that these went beyond his own efforts, and to reevaluate his own writing, to transform and strengthen it along the lines suggested to him by Mozart's compositions.

To piano music Mozart contributed seventeen sonatas, together with
some shorter compositions (including variations, rondos, and fantasias)

which are hardly less remarkable. Violin music was enriched by his forty-two sonatas for violin and piano, with which the violin sonata arrives at structural and artistic maturity. And his output in chamber music was awesome for quantity as well as quality, many of the works landmarks in chamber music history: twenty-six string quartets, together with quartets for flute, violin, viola, and cello, and one for oboe, violin, viola, and cello; seven string quintets (two violins, two violas, and cello), as well as one for horn and strings (violin, two violas, and cello) and the extraordinary one for clarinet and strings; seven piano trios, as well as several string trios (violin, viola, and cello), and a clarinet trio (clarinet, viola, and piano).

Mozart's childhood exploits in music are almost beyond belief. He was born in Salzburg, Austria, on January 27, 1756. He was the son of Leopold, an excellent violinist employed in the archbishop's court and the author of the first important treatise on violin playing. More in play than in seriousness, Herr Leopold began giving Wolfgang lessons on the clavier when the child was four. But the father soon discovered to his astonishment that making music was no child's play for Wolfgang but deadly serious business. The child felt such pain at discordant musical sounds that sometimes he went into a faint. He was born with perfect pitch, a spongelike memory, and a seemingly infallible musical intuition. Without taking a violin lesson he could tell when a violin was the slightest bit out of tune. He needed only elementary instruction to play both the clavier and the violin well. So remarkably developed was his musical intelligence that a single lesson was enough for him to master a composition. He heard a piece of music once and could forthwith play it faultlessly. He could read music at sight as if he had practiced it for hours.

The first piece of music he ever wrote was for the clavier—the Minuet in G major, K. 1, when he was five. (The letter *K*. stands for Köchel, who, in 1862, compiled the first complete chronological catalog of Mozart's works. The number after the letter is the place of the composition in this catalog.) Within the next year Mozart wrote three more minuets. They have become familiar beginning pieces for piano students. An Allegro, an Andante, a set of sundry pieces, and several sets of variations, all for the clavier, had been written by the time Mozart was ten, together with his first sixteen sonatas for violin and clavier, his first symphonies, and his first choral compositions.

Here, then—as the father soon came to realize—was a musical attraction to impress all of Europe. Dressed in the elegant fineries of a nobleman (velvet jacket, silk breeches, silk hose, a powdered wig), little

Wolfgang Amadeus was put on exhibition in the royal courts in Munich, Vienna, Paris, and London. His older sister Maria Anna (affectionately known in her family as Nannerl), a gifted performer on the clavier, was a supplementary attraction, but the spotlight was focused on Wolfgang Amadeus. He played the clavier, the violin, and the organ. One then prominent musician had him perform this composer's concerto at sight, a performance that led the man to burst into tears. Wolfgang Amadeus went through a variety of musical stunts. Here is how an advertisement in Frankfurt, Germany, announced his public appearance in 1763: "He will play a concerto for the violin, and will accompany symphonies on the harpsichord, the manual or keyboard being covered with a cloth, with as much facility as if he could see the keys; he will instantly name all the notes played at a distance, whether singly or in chords, on the harpsichord or any instrument, bell, glass, or clock. He will finally improvise as long as desired, and in any key, on the harpsichord and organ."

Wherever he went he was the object for adulation, the recipient of gifts of gold and precious jewels. Nobody was of too high a station or too sophisticated in musical values not to be overwhelmed by his miraculous musical powers.

Mozart's first four violin sonatas (K. 6–9) were published in Paris, and six more (K. 10–15) in London. Precocious though they are in the neatness with which the child can put his musical ideas down on paper, they are nevertheless just museum pieces today—of greater interest to us because they came from a child than for their actual musical content. They assign principal importance to the clavier, with the violin virtually assuming the role of an accompaniment. It would take Mozart more than a decade before he mastered the art of writing either a violin sonata or a sonata for the piano. First he would have to spend several years studying the published music of various instrumental composers—first, Carl Philipp Emanuel Bach, and later on, Joseph Haydn.

His success throughout Europe continued for several years and through a number of tours. In London, late in 1764 and early in 1765, he introduced his first symphonies at a public concert at the Vauxhall Gardens. One year later he was invited to give concerts of his own music in Amsterdam and was commissioned by the electress to write six new violin sonatas (K. 26–31). He also made an extended tour of Germany, where, for a twelve-day period in a single city, he gave a concert practically every night. In Vienna, in 1768, Mozart's little comic opera *Bastien and Bastienne* was performed privately. There he was also commis-

sioned by the Austrian emperor to write another opera (*La Finta*
semplice), which was kept from the stage only because the opera performers were humiliated at the idea of appearing in the work of an elev-
en-year-old boy. In Italy, when he was fourteen, he completed his first
string quartet, in G major, K. 80, which he wrote in a single evening;
and in that same country, between 1772 and 1773, he wrote six more
string quartets, K. 155–160. Meanwhile, in 1769 and again in 1770, he
caused a furore in Verona with his concerts. In Bologna he became the
youngest musician ever to be elected a member of the Accademia Filarmonica. In Milan he was commissioned to write a full-length serious
opera in the Italian style: *Mitridate,* a triumph when given in that city
on December 26, 1770.

In his compositions, Mozart thus far had proved most original and
precocious within the realm of opera. In his instrumental music, amazing though it was as the work of a boy, he was still derivative; in his
string quartets, for example, he was an echo of the Italian instrumental
composers of that period. But between 1772 and 1780 his genius began
to shine through the pages of his music. What a productive period this
was for young Mozart! Symphonies and other orchestral compositions,
concertos, violin sonatas, piano sonatas, as well as other piano compositions, masses, chamber music, operas, vocal pieces all poured from him
with an abundance, spontaneity, and originality to inspire awe and in-
credulity.

It was during the latter part of this period that we encounter Mozart's first masterworks for solo instruments and the first chamber music
works that are recognizably Mozartean. What he had learned from the
Italians, from Carl Philipp Emanuel Bach, and subsequently from
Haydn filtered through his imagination to become something fresh, new,
and invigorating. By now he had become a master of the sonata form
and the *galant* style, as well as of the techniques for writing for the piano and for the violin. He was now able to give voice to his own
thoughts and emotions in the manner that suited him best, a manner
that time and again departed sharply from accepted procedures. He
broke rules and he created his own laws whenever artistic necessity demanded that he travel into territories of musical creativity heretofore
unexplored.

If any one piano sonata can be singled out as the best known it is
that in A major, K. 331 (1778), nicknamed *Turkish*. Here Mozart side-
steps the sonata tradition that he had previously accepted and that he
would readopt in later works. He begins the A major Sonata not in the

allegro sonata form, but in a tempo marked andante grazioso, and in the form of theme and variations. The theme, an elegant two-part melody, is the essence of rococo writing. Six variations, in which the basic melody always remains identifiable, follow. The second movement is a minuet, through whose classical design Mozart allows himself the indulgence of feeling in a romantic vein. The closing movement, marked allaturca allegretto, is the one that earned for the whole composition its descriptive title of *Turkish.* Its brisk melody is in the intervallic and chromatic style then identified in Austria as Turkish.

There is depth of feeling (a carry-over and enrichment of Carl Philipp Emanuel Bach's *Empfindsamer Stil,* expressiveness) in some of the other piano sonatas of these years: in the noble Adagio of the F major Sonata, K. 280 (1774); in the fervor of the A minor Sonata, K. 310 (1778)—in the dramatic tension of the first movement, and the contemplative loveliness of the second movement (with its magical effect brought on by change of key from minor to major). In the finale of the F major Sonata, K. 332 (1778) we come upon delightful pleasantries that are Mozartean in the lightness of touch and gaiety of mood.

In 1778 Mozart wrote seven violin sonatas in which (after eighteen earlier efforts) he begins to touch greatness. Here the violin is finally accorded that prominence in the overall design which it would henceforth enjoy with Mozart and later composers. These sonatas are filled with those wondrous lyrical passages so ideally suited for the violin, while the piano contributes rhythmic vigor and harmonic richness. Both instruments, however, are partners in sharing the center of musical interest. Typical of this group—the first Mozart violin sonatas still receiving frequent hearings—are the Sonatas in C major, K. 296, and B-flat major, K. 378. The C major Sonata was written in a single day.

The years of 1777–78 brought the first chamber music in which Mozart's personal manner of developing his musical ideas, the effervescence of his spirit, and his beguiling lyricism can be discovered. Commissioned by two flutists, Mozart completed three quartets for flute, violin, viola, and cello, K. 285, 285b, and 298. This is delightful music, but not half so important or so imaginative as the quartet for oboe, violin, viola, and cello in F major, K. 370 (1781), one of the most perfectly realized chamber music compositions Mozart wrote. This, too, was written with a specific performer in mind, in this case an oboe virtuoso from Munich. When introduced in Munich on January 29, 1781, this quartet led a distinguished horn player of the city to exclaim, "I must own that I

have never yet heard any music which made such a deep impression
upon me!"

Would not one imagine that a composer to whom the creation of musical beauty came as naturally as breathing would be held in the highest esteem by his employer? Regrettably, this was not so. A new archbishop had taken office in Salzburg who treated Mozart as if he were a lackey and paid him a miserly salary for his musical services. The fact that Mozart was treated contemptuously by his employer, that Mozart detested working at the archbishop's court and resented the treatment he was given, has led some writers to leap to the conclusion that the richly productive Salzburg years in the 1770s were unhappy for the young composer. This belief, however, does not seem justified. Mozart loved composing. He did it with such little effort that creation, far from causing him any anguish, brought only joy. Besides, Mozart was no recluse or ascetic. He could delight in a new velvet jacket, in drinking punch, in dancing.

Then there were opportunities for travel, which Mozart enjoyed especially because they took him away from his disagreeable job at the archbishop's palace and also because they invariably brought him the recognition that Salzburg failed to give him. He paid a return visit to Vienna in 1773, then went on to Munich in 1774 to help produce a new comic opera, *La Finta giardiniera.* In 1777 he went to Augsburg (where he carried on a flirtation with his cousin Bäsle), to Mannheim (where he fell in love with Aloysia Weber), and to Paris (where he hoped to repeat the triumphs of his childhood and early youth but failed). In 1781 he attended the premiere of his serious opera *Idomeneo* in Munich.

In 1781 Mozart broke permanently both with his employer, the archbishop, and with his native city of Salzburg. The break with the archbishop came after some heated verbal exchanges in which the employer hurled abuse at Mozart and Mozart responded in kind. The archbishop threatened to dismiss him; Mozart replied hotly that his resignation in writing would be dispatched to the archbishop the following morning.

A free man at last, Mozart transferred his permanent home to Vienna. On August 4, 1782, he married Constanze, sister of the Aloysia with whom he had been emotionally involved a few years earlier.

Life in Vienna promised much for Mozart's success. The emperor called him to his palace to have him compete with Vienna's most honored pianist, Muzio Clementi, and pronounced the competition a draw.

This decision immediately placed Mozart on a level with the greatest pianist of his time. The emperor further commissioned Mozart to write an opera, *Die Entführung aus dem Serail* (*The Abduction from the Seraglio*), produced in the summer of 1782 so successfully that the people of Vienna were humming its airs, and Prince Kaunitz was going around saying that a genius like Mozart came along only once in a century.

But though Vienna promised much, it fulfilled little. Continually Mozart encountered the opposition of powerful musicians, in and out of court, who saw in him a serious rival. They joined forces to obstruct his progress. If the emperor himself had not intervened, *The Abduction from the Seraglio* premiere would have been sabotaged. Then, when another of Mozart's incomparable operatic masterworks—*Le Nozze di Figaro* (*The Marriage of Figaro*)—was produced in 1786, those enemies used guile and machinations to turn its initial success into failure and forced the opera from the boards.

But while some of Vienna's leading musicians were solidly lined up to destroy him, Mozart did find an ally in a musical giant: Joseph Haydn. They met personally for the first time in 1781, soon after Mozart had settled in Vienna. Haydn—the respected Kapellmeister from Esterháza, and already the most famous composer in Europe—was then forty-nine; Mozart, still struggling to get the rewards his genius deserved, was only twenty-five. Haydn and Mozart had long known each other's works and had admired them and been stimulated by them. Since childhood, Mozart had been studying Haydn's symphonies and had absorbed many a valuable lesson that he forthwith applied to his own orchestral music. Mozart, openhearted, passionately in search of understanding, turned to the older man, learned from him freely, and always felt himself in Haydn's debt. From Haydn he learned perfection of the classic sonata form in which transparency, neatness, and clarity dominated. Then, on the steps of what he had acquired from Haydn, Mozart went on to climb heights above Haydn's own achievements. When Haydn came into contact with the mature Mozart compositions of the 1770s he knew that here was a creative genius more daring, more imaginative, more prophetic than he himself was. He was not too proud to study the music of a man so much younger, and so much less famous, than he, or to assimilate many of Mozart's structural, technical, and aesthetic innovations. The richer strains that flow in Haydn's music after the early 1780s—music that is less stylized, less formal, more emotional, subtler in detail, more dramatic, and more experimental—were made

possible only because Mozart had opened for him new horizons which
Haydn did not hesitate to explore.

The *Sun* Quartets of Haydn, which Mozart came to know in 1782, impelled the younger man to break his silence in quartet writing, which had lasted nine years. Now from Haydn he had uncovered the secret of writing string quartet music in which the four instruments were brought to life, individualized, yet at the same time unified under a common will. He wrote the String Quartet in G major, K. 387, beginning where Haydn had stopped, but going far beyond Haydn in the soaring flights of his inspiration as well as in the most striking originality in working out his musical ideas. He wrote five more quartets in the next three years. In gratitude to Haydn for having taught him how to write string quartets, Mozart dedicated all six quartets to the older master.

Three of these six quartets were played for the first time at Mozart's apartment in February of 1785. Haydn played first violin, and Mozart, the viola. Mozart's father, on a visit to Vienna, was also present. As the four players went from one quartet to the next, Haydn would shake his head with disbelief at the grandeur of this music, and his eyes would blink with puzzlement at Mozart's iconoclastic methods, which he did not completely understand. Again and again the unexpected happened in this music, yet always it had about it an inevitability that made it unthinkable to have this music written in any other way. Haydn marveled at the polyphonic skill in the G major Quartet and how skillfully contrapuntal passages were woven within a homophonic fabric. He was profoundly moved by the pathos, which at times lapsed into total despair, in so many of the pages of these quartets. He marveled at the way Mozart continually introduced fresh ideas with inexorable logic, and how magically the feeling and mood of an earlier melodic subject became transformed through subtle changes of key and rhythm. He marveled at the way Mozart achieved unity in the A major Quartet, K. 464 (1785) by having themes from the first movement reappear throughout other movements in altered forms; the way Mozart sprinkled his writing with unexpected sharps and flats and startling transitions of keys, as in the first movement of the D minor Quartet, K. 421 (1783); the bewildering obscurity of tonality with which the Quartet in C major, K. 465 (1785) opened—hence the name *Dissonant* Quartet. All these were beyond even his comprehension.

Haydn could only express the thought that if this was the way Mozart wanted to write, this was the way this music *had* to be written. That these six works were the greatest quartets thus far conceived, exceeding by far his own string quartet efforts, was something Haydn knew with finality. "I tell you before God and as an honest man," he told Mozart's father, "that your son is the greatest composer I know, either personally or by name."

Mozart also rose to unparalleled heights for his time in his solo instrumental music. In 1782 he wrote two fantasias for the piano: the C major, K. 394, and the D minor, K. 397. Both were inspired by and contain the structural breadth and the powerful dramatic thrusts and contrasts of the great organ fantasias of Johann Sebastian Bach, which Mozart had been studying. Mozart's principal fantasia for the piano is the one in C minor, K. 475 (1785), which he intended as a preface to his Piano Sonata in C minor, K. 457 (1785). Mozart had both compositions published in a single volume because he wanted them to be played together. They represent perhaps the summit of Mozart's literature for solo piano. Nowhere else in his piano music do we find such powerful and contrasting emotions as in these two compositions. At turns lyrical, anguished, tender, noble, introspective, and passionate, these two works seem to run the entire gamut of Mozart's expressivity. It is surely regrettable that the fantasia and the sonata are now so often played separately, since together they form a splendid monument with few parallels in piano music.

Mozart's last three sonatas for solo piano were the C major, K. 545, B-flat major, K. 570, and D major, K. 576 (1788–89). Claudio Arrau, one of the foremost pianists of our time, regards Mozart's last two solo piano sonatas as a kind of summation of what Mozart had accomplished in this form. "Mozart strips his pianistic fabric to almost bare, naked outlines," Arrau wrote, "and with their tone of abstract remoteness and lonely farewell, makes a last plunge into the aching roots of being in this world." Both sonatas have slow movements filled with desolation, which from time to time is relieved by moments of quiet resignation.

Mozart's violin sonatas, written between 1784 and 1787, are among his best. That in B-flat major, K. 454 (1784), was intended for one of Mozart's pupils. It was conceived so hurriedly that the performer did not have the time to study the music thoroughly before the concert, and the piano part was not even down on paper yet. At the performance, Mozart improvised his piano accompaniment (which he later wrote down). This, however, was not an unusual procedure for Mozart. Mozart habitually had his music thoroughly clear in mind in every detail before he committed it to paper. Despite the spontaneous method of its composition, there is nothing in this masterwork to give a clue to the hurried way in which it came into being. The Sonata in E-flat major, K. 481 (1785), is more ambitious in design than most of Mozart's earlier violin sonatas. The music of the first movement has dramatic and at times tragic implications; the second movement, adagio, is a rondo; the third movement is a set of six variations on a theme. The Sonata in A major, K. 526 (1787), is generally agreed to be his greatest violin sonata. It begins nervously with a first theme in irregular rhythms and accents before yielding to a more relaxed second subject; but it is the first theme that interests Mozart for the purposes of development. The second movement finds the violin and piano engaging in an eloquent dialogue. An elaborately conceived rondo brings the composition to a majestic conclusion. Mozart's last violin sonata, in F major, K. 547, was written in 1788.

Between 1785 and 1786 Mozart became the first composer to write compositions for a piano quartet (piano, violin, viola, and cello) in the style and manner we have come to expect in this form. He did so with the Quartets in G minor, K. 478, and E-flat major, K. 493. He was also the first to bring significance to the string quintet (two violins, two violas, and cello) and the clarinet quintet (clarinet and string quartet). His first string quintet was that in B-flat major, K. 174 (1773); his first eminent ones were the two that followed in 1787, the C major, K. 515, and the G minor, K. 516. His greatest string quintets were the two that appeared between 1790 and 1791: the D major, K. 593, and the E-flat major, K. 614. The Clarinet Quintet in A major, K. 581, came in 1789. All reveal the consummate mastery of technique and the luminosity of inspiration that characterize Mozart's chamber music at its best. What emotional impact Mozart carries over even to the most intricate contrapuntal passages in his last string quintets! How poignant is the romantic song in the second movement of the Clarinet Quintet where the mellow voice of the clarinet is heard chanting over the whisper of muted strings!

Mozart also wrote an outstanding composition for the combination of clarinet, viola, and piano: the Clarinet Trio in E-flat major, K. 498 (1786). This masterwork is believed to have been written while Mozart was playing a game of skittles, the reason it bears the sobriquet of *Kegelstatt* Trio (*Skittle* Trio). This trio, and the Clarinet Quintet, have historic as well as aesthetic importance, for they are the first significant compositions to lift the clarinet out of the orchestra and place it in a chamber music ensemble. It took a number of fortunate coincidences for the clarinet thus to achieve so important a status. It had to achieve an advanced stage of structural development, which had happened by Mozart's time. It had to find a performer of extraordinary attainments to prove its artistic and technical capacities. That performer was Anton Stadler (1753–1812). And the clarinet had to have at hand a composer with the rare capabilities of Mozart to write for it music of such surpassing eloquence. It was for Anton Stadler that Mozart created not only the Clarinet Trio and Clarinet Quintet, but also a no less extraordinary concerto for clarinet and orchestra (in A major, K. 622, in 1791).

Mozart completed his last three string quartets—K. 575, 589, and 590—between 1789 and 1790. He wrote them on a commission from the king of Prussia, and so they are referred to as the *Prussian* Quartets. The king was an amateur cellist. Bearing this in mind, Mozart assigned a particularly important role to the cello in each of these compositions —so much so that the first of these, in D major, is frequently referred to as the *Cello* Quartet. The second is in the key of B-flat major, and the third in F major. The last of these was written eighteen months before Mozart's death, and although he was experiencing many difficulties, Mozart, with his uncommon ability to separate his personal life and feelings from his creative ones, is almost consistently light of heart and bright of spirit in this, his farewell to the string quartet.

But he was neither light of heart nor bright of spirit in his last years. He had good reason to be distressed. When, at long last, he received a post at the Austrian court, in 1787, he was paid such a miserable salary that it was not enough to support him and his family. More than ever he had to borrow money from his friends (promising to repay them with interest) to make ends meet. All around him in Vienna were powerful rivals indefatigable in placing obstacles in the way of his success. Only the city of Prague gave Mozart the acclaim he deserved. There his operas *The Marriage of Figaro* and *Don Giovanni* (the latter written for and given its world premiere in the Bohemian capital) enjoyed triumphs, and their composer was adulated.

Not sickness nor futility nor despair could defeat him as a composer. Only death could. Mozart died in Vienna on December 5, 1791, and was buried in a pauper's unmarked grave, with only a scattered handful of mourners paying him their last respects.

Haydn was in London when he heard the news of Mozart's death. The extent of Haydn's grief can be measured by the fact that when he prepared to return to Vienna he suddenly burst into tears because Mozart would no longer be there to greet him. Even as late as 1807 Haydn invariably cried when Mozart's name was mentioned. "Forgive me," he would say. "I must always weep at the name of my dear Mozart."

Domenico Scarlatti at the cembalo.

Carl Philipp Emanuel Bach.

Opposite, Mozart at the clavecin, a painting by J. S. Duplessis in the collection of the Louvre.

A page from the Mozart Piano Capriccio in C major. An autograph manuscript.

5

A Colossus Bestriding the Worlds of Classicism and Romanticism

Ludwig van Beethoven

Beethoven was about thirteen years old when he wrote his first compositions. One was a string quintet he never published. All the others were for the piano, the first of which is a set of variations, and the remainder, a minuet, a rondo, and three juvenile piano sonatas not included among the thirty-two with which he is now credited. It was as a pianist rather than composer that Beethoven later realized his first successes as a musician—in 1792, after he had made his home permanently in Vienna.

These facts are not without significance, since they underline not only that the piano was Beethoven's instrument but how, from his beginnings, the piano dominated his musical career. With Beethoven, the piano almost appears as an extension of his physical being. Through it he gave voice to his rebellions, his independence of spirit, his inner conflicts, his stormy or resigned mood, and his most cogent thoughts. At the piano he would be in a kind of trance as he allowed his fingers to translate dreams and fantasies into tones. The keys of the piano helped unlock his soul. This expressivity is the reason why he had no equal in the art of extemporization. In the early 1800s pianists delighted audiences with spontaneous elaborations on some melodic theme. In this Beethoven was unique, as his contemporaries and rivals readily conceded. His rivals flaunted their technical powers and their astuteness in handling melodic material. But with Beethoven—as he permitted his imagination freedom —he laid bare his inner self. Of course, extemporization is spontaneous invention that dies after it has been heard. But we do have Beethoven's piano music—and, most significantly, his thirty-two piano sonatas—in which we find revealed every facet of Beethoven's personality.

His was, for his time, a new kind of piano performance, just as his was a new kind of piano writing. When Mozart played the piano, and wrote for it, he seemed to hear the sounds of the harpsichord reverberating in his inner ear. Beethoven thought and wrote exclusively in terms of the piano, whose range of sonorities and dynamics were at that time being continually extended. He was lavish with big sound effects and climaxes, rich harmonic colors, forceful dynamics—almost as if he were trying to make the piano into an orchestra.

When he improvised, his hands would rest on the keys awhile. He would then strike a few discords, sometimes playfully, sometimes in controlled rage. Then, once finding his theme, he would transport hearers with his musical wanderings, his cataclysmic power, his personal revelations. When he played his own formal compositions he would produce thunder and lightning with stormy passages. His fiery eyes blazed as he played. His strong, pockmarked face became disfigured, sometimes by anguish, sometimes by fury, sometimes by a beatific expression as if he had had a vision of a new world. His strong jaw seemed to jut out more noticeably than ever.

In his piano playing and in his piano writing he was the reflection of a new age, aflame with the spirit of revolution that had overturned France and whose impact was felt all over Europe. Beethoven was the true republican. He had absorbed the writings of Jean Jacques Rousseau, who had violently attacked oppression and inequality among men. Diderot's satire on contemporary society and his call for freedom struck a responsive chord with Beethoven. The old ways—with their glorification of nobility and aristocracy and the demeaning of human rights and decencies for the masses—were soon to be overthrown. Beethoven was the musical spokesman for the rebellion against the status quo.

But he was born and grew up in the aristocratic era to which Haydn and Mozart belonged and to which he, too, at first submitted. His birthplace was the German city of Bonn, on December 16, 1770. There his father, a chronic drunkard, was a singer in the choir of the elector. Raised as a musical prodigy by a ruthless, dictatorial parent who hoped

73

to reap a profit from his son the way Mozart's father had done, the child Beethoven was subjected to physical abuse and mental torture while receiving his early training at the piano. That Beethoven did not turn from music with disgust is only because he was born to create it. To survive he needed music, just as he needed food and air.

Though he made excellent progress with his piano studies, he was totally incapable of rivaling Mozart's spectacular musical feats or competing with Mozart's fetching personality and appearance. For the child Beethoven, like the later grown man, was awkward, uncouth, disheveled, even ugly. He completely lacked the charm that had been such a strong attraction of the child Mozart. Beethoven's father soon reconciled himself to the sorry truth that his son could not be converted into a profitable investment. Once this conclusion was arrived at, the father loosened his strangling grip on the boy, who now acquired a sensitive and sympathetic teacher in Neefe, the court organist. Neefe soon reported in a magazine that his pupil "plays the piano with wonderful execution."

Beethoven's earliest piano compositions are not music of consequence, for even in his creative precociousness Beethoven was no Mozart. But it was good enough to attract interest among some of the rich and powerful in Bonn. Count Ferdinand von Waldstein and Frau von Breuning became his patrons. The elector, who had appointed him assistant court organist in 1784, made it possible for young Beethoven to pay a brief visit to Vienna in 1787 and play for Mozart. Mozart was not overly impressed by Beethoven's compositions, which, truth to tell, were not outstanding. But when Beethoven improvised on a theme provided by Mozart, the latter exclaimed prophetically, "This young man will leave a mark on the world."

Back again in Bonn, Beethoven grew more ambitious in his compositions. Between 1783 and 1790 he wrote three piano quartets, a piano trio, music for a ballet, and two cantatas. Haydn, now advanced in years as well as fame, heard one of Beethoven's choral works and was impressed. He urged Beethoven to come to Vienna and be his pupil.

With funds provided by his patrons, Beethoven went back to Vienna in 1792, never again to return to Bonn. Determined to make his mark with Viennese nobility, to whom he came bearing letters of introduction, he bought a handsome coat, silk hose, shining boots, and a wig. Before long he abandoned these niceties, preferring to wear the pedestrian clothes with which he had come to Vienna, and to leave his disordered mane uncovered. This discard of aristocratic refinements in dress is symbolic. Already Beethoven was breaking with the customs of his time, ready to stand in open rebellion against a society glorifying aristocracy. This attitude is the basic reason why the few lessons he took with Haydn went so badly. Haydn belonged to and accepted the old order. Beethoven was a child of a new age. The two clashed continually.

This attitude of Beethoven's is also why, though the palace doors swung wide open to him and welcomed him in spite of his unsightly appearance and uncouth demeanor, he reacted with ill-mannered and hot-tempered responses. Convinced of his musical powers and certain of his artistic destiny, he felt he was the equal of kings and princes. He made it quite plain to Prince Josef Franz Lobkowitz, one of his earliest wealthy patrons, that their friendly relationship could continue only if the prince regarded him of "equal birth." Those whose standards of life and music he could not accept he openly scorned, however high their station. He demanded from nobility the same fierce belief in his genius that he himself had. "With men who do not wish to believe in me," he proudly told Prince Lobkowitz, "because I am yet unknown to universal fame, I cannot, and will not, associate." To Prince Karl Lichnowsky, another Viennese patron, he said arrogantly, "You are only a prince. I am Beethoven." No musician before him had ever dared thus to throw the glove of defiance in the face of aristocrats and aristocratic patronage. But the more perceptive among the noblemen—Prince Lichnowsky, Prince Lobkowitz, and, most of all, Archduke Rudolph—tolerated Beethoven's tempers, pride, and impudence because they sensed that Beethoven had not overestimated himself. They came back to him after each of his stormy moods and insults to offer faith, love, and financial support.

Already in 1793 the newspapers in Vienna were saying that Beethoven was "beyond controversy one of the foremost piano players." Beethoven was a sensation when he made his first public appearance, at a concert for charity in 1795. "He is a giant," said one of the critics, referring to Beethoven's pianism and not to Beethoven's music, even though the program included one of Beethoven's first two piano concertos. Carl Czerny said, "Nobody equaled him in the rapidity of scales, double trills, skips." And here is how Czerny described Beethoven's extemporization: "Apart from the beauty and originality of the ideas there was something extraordinary in the expression." Bravura, virtuosity, domination over the keyboard, character, feeling, anger, poetic insight —all this Beethoven brought to his piano playing.

And all this he would eventually bring to his compositions, but for a while—like a child clinging to his parents for protection—he looked backward rather than forward, and wrote in accepted and traditional   75 styles. He did so in the six minuets for piano he wrote in 1795 (published long afterward as op. 167), which are deserving of mention because the second of these, in G major, is possibly the most famous minuet ever written. (It has been transcribed for every possible instrument or combination of instruments.) He did so in his early chamber music: the wind Octet in E-flat major, op. 103 (two oboes, two clarinets, two bassoons, and two horns), in 1792; and the Septet in E-flat major, op. 20 (for clarinet, horn, bassoon, violin, viola, cello, and double bass) (1799–1800); the Sextet in E-flat major, op. 81b, for two horns and strings (1795) and wind Sextet, also in E-flat major, op. 71 (two clarinets, two bassoons, and two horns), in 1796; and his first published work, a set of three piano trios, op. 1 (1795). And he did so again in the first three of his thirty-two piano sonatas, gathered in op. 2 (1796). In spite of his former sharp differences with Haydn in their teacher-student relationship (had he not said that "although I had some instruction from Haydn I never learned anything from him"?), Beethoven dedicated these, his first adult sonatas, to the master whose music he had always admired and from which he had so greatly profited in his earlier years. While in Beethoven's first sonata, in F minor, the composer leans for support on Carl Philipp Emanuel Bach, in the next two (A major and C major) the influence of Haydn is unmistakable.

Beethoven had also learned many a lesson from the music of Muzio Clementi (1752–1832), whose sixty or more solo sonatas and sonatinas have since become so valuable as instruction material for young pianists. (A sonatina is a miniature sonata. It is less ambitious in structure and requires only a modest technique for performance.) True, Clementi never had the powerful originality or the vast invention of either a Haydn or a Mozart. But the clarity of Clementi's sonata form, the precision of his technique, the neatness of his keyboard writing were things Beethoven emulated in his earliest piano works. Beethoven's two simple sonatinas, op. 49 (1796), are particularly derivative of Clementi, who had been one of the first composers to write piano sonatinas.

Before the century had ended—in the year of 1798—Beethoven wrote his first piano sonata in which derivative influences begin to dissipate at the touch of his forceful personality. It is the Sonata in C minor, op. 13, to which Beethoven himself gave the title of *Pathétique* (*Pathetic*). Here the brooding melancholy occasionally encountered in the slow movements of some of his earlier sonatas (and with particular poignancy in the Sonata in D major, op. 10 no. 3) develops into an anguish whose presence is instantly felt in the introductory slow and somber section of the first movement. Ever-changing dark chromatic chords give suggestions of discord and unrest. Once this solemn introduction is over, Beethoven allows his turbulent emotions to spill over into an electrifying Allegro. Sobriety returns in the second movement, but more in a mood of reflection than pain, but the restlessness of the first movement stirs anew in the concluding rondo.

A visit to Berlin in 1796 led Beethoven to write two sonatas for cello and piano for the king of Prussia (F major and G minor, op. 5), which Beethoven and the court cellist performed for the king at the royal palace. Beethoven here makes significant forward strides for solo cello music. Neither Haydn nor Mozart had written any music for cello and piano, though, of course, they did use the cello in chamber and orchestral music. Johann Sebastian Bach had written sonatas and suites for the unaccompanied cello, and so did several Italian composers who followed him. The most important cello music after Bach came from Luigi Boccherini (1743–1805), an outstanding cello virtuoso as well as a highly prolific composer. In his six cello sonatas—and in an excellent cello concerto (B-flat major), still very much alive in the symphonic repertory—Boccherini developed classical structures for the cello, and a style that was grateful to it, which helped to make it an important solo instrument. With Beethoven, the cello assumes even greater significance. It is true that, in his first two cello sonatas, Beethoven's writing for the cello is still elementary in performing techniques; he does not as yet comprehend what the instrument can do best. It would take Beethoven a dozen years more to write another cello sonata, but when he did so he created what is without doubt the greatest cello sonata up to that time.

More impressive than his first two cello sonatas are the first three he wrote for the violin and piano at about this time. They are found in op. 12 (D major, A major, and E-flat major) and were completed in 1797. Where in the cello sonatas the stringed instrument plays a subsidiary role to the piano, in the three violin sonatas the violin is given a more prominent assignment. There is a good deal of spirited virtuoso writing in these compositions, even though he still insisted on identifying them as "sonatas for piano and violin," instead of vice versa.

The year of 1800 was momentous for chamber music, for it was then that one of foremost composers of string quartets completed the first six of his sixteen string quartets. These six, op. 18—dedicated to Prince Lobkowitz—are called the *Lobkowitz* Quartets.

Time and again in the op. 18 quartets the rebel in Beethoven begins to oppose the older order. In his later masterworks, Beethoven favored using a brief fragment—a melodic phrase, or a rhythmic pattern—and building it to monumental proportions. He already did so in the first movement of his first quartet, in F major. A two-bar motive is used over a hundred times, but with all kinds of elaborations, amplifications, and transformations. On the listener the effect is like that of a hurricane compared to the gentle spring breeze of a Haydn or Mozart first movement. In this first quartet we also encounter Beethoven's tendency to sound a tragic note in his slow movements. In the brusqueness and virility of his scherzo movement, and in the energy of the finale, the giant is beginning to reveal his muscular strength.

The second quartet, in G major, has the name of *Komplimentierung* or *Compliments* because the main subject of the first movement has courtly grace. Beethoven's later tendency to brush aside convention makes itself felt in the way in which, unexpectedly, a scherzo section is introduced into the slow movement. The fourth quartet, in C minor, is also a departure from normal practice: a slow movement is dispensed with, since a scherzo is used as a replacement to separate the first movement from the minuet third movement. In the sixth quartet, B-flat major, the tragic muse in Beethoven once again comes into the spotlight in a short slow introduction to the finale, above which in the score Beethoven wrote *"La Malinconia"* ("Melancholy").

But there is nothing to suggest Beethoven the iconoclast in the graceful and pleasing music of the Septet in E-flat major, op. 20. This is a six-movement work in the light and charming style of the Baroque divertimento of Haydn or Mozart. This septet became very popular because in listening to it Beethoven's audiences were here traveling on familiar ground. It is typical of Beethoven that he should have deeply resented this success. Few were more critical in properly evaluating his own work than Beethoven.

Beethoven's creative life has been conveniently divided by historians into three periods. The first, the time in which he completed all the works described above, ended roughly in 1801. In this stage he was learning his trade, allowing himself to be influenced by the great composers who had preceded him, yet at the same time experimenting with ways and means of letting his own individuality express itself. After 1801 the voice that spoke his music and the hand that wrote it were those of Beethoven and Beethoven alone.

As a human being he changed greatly during this second period. As the years passed, and as he became increasingly assured of his creative powers, he grew prouder, more defiant, more rebellious. He had not only proved himself as a composer to himself (his severest critic) but to the marketplace as well. He had more requests from publishers than he could fill, and he was in a position to dictate the financial terms. Yet he knew—and he said so—that this was just the beginning. "I live only in music," he once said as he was passing on into this second creative period, "and I have scarcely begun one thing when I start on another." His now prodigious achievements made him intoxicated with life. "Oh, life is so beautiful," he exclaimed, "would I could have a thousand lives."

He was like a man possessed. He would move from one apartment to another as if driven by devils; sometimes he paid rent for three or four apartments at once. He looked like a wild man as, even in thunderstorms, he walked briskly through the Viennese forests he loved dearly, his hands clasped behind his back, his mind storming with musical sounds. He was completely indifferent to his appearance, which was untidy, just as he was little concerned with the state of disorder in his home. Only one thing concerned him: his destiny as a composer.

For a time it seemed that Fate would crush him completely. That sense most precious to musicians—hearing—was failing him. As early as 1800 he began to realize he was going deaf. By 1802 he knew that the world of sounds would forever be muted for him. He poured out his grief in a verbal document that was an agonized cry of despair—the *Heiligenstadt Testament,* written in the outlying Viennese district of Heiligenstadt where Beethoven was then living. Henceforth he would draw his will to live from work. He would *not* be defeated, he exclaimed again and again. He *would* fulfill the destiny for which he had been born. He was indeed (as Wagner once said of him) "a Titan wrestling with the gods." And so, forced by destiny to look inward, to find his inspiration in inner resources, he entered upon a new phase as composer, his second period. Deaf to the tones of other people's music—and incapable of physically hearing what he was scribbling on paper—he achieved an independence with which the art of music became permanently changed.

Lyricism as such, beauty of sound, elegance of form—these did not interest him. *His* music had to be the means of projecting mighty tonal dramas reflecting the storms that raged within him. It had to be able to give voice to abstract ideas. Beethoven felt the need to extend the expressiveness of music beyond that of the late Haydn and Mozart to a point where, without using a program, it would convey poetic concepts. He would build mighty monuments, starting out sometimes with one or two bricks or, to change the metaphor, the germ cell of a theme would evolve into a mighty living tonal organism. He had to work out his profound ideas and his overwhelming emotions within gigantic architectonic designs.

What acute, agonizing pains attended the birth of each of his masterworks! How long and hard did he labor on each composition to reach musical truth as he saw it! All this finds proof in the notebooks he kept through the years in which he stored musical ideas and motives, where he endlessly experimented with how best to make them effective. He would struggle with his thematic material for years until it acquired the form and shape that satisfied him. His sketchbooks are filled with numerous ways in which a theme could progress and the many different guises it could assume. Now we come upon one version, now another. Again and again Beethoven changed, revised, refined, eliminated, added —only to be still dissatisfied. The torment that went into this sustained creative process is revealed in the way those sketches appear to the eye: scratched-out phrases, crossed-out notes, sloppily superimposed notes, all an ugly angry mass of blots and blotches. The search ended, he would use his materials with a power and an exalted inspiration that were to make him the greatest dramatist and the greatest poet that instrumental music has known. His music projects tonal thoughts, ideas, and ideals—together with torrential emotions—hitherto unrealized even by the great Mozart, and since Beethoven probably never surpassed.

As we pass into the second of Beethoven's three periods we are entering a new world of music, for Beethoven had made a leap from Classicism toward the Romantic future. What an amazing output sprang from this second period! Symphonies, concertos, overtures, and the opera *Fidelio* were supplemented by his wonderful quartets and sonatas. To chamber music he added the three string quartets in op. 59, the op. 74 and op. 95, and the two piano trios, op. 70. For the piano other towering masterworks are found, including the *Moonlight, Waldstein,* and *Appassionata* sonatas. For violin and piano he wrote the *Kreutzer* and the G major sonatas; for cello and piano, the A major Sonata.

The first of Beethoven's piano sonatas of interest during this second period was also the first one ever to use a funeral march as one of its movements. This is the Sonata in A-flat major, op. 26 (1801), for piano. The funeral march appears as the third of four movements, its heading bearing the words "For a dead hero." This funeral music—a slow, stately melody accompanying a procession, the music soon imitating the sounds of drum rolls and cannon shots—has been transcribed both for the orchestra and for the band.

To the general music world possibly no sonata by Beethoven is more beloved than the so-called *Moonlight:* the Sonata in C-sharp minor, op. 27 no. 2 (1801). It was not Beethoven but a German critic who contrived the title of *Moonlight* for this music, because the tranquil melody of the first movement over accompanying triplets in the bass brought to the critic's mind the picture of moonbeams streaming across a lake. Beethoven himself designated this work as a sonata *"quasi una fantasia"*— "somewhat like a fantasia." He did so because the first movement has a fantasia-like character, is not in the sonata form, and is in a slow rather than fast tempo. The romantic nature of this first movement has tempted some Beethoven authorities to suspect that this music was a love offering from Beethoven to the Countess Giulietta Guicciardi, to whom he dedicated the work. The tranquillity of the first movement yields to delicacy in the second movement and to violent outbursts in the finale.

The Sonata in D major, op. 28 (1801), was given by a publisher the name of *Pastoral*—with good reason. Its first and last movements are bucolic—reflections of Beethoven's profound love of nature. This is a four-movement work whose second movement has a solemn beauty and whose third movement is a scherzo with some humorous implications and with a waltzlike melody as its principal subject.

With the Sonata in D minor, op. 31 no. 2 (1802), Beethoven's tempestuous nature begins to erupt more forcefully than ever before. Beethoven controls the storm for just a measure and a quarter in the introductory Largo before he permits it to break loose. The same kind of upheaval is experienced in the last movement, in which a four-note motive from which the main theme is derived is believed to have been suggested to the composer by the sound of galloping horses. The other side of Beethoven's dual personality—the meditative and the poetic—appears in the slow movement.

By 1804 Beethoven had to accept the grim truth that he would be deaf for the rest of his life. He was tossed back and forth between defiance and rage against an implacable fate and resignation to the inevitable. This struggle, alternating with resignation, are the hallmarks of his Violin Sonata in C minor, op. 30 no. 2 (1802), and even more strongly of the two greatest piano sonatas of his middle period: the Sonata in C major, op. 53, and the Sonata in F minor, op. 57, both of which were composed around 1804. The first is dedicated to one of Beethoven's benefactors, Count von Waldstein, and is called the *Waldstein* Sonata; the other has acquired the name of *Appassionata* because of its passionate moods. Both are mighty tonal dramas for the piano. The *Waldstein* opens with a towering rage. Here the music seems to be repeating in tones what Beethoven had then put to words: "I will seize Fate by the throat!" But Beethoven also said, "Plutarch taught me resignation," and so once the passions have been dissipated, there comes a resting point with a hymn-like passage. The slow movement is the voice of a man who has found peace with himself, a three-part song in an exalted mood. Beethoven had originally completed a different slow movement for this sonata, but discarded it because he found it too slight and superficial to be placed between the epic flanking movements, the last of which generates the same motor energy and releases the same strength and power we find in the first movement. The discarded movement was published independently as *Andante favori,* in F major, op. 170.

Beethoven's tendency to build mighty musical schemes out of germinal thematic ideas recurs in the *Appassionata* Sonata, where the first three notes of the theme with which the work opens reflectively become the nucleus of a grandiose movement. It is interesting to recognize that the background of this opening reflective theme are four notes in the bass, not much different from the celebrated four notes that open the Fifth Symphony. That four-note motive must have meant much to Beethoven. We find it scrawled through the pages of his notebooks with numerous changes; now we encounter one version, now another. He used it not only in the Fifth Symphony and the *Appassionata* Sonata but also in the opening phrase of his Piano Concerto no. 4 and in the String Quartet, op. 74. In all probability this terse, spirited statement was Beethoven's proclamation of defiance against a fate dooming him to permanent deafness.

The forces of conflict that sweep like a whirlwind through the opening of the first movement of the *Appassionata* arrested by a chorale-like theme. A rapturous melody in the second movement receives variations, the melody being repeated after the variations are over. Violent chords introduce a febrile finale, which before the end of the sonata lapses into resignation with a new hymn-like theme in the minor mode.

In writing for the piano, Beethoven did not concentrate exclusively on the sonata. In spite of the fact that his mighty brushstrokes called for large canvases, he did manage to sketch out some delightful small pieces. It was with Beethoven that the form of the bagatelle became prominent. The word *bagatelle* means "a trifle," and a piece of music with the designation of bagatelle is an unpretentious little composition, slight both in form and in content. Beethoven wrote twenty-seven such pieces. He first used this form in his *Seven Bagatelles,* op. 33, which he completed in 1802. As late as 1823 he was still writing music in this form (op. 126). Beethoven's bagatelles belong with the literature used to train young pianists. None of these is more often utilized than the one named *Für Elise* (*For Elise*), op. 173 (1810). Other little pieces by Beethoven include seven *Écossaises*—a dance in 2/4 time—also twelve *Contratänze* (Country Dances), some little waltzes, and some rondos.

With the Sonata in A major for cello and piano, op. 69 (1809) we come upon Beethoven's first masterwork for cello and piano. This sonata begins with a passage for the cello unaccompanied, almost as if Beethoven were determined here and now to proclaim the full emancipation of this instrument. From then on in the sonata, and most especially in the brief, undeveloped Adagio cantabile that serves as a substitute for the usual slow movement, the mellow voice of the cello is allowed to sing out fully and richly.

It took Beethoven six years after that to return to the cello. In 1815 he completed his last two cello sonatas, the C major and D major, op. 102. The slight departure from structural norm that had characterized the mighty A major Sonata becomes even more prominent in the C major. There are only two movements, each preceded by a thoughtful slow preface. The material is treated in a rhapsodic manner. The D major is in three movements, with the middle Adagio being the only fully evolved slow movement encountered in any of his cello sonatas—a tender interplay between the cello and piano. In these two sonatas, as in the A major, the writing for the cello is masterful.

The most favored of the ten sonatas for violin and piano by Beethoven is that in A major, op. 47 (1803), dedicated to a distinguished violin virtuoso of Beethoven's time, Rudolph Kreutzer (the reason why this work is called the *Kreutzer* Sonata). So advanced is the style and technique of this masterpiece that Kreutzer refused to play it, insisting that the music was "outrageously unintelligible." It is the only Beethoven violin sonata opening with a slow, contemplative introduction before nervous energy is allowed to erupt. The second movement is a theme and variations, the theme being an elegant melody which repeatedly changes character like a chameleon in the ensuing variations, as now the violin and now the piano attracts central interest. There is such stirring theatricalism in the finale that it inspired Russia's great writer Leo Tolstoi to write a story of passion and jealousy that he called *The Kreutzer Sonata*.

Beethoven's last violin sonata was that in G major, op. 96 (1812). The passions of the *Kreutzer* Sonata give way to a delicacy of style, a lightness of touch, and subdued emotions. The music sounds as if the composer were having an intimate conversation with his audience.

If we were to try to put a finger on the one attribute above all others that sets Beethoven's music apart from that of his predecessors or contemporaries, we would have to select his capacity to make abstract music express to an unusual degree ideas and ideals, soul states, poetic concepts. With Beethoven, music becomes far more than beauty of sound or expression of emotions; it has been transfigured into experiences of the soul.

The above holds true for all of Beethoven's masterworks beginning with those of his second creative period, but particularly so for his string quartets, into which he seemed to pour his noblest thoughts and highest spiritual values. We need but listen to the slow movements of the Quartet in F major, op. 59 no. 1, and the Quartet in E minor, op. 59 no. 2, to understand what Beethoven's friends meant when they said that when the creative spirit moved him he entered into a kind of *"raptus"*— rapture or ecstasy. These quartets are two of three collectively known as the *Rasumovsky* Quartets (1806), written on a commission from Count Rasumovsky, the Russian ambassador to Austria. In all three quartets there is a new-found freedom of expression, a new kind of expressivity that justifies the composer's remark that this was music "for a later age." In none of his other music of this period (be it for orchestra, for piano, or for solo instrument and piano) was he more personal, more subtle, and more revelatory.

Because he wrote these quartets for a Russian, Beethoven introduced in two of the three works Russian melodies. All the movements of the first quartet are in the sonata form, with a Russian melody entering in the finale. The Russian element intrudes into the second quartet, where, in the trio part of the scherzo, Beethoven quotes a folk tune which that later Russian master, Mussorgsky, quotes in his folk opera *Boris Godunov*. The third quartet, in C major, has such dramatic power that it has won the sobriquet of *Heroic*. Here one of the high points of musical interest comes in the fugue of the finale, where polyphonic writing seems to reflect and interpret, to borrow a statement by musicologist Paul Bekker, "the occurrences of a world far removed from actuality, a world

. . . which is an abstract representation of an actual region of the intellectual and emotional life."

Beethoven's chamber music masterworks of this second period include two piano trios, D major and E-flat major, op. 70 (1808), his first compositions for the combination of piano, violin, and cello in several years, and the Piano Trio in B-flat major, the *Archduke,* op. 97 (1811). The last, dedicated to the Archduke Rudolph, is the greatest of the three. Here, too, as in the slow movements of the first two *Rasumovsky* Quartets, Beethoven enters an awesome world of the spirit, for example in the tender melody for the piano with which the first movement opens and in the exalted religious character of the third movement, a sublime melody followed by five variations.

Two sonatas for cello and piano, C major and D major, op. 102 (1815), are the only significant works completed between the years of 1813 and 1816. The prodigious output of the preceding decade had come to a halt. Some writers try to explain this sudden drying up of Beethoven's creativity by the unhappy circumstances then surrounding his personal life. His deafness made it impossible for him to appear in public any longer as a pianist in his compositions. He had also withdrawn himself completely from the social world. Emotionally parched by his failure to find a woman to share his life, he committed to paper an anguish that tears the heart of the reader, a document now described as Beethoven's "letter to the immortal beloved." He secreted it in a hidden desk drawer and not until after his death was it discovered. Who his "immortal beloved" was and precisely when the document was written are matters that have long encouraged conjecture.

In addition, during this period, Beethoven was harassed by legal complications brought on by his insistence on trying, after his brother's death, to adopt his nephew over the boy's and his mother's protests. Victorious in court, Beethoven found himself defeated in his own home, for the nephew turned out to be a thorough wastrel.

Crushed by mounting pressures and frustrations, Beethoven became more disagreeable and unreasonable to friends, more volatile in his moods, more irrational in his behavior than ever. He drove away one of his closest friends over a trifle, even though that friend had only recently nursed him through a serious illness. In a café, when a waiter brought Beethoven a dish he had not ordered, Beethoven hurled the food at the waiter's head while screaming insults.

Yet the temptation to blame Beethoven's temporary musical silence between 1813 and 1816 on his personal problems and outside influences should be scrupulously avoided. Never before had his despair, tragedies, frustrations, and disappointments in life and love stultified his inspiration. Closer to the truth lies the belief that, having expended such Herculean efforts in composition between 1802 and 1813, his musical resources needed a temporary quiescent period for revitalization and regeneration.

And how revitalized, how regenerated they became! After 1818, Beethoven's creative strength was renewed, his imagination inflamed, his powers extended. He now entered upon the third and last period of his career as composer. It was as if he was reborn—so different now was the music he wrote. The former angry thunder is more often than not replaced by philosophic or religious meditation. His writing is less personalized than that of his second period, more abstract, and certainly more elusive to comprehend. An other-worldly calm and a new kind of spirituality enter his music, as more than ever before he shatters whatever structural limitations and rules impede the flow of his thoughts.

His music is now the voice of one who has visions of a wondrous new world. Upon the perceptive listener it comes as a kind of revelation to which words can never provide an altogether satisfactory interpretation. More and more revolutionary do his methods become. The music of this last period is filled with strange progressions, iconoclastic harmonic textures, startling modulations, stark intervals, harsh accents. Theme breaks in on theme; fragments of themes follow one another, varied, transformed, willfully interrupted, recalled. The old standard type of coherence is abandoned for a more subtle and a more vague type of unity. For its time, this represented anarchy; for a much later generation it brought visions and dreams divorced from actuality.

Beethoven entered upon his third period with the Sonata in A major, for piano, op. 101 (1816). This work is the first of Beethoven's last piano sonatas, the other four being the B-flat major, op. 106 (1818), the E major, op. 109 (1820), the A-flat major, op. 110 (1821), and, last of all, the C minor, op. 111 (1822). In his manuscripts for two of these sonatas Beethoven uses the word *"Hammerklavier"* instead of "pianoforte." *"Hammerklavier"* is the German word for "pianoforte," but Beethoven had previously used the latter term. The reason for this change of terminology is that in the late 1810s a wave of Germanic nationalism flooded Austria. In this spirit Beethoven preferred a German word for the instrument for which he was writing these sonatas; he even used German tempo markings for his A major Sonata. The other four sonatas, however, revert to Italian markings.

The A major Sonata is dedicated to Baroness Dorothea Ertmann, a gifted pianist who was his close friend. She was the woman whom Beethoven comforted upon the death of her child—not only with words and physical gestures but also by sitting at the piano and playing for over an hour. "He told me everything," she later recalled, "and at last brought me comfort." Some see in the tenderness of the Adagio movement (marked "slow and full of feeling") Beethoven's recollection of this episode. This sonata is unusual in several respects. It is remarkably concise, the first movement extending for only two pages, while the third-movement Adagio is just nineteen measures long. Between the first and third movement comes vigorous march-style music. Another distinctive feature is its extensive use of polyphony. Canonic imitations are found in the trio section of the second movement; in the last movement, the opening theme provides the subject for a later four-voiced fugue. Something else sets this sonata apart from earlier ones. In the Adagio, Beethoven suddenly refers to the opening of the first movement.

Though two sonatas are written for the *Hammerklavier,* only one is actually named the *Hammerklavier* Sonata—the B-flat major. This is the most gigantic structure among the Beethoven sonatas—so huge in design, so spacious in line, so elaborate in its developments, and so orchestral in sonority that it has been called a "symphony for the piano." (Indeed, it has been transcribed for the orchestra where it *does* sound like a symphony!) Thunderous chords that open the work warn us of the cyclonic force that will soon be released. The adagio is the longest such movement Beethoven ever wrote, and one of the most soul-searching in his piano literature—filled with discords, changing tonalities, leaps from the lowest notes of the bass to the highest treble, all creating an almost intolerable tension. "The pain that tears the heart no longer has the word here," said the famous pianist-conductor Hans von Bülow of this music, "but—as it were—tearless resignation rigid as death." This regal work finds an appropriate crown. In the finale there first comes an expansive fantasia section; after that a three-voiced fugue is based on a eleven-measure subject; then a series of trills pierce through the surface of the listener's consciousness like an electric drill; finally a gentle melody brings solace, and resounding chords and trills, exultation.

The *Hammerklavier* Sonata is a mighty drama played on a giant stage. Both the E major and the A-flat major sonatas are of more modest dimensions, though the restless search for things of the spirit remains ceaseless. Beethoven's last piano sonata, in C minor, is among the noblest of the thirty-two. It has just two movements. The first has a majestic opening before an atomic explosion ensues, a climax being reached with a powerful fugue. The second movement, on the other hand, is a gentle Arietta, followed by variations, and ending with a surpassingly calm coda. The last word Beethoven spoke in his piano sonatas, then, carries the message of resignation and peace.

The C minor was Beethoven's last sonata, but it was not his last work for the piano. In 1823 he wrote the *Thirty-three Variations on a Waltz by Diabelli*, op. 120. Throughout his life, Beethoven had written many individual compositions for the piano using the form of theme and variations. This is the greatest of them all. Hans von Bülow said that "the whole image of the world of tone is outlined here, the whole evolution of musical thought and sound fantasy, from the more contained contemplation to the most abandoned humor—an unbelievably rich variety." The melody was of no great consequence, a little waltz tune by the Viennese publisher Diabelli. He submitted his piece to various composers (including Beethoven and Schubert), asking each to write one variation. He intended to publish all these variations as a single composition. Beethoven, however, refused to confine his invention to a single variation. He wrote thirty-three. In the last one he passes from a minuet to that abstract, remote kind of music that so characterizes the writing of his last period. He was thus reviewing his career as a composer for the piano in capsule form. Robert Schumann was convinced that Beethoven had intended this as a way of bidding his admirers farewell, that when he wrote this last variation, Beethoven knew that never again would he write anything for the piano.

Beethoven completed five quartets during this, his third and last creative period. As in his piano sonatas, totally new structural and technical procedures are introduced as the composer seeks to tap ever profounder, ever more poetic, ever more religious, and ever more philosophic veins of musical thought. There are here awesome pages that make us feel the composer has gazed into the infinite and has uncovered the mysteries of life and death: the mysticism of the theme and variations movement of the Quartet in E-flat, op. 127 (1824); the heavenly radiance of the Cavatina of the Quartet in B-flat major op. 130 (1825); the philosophic introspection of the slow fugue which opens the Quartet in C-sharp minor, op. 131 (1820); the religious fervor of the slow movement of the Quartet in A minor, op. 132 (1825).

In three of the five quartets, Beethoven abandons the four-movement format, to give more room for the outflow of his rapidly changing musical ideas. The Quartet in A minor has five movements; the Quartet in B-flat major, six movements; that in C-sharp minor, seven. The classic practice of presenting principal themes formally and then developing them gives way to a new method where one musical thought follows another in rapid succession, where one fragment is superimposed on another. Earlier concepts of lyricism make way for brusque statements, short revelations, themes with strange intervallic structures. All this and more—as J. W. N. Sullivan, a distinguished scientist who wrote penetratingly about music, explained—reaches "a state of consciousness surpassing our own where our problems do not exist and to which our highest aspirations . . . provide no key."

Beethoven must have been fully aware that with the Quartet in F major, op. 135 (1826) he was writing his last complete string quartet. Above the notes of the slow introductory theme of the finale he wrote: "Must it be?" And in the fast section he added, "It must be!" over the first principal theme.

The last music created by Beethoven, however, was not the op. 135 quartet but the finale of the op. 130. When he submitted the original version of the op. 130 quartet to his publisher, its last movement was a huge, complicated fugue. The publisher finally convinced Beethoven that music like this was much too difficult and abstruse to serve as the concluding part of a string quartet. Beethoven eventually wrote a new finale, the one that is now used when this quartet is played. The fugue was published separately as *Grosse Fuge* (*Great Fugue*) in B-flat major, op. 133. This is a giant work that begins with an "overture" and a variation of its motto subject, before the fugue itself—one of immense dimensions—is presented. The closing part of this work is a summation of the main ideas previously stated.

Death silenced Beethoven forever on March 26, 1827—much too soon when we remember he had not yet reached his fifty-seventh birthday but not soon enough to have kept him from scaling the Olympian heights of musical expressivity and thereby inaugurating a new age for music.

Inspired Romantics

Franz Schubert, Robert Schumann,

Felix Mendelssohn

The intensified dramatic and poetic expressivity that Beethoven brought to music marked the beginnings of musical Romanticism. During the Romantic era, subjectivity—the free expression of personal feelings—dominated musical composition. The Romantic composer was so concerned with the release of emotions that he did not permit the constrictions of form to arrest the tide. This subjectivity expressed itself in beautiful melodies, lyricism being a strong point with most of the Romantics.

The Romantic era gave new importance to the shorter forms of piano music (though the larger structure of the sonata was by no means neglected). New short forms were devised, suitable for the projection of the subjective sentiments and Romantic effusions. Some of these forms established a mood; some suggested a verbal or pictorial program; some bore descriptive titles; some were just casual items with no extramusical implications; some were in the style and idiom of folk dances. All this literature is grouped under the heading of "character pieces." Schubert wrote impromptus and *Moments Musicaux;* Mendelssohn, *Songs Without Words*. Schumann devised large forms in which a number of short character pieces, each carrying its own title, are bound together by a central nonmusical unifying subject. The writing of character pieces remained a major preoccupation of such other masters of Romantic piano music as Chopin, Liszt, and Brahms.

Beethoven was a pioneer in writing short pieces for the piano when he wrote bagatelles, Écossaises, and other trifles. These, by no stretch of the imagination, can be placed with Beethoven's important compositions. It was Franz Schubert who was destined to be the first composer to raise the short piece for the piano to a high artistic position. Schubert wrote larger works for the piano, too, including sonatas. But his work in piano music is predominantly within the shorter forms, including not only his six *Moments Musicaux* and eight impromptus, but also Écossaises, German dances, waltzes, Ländler (an Austrian peasant dance predating the waltz), minuets, and *Klavierstücke* ("piano pieces"). In addition, Schubert was the first composer to create important music for piano duet.

Above everything else he was the supreme genius of melody—the greatest composer of songs the world has known. Beautiful melodies spring from all his compositions, large and small, in a geyser eruption. This incomparable lyricism was responsible for making him such a remarkable creator within the shorter forms: melody, like a pure diamond, shines brightest in an unpretentious setting.

Whether in the shorter forms or the larger ones—whether in piano, orchestral, chamber, or vocal music—Schubert possessed a lovable charm uniquely his. It is a charm that is characteristically Viennese, best identified by the German word *Gemütlichkeit,* meaning a spirit of good feeling. After all, Schubert was the only one among the masters of classical music who was born and lived almost all his life in Vienna. He was Viennese through and through. The same qualities that so endeared the city of Vienna to the rest of the world overflow in his music. Vienna was a city of gracious living, filled with the zest that its citizens always brought to living. The warm, gentle breeze—called the *Föhn*—was sensuous, filling Vienna's air with intoxication. In the early spring (the carnival season) and the autumn, the spell of the *Föhn* was irresistible. The Viennese, of course, often knew the meaning of unhappiness, and often lamented his fate and cursed his luck. But then he would breath in the *Föhn* deeply, listen to the serenade music played in the streets or to the infectious popular music of the cafés, engage in flirtations and gossip, consume delectable Viennese food and drink, and come to realize that, after all, life was good. Thus, for every true Viennese, his city was a source of exhilaration. The Viennese coined a word characterizing life in Vienna: *Flott,* meaning zest, buoyancy, ebullience.

These two German words—*Flott* and *Gemütlichkeit*—are as good as any with which to describe Schubert's music, which is so identifiably Viennese. Except for those pages in which Schubert plunges to the depths of despair, his music is as light-footed as a Viennese waltz, as succulent as Viennese pastry, as full of the love of life as a Viennese carnival, as heady as Viennese May wine. And because he was Viennese, this kind of music could pour opulently from his ever-busy pen while he himself knew little else but poverty, frustrations, suffering and—in his last years—physical pain and despair.

He was born in the outskirts of Vienna on January 31, 1797. When he was eight he began taking lessons on the violin from his father, a schoolmaster who owned a schoolhouse. The father, marveling at the rapidity with which Franz learned music, soon had the boy study the piano with an older brother, Ignaz, and singing and counterpoint with a church choirmaster, Holzer. "When Franz had been studying the piano with me for barely a month," Ignaz recalled in later years, "he informed me he needed no more of my teaching and wished to get on by himself. And, indeed, he had made such progress that I was forced to acknowledge him a master who far surpassed me, and whom I could never hope to overtake." Holzer said, "If I wanted to teach him something new—he already mastered it. Consequently I could not give him any real instruction, but could only talk with the lad and quietly admire him."

Between 1808 and 1813 Schubert continued his music study at a seminary training boys as court singers. When he was thirteen he wrote his first composition: a fantasy for piano duet. A Mass followed. Now there came an onrush of compositions, including his first string quartet (1812). He finished one work after another with amazing speed. Ideas came to him quicker than his fingers could move to get them down on paper. One of his teachers at the seminary remarked, "I can't teach him anything. He's learned it all from God himself." During this period he wrote the String Quartet in E-flat major, op. 125 no. 1 (1813)—the first in which Schubertian charm and Schubertian lyricism is encased in a Haydnesque mold—and his first masterpiece in the song form *Gretchen am Spinnrade,* op. 2 (1814).

At this point the opus numbers attached to Schubert's compositions should be explained. With other composers, the opus number is usually an indication of the chronological order of a piece of music in a composer's overall output, but not so with Schubert. Schubert's opus numbers were added by publishers long after the composer's death and refer more to the order in which these works were published than when they were written.

For four years, between 1814 and 1818, he worked off and on as a teacher in his father's schoolhouse. Neither his heart nor his mind was on teaching. He neglected his students as he spent his time in class scribbling music notes on paper. Nothing outside composition seemed to interest him. Within an eight-day period in 1814 he completed the String Quartet in B-flat major, op. 168. In 1815 he wrote his ninth string quartet and two piano sonatas, together with numerous shorter piano pieces, two symphonies, and many songs, including the immortal "Erlkönig," op. 1.

He quit schoolteaching for good in 1818. Except for two temporary summer assignments as a piano teacher for the Esterházy family in Hungary, he never again held any kind of a job. An irresistible inner urge compelled him to dedicate himself entirely to music. Generous friends, who never wavered in their conviction that he was a genius, gave him a roof, food, spending money. Now he lived with one friend, now with another. He would start composing at six in the morning and continue without a break until noon, puffing at pipes as he wrote. When he finished a composition he played it for whatever friend was nearby. At praise his eyes would shine behind the eyeglasses that he wore constantly (even when sleeping), and his round, cherubic face would beam. He could finish the movement of a large work in a matter of hours, and a song or a short piece for the piano in the time it took him to scratch it out on paper. The American composer and musicologist Daniel Gregory Mason put it well when he said, "One rubs one's eyes. Compared with Schubert's pen, Aladdin's lamp seems a poor affair."

There were gay times, particularly during those evenings with his friends when he and others performed his compositions. These gatherings came to be known as *Schubertiaden* (Schubert evenings) because he and his music were the central points of attention and interest. The music over, Schubert and his friends (in true Viennese fashion) would drink wine or coffee, exchange light talk and jests, and indulge in pranks and games.

But as the years passed—and his manuscripts kept piling up to mountainous heights—there was also for Schubert much sadness. He could not ignore that he was entirely dependent on the charity of friends, incapable as he was of earning any money. The world outside his own immediate circle ignored his music shamefully. By the time Schubert was twenty-one, though he had already written some five hundred compositions, only three of them had been performed publicly, and these at unimportant places. Only one piece of music, the song "Am Erlafsee" had been published, and that only in a periodical.

When finally a few important performances of his music did take place, they failed to enhance either his reputation or his financial situation. Two stage works with his music were produced in 1820 in major theaters, and a third theater introduced his incidental music to the play *Rosamunde,* op. 26, in 1823. All three were failures, mainly due to the execrable texts for which Schubert had written his music. And when a volume of his songs appeared in 1821, it was only because several friends raised a subscription to pay for the printing.

His poverty, his inability to get a hearing, his failures all combined to bring on a gloom that darkened the remaining years of his life. "Each night when I go to sleep," he wrote to a friend, "I hope never to awaken, and every morning reopens the wounds of yesterday." Yet he kept on writing music of all kinds, his invention and imagination growing increasingly fertile. Not even the degeneration of his health in his last years could keep him from his work, with one masterpiece following another, each more wondrous than the other.

Just once did he know the sweet taste of success. An all-Schubert concert on March 26, 1828, excited the enthusiasm of a crowded auditorium and led critics for the first time to become aware of his greatness. But this victory came too late. His physical resources had been depleted. He died at his brother's home in Vienna on November 19, 1828. Just before his death he was feverishly putting the final touches on his last masterpiece, the lugubrious song cycle *Die Winterreise (Winter's Journey),* op. 89. Schubert's own winter journey was over.

In writing for solo piano, Schubert added nothing to keyboard technique, but he did contribute an incomparable wealth of the most tender and the most ingratiating melodies and sentiments, Viennese to the core. With the exception of several significant sonatas, his shorter works were his best.

Beginning with 1816, and continuing on for the next eight years, Schubert compiled practically a library of his waltzes, German dances, and Ländler. One facet of Romanticism in music was to seek out national sources for material. Schubert proved himself a legitimate child of musical Romanticism in these pieces, all rooted deeply in the soil of Austrian peasant and popular dance music. Schubert's greatest piano waltzes came late in life: the *Valses sentimentales,* op. 50 (1825) and the *Valses nobles,* op. 77 (1827). These are among the first compositions in which several waltz tunes are combined into a single integrated work. (The first such was Carl Maria von Weber's *Invitation to the Waltz,* for the piano, in 1819.) Weber and Schubert were the inspiration for Vienna's waltz kings—of whom Johann Strauss II was the most celebrated—when they wrote their waltz sequences for orchestra. In fact, the influence of Schubert's two waltz masterpieces penetrates right into the twentieth century, to reach Maurice Ravel, who used them as the source of inspiration and emulation for his own *Valses nobles et sentimentales.*

Schubert's best short pieces for the piano are the six *Moments Musicaux (Musical Moments),* op. 94, between 1823 and 1827, and the eight impromptus, op. 90 and 142, in 1827. Schubert invented the term *"Moment Musical"* for a brief, lyrical piece in song form. Each of his little pieces is a tonal delicacy, of which the highly popular one in F minor (the third in the set, sometimes labeled *"Air russe,"* or "Russian Dance") is characteristic.

An impromptu is a composition giving the feel of an improvisation, —music that seems to have been created spontaneously. It is also in the song form and highly melodic. Schubert was not the first composer to write impromptus, but he was the one who made this form famous in piano literature. The methods pursued by Schubert in his impromptus vary. Sometimes he begins with a declamation before presenting two melodies that are subjected to variations (C minor, op. 90 no. 1). Sometimes he is eloquently lyrical (G flat major, op. 90 no. 3). Sometimes he stresses virtuoso writing (F minor, op. 142 no. 4). One of his most highly esteemed impromptus is that in B-flat major, op. 142 no. 3, in which one of his heavenly melodies is followed by five variations. Schubert himself liked this melody so much that he had also used it in his incidental music to *Rosamunde* and in the slow movement of his A minor String Quartet.

It took Schubert a long time to achieve distinction as a composer of piano sonatas, of which he composed twenty-two. For a long time too he was dissatisfied with his sonatas. The first in which he liberated himself from the bonds that had tied him to Haydn and Mozart is his thirteenth, in A major, op. 120 (1819). It is a short work, and its structural dimensions are modest. But it is rich with lyricism, the soaring melody of the first subject in the opening movement spreading archlike over nineteen measures.

Few of Schubert's sonatas are performed frequently because more often than not his writing was diffuse, his sense of the sonata form weak, his ability to vary and develop his wonderful melodic material limited. Scale passages, chord sequences, changing dynamics are conveniences to bridge one melody to another, as a substitute for the expansion and transformation of material already used. These shortcomings tend to induce monotony, which is temporarily relieved only when a wonderful new melody springs to life. But with experience, Schubert learned to develop his harmonic writing, to pay increasing attention to rhythm, to achieve poignant effects through key changes. Such developments are met in the Sonata no. 17 in D major, op. 53 (1825) and the Sonata no. 18 in G major, op. 78 (1826).

Schubert's greatest piano sonatas are the three written in 1828, the last year of his life: the C minor, A major, and B-flat major (no opus numbers). By now he had learned from Beethoven how to build his melodic material into impressive structures; how to achieve expressiveness by means other than melody; how to be varied and expansive in his developments. He had learned to thunder as well as sing, and he could also whisper gentle confidences in exquisite *piano* or *pianissimo* sections. He was now able to be emotional as well as tender and charming, dramatic as well as whimsical. Like Beethoven he arrived at effective contrasts by passing from the sobriety of introspection and the poignancy of soul-searching to passionate outbursts and powerful thrusts. The leaping arpeggio figures and eruptions in the finale of the C minor Sonata, and the power that surged through the coda of the first movement of the A major; the mystery created in the first movement of the B-flat major and the violence erupting in the finale of this sonata—all this is more Beethovenian than Schubertian. But there is also a good deal of Schubert in these sonatas as well. Only Schubert could have fashioned the lyric line of the second theme in the first movement of the A major sonata and the poignant poem that unfolds in the slow movement of the B-flat major sonata, to mention only two of several melodic treasures.

Schubert produced another large work for piano, but in a form other than the sonata. It was the Fantasy in C major, op. 15 (1822), which bears the name of *Wanderer* because it makes such extensive use of the dark, haunting theme from the song of the same name (op. 4 no. 1, in 1816). This composition is in four extended sections played without interruption. The first part is in the sonata form, that is, it has a first and second theme, but without a recapitulation section; here the rhythmic pattern of the song is found in the main theme, while the second theme bears no relation to the song. In the second part a portion of the song is presented in modified form, sounding ominous with its dark-hued harmonies. To lighten the mood Schubert progresses in his third section to a scherzo, which begins with a bouncy tune, continues with another characteristically lighthearted Viennese melody, and concludes in the final section with a fugal episode on a subject based on the opening bouncy theme.

Schubert wrote much for piano four hands—that is, two pianists at a single keyboard—two compositions of which are among his keyboard treasures. The Sonata (or Duo) in C major, op. 140 (1824), bears the descriptive word *Grand* in its title, because it has such a symphonic breadth. (This sonata was orchestrated by the Hungarian violinist Joseph Joachim.) Mystery surrounds this composition. During a visit to Bad Gastein in Austria, Schubert wrote a symphony that has been lost; some musicologists suspect that this four-hand piano duo is Schubert's arrangement of this symphony. Most others, however, insist that this is not the case at all, that Schubert had always intended the sonata as a piano composition. In any event, as a composition for the keyboard, this sonata comes off with enormous effect through the richness of its sonorities, the fullness and variety of its harmonies, the magical effects achieved through modulations, and the richness of its lyric content. Such an evaluation can also be given to Schubert's wonderful Fantasy in F minor, op. 103 (1828), for piano four hands. In four movements, played without pauses, it opens with best foot forward with a melody of sweetness, purity, and enchantment unmistakably Schubertian and unmistakably Viennese. This melody recurs throughout the composition, heard for the last time in the final coda. The second movement is so romantic that the musicologist Alfred Einstein described it as a "declaration of love," without trying to identify for whom this declaration might have been intended.

A Schubert semi-classic that became famous in orchestral transcription is also for piano duet: the *Marche militaire* (*Military March*) in D major, the first of three marches in op. 51 (in or about 1826).

Of Schubert's sonatas for violin and piano, the one richest in melodic content and the most spacious in form is the A major, op. 162 (1817). Schubert never wrote a sonata for cello and piano. The one occasionally played by these two instruments was written not for the cello but for a now obsolete instrument with the strange name of "arpeggione." This is the Sonata in A minor (1824). An "arpeggione" is a six-string fretted instrument shaped like a guitar, but held between the legs like a cello, and played with a bow. It has rich mellow tones, much like the cello, for which Schubert's music is so admirably suited. The Spanish cellist Gaspar Cassadó provided this work with an orchestral accompaniment when he adapted it into a concerto.

With the exception of his tuneful Quintet in A major, op. 114 (1819), Schubert's greatest chamber music came at the end of his life. The A major Quintet calls for the unusual combination of piano, violin, viola, cello, and double bass—the only famous quintet to use a double bass. It is in five movements. In the fourth Schubert borrows the melody of one of his famous songs—*"Die Forelle"* (*"The Trout"*), op. 32 (1817)—as the subject for six variations; this explains why the quintet is nicknamed *Die Forelle*. Schubert wrote this work after having made a walking tour of the Steyr countryside in Austria. The joy these beautiful landscapes brought him is caught in this exuberant music, from the rippling arpeggio opening of the first movement through the Austrian and Hungarian folk-type melodies in the finale.

Schubert's three greatest string quarters came between 1824 and 1826. The A minor, op. 29 no. 1 (1824) is the only one of Schubert's quartets published during his lifetime. It is one of the most beautiful he ever wrote. The sweet sadness of his lyricism pierces the heart like a blade, particularly the glorious melody of the second movement (which, as we already remarked, Schubert also used for a piano impromptu and in his incidental music to *Rosamunde*). The D minor Quartet (1826—no opus number) is named *Der Tod und das Mädchen* (*Death and the Maiden*), a Schubert song of the same name (op. 7 no. 3, in 1817) being used in the second movement for variation treatment. This theme of struggle with death, which is the subject of the song lyric, seems to pervade the entire quartet; the shadow of death stalks menacingly through all four movements. The G major Quartet, op. 161 (1826), was Schubert's last string quartet. This, for the most part, is music of conflict rather than sorrow. In the slow movement the beatific mood is interrupted by two turbulent episodes.

Schubert's last chamber music works are his two piano trios—B-flat major, op. 99 (1826), and E-flat major, op. 100 (1827)—and the String Quintet in C major, op. 163 (1828). The piano trios are the only ones Schubert wrote. Each is a masterpiece, each boasts Schubert's incomparable melodies, seductive charm, and uncommon instinct for touching moments of magic through subtle changes of mood through dynamics or tonality. The B-flat major is the brighter-faced of the two; the E-flat major is the more solemn, particularly in its second movement, which

sounds like a funeral march, a condensed version of the melody of
which returns toward the end of the finale.

The String Quintet in C major is for the unusual combination of two
violins, viola, and two cellos, which has not been significantly used since
Schubert. This is one of the most tragic compositions in all chamber
music. From beginning to end it reflects the physical and mental torment
Schubert suffered in the last year of his life. So somber is this music that
it can well serve as Schubert's own requiem. The opening measures are
but the preface to a first movement filled with the most elegiac
sentiments—sentiments that plunge into dark despair in the grief-
stricken second movement. Only in the finale is there relief from mor-
bidity and pessimism. Suddenly, inexplicably, the music leaps spiritedly
and buoyantly. Having spoken of his despair, Schubert proved himself to
be the true and typical Viennese by recognizing that life must not be rejected, that it was still capable of bringing treasurable rewards.

Since Schumann belongs with the greatest masters in music, it is sur-
prising to find how circuitous a route he took before becoming a composer. Born in Zwickau, Germany, on June 8, 1810, the son of a
publisher-bookseller, Robert's first major boyhood interest was literature
(though he had begun to study music early). He devoured the Greek
classics and the Romantic poets. He formed a literary society of youngsters discussing great literature. Some of his own early literary efforts
were published.

Then it seemed he would become a lawyer. Upon completing his
high school education in 1828, Robert was driven by his strong-willed
and practical mother (his father was now dead) to enroll in the University of Leipzig for the study of law. By late 1829 Robert realized that
law was not for him, that more than anything else he wanted to become
a musician—specifically a piano virtuoso. He made his home with his
piano teacher, Friedrich Wieck. Determined to become the greatest pianist of his time, Schumann threw himself without reservations into piano
study. "I shall within six years be able to challenge any pianist," he
wrote to his mother in November of 1829. His teacher was equally optimistic. In 1830, Wieck wrote to Robert's mother: "I pledge myself to turn
him into one of the greatest pianists." In his impatience to develop his
digital technique he devised an artificial method for strengthening the
weak fourth finger, a process that brought on an incurable paralysis of
the hand. Schumann's hopes of becoming a world-famous pianist
crashed into ruins.

He could not abandon music; it had by now become the center of his life. It was at this juncture—in the year of 1832—that he decided to become a composer.

He had already published a highly talented work for the piano: *Abegg* Variations (or to give it its official title, the *Variations on the Name Abegg*), op. 1 (1830). Abegg was a young lady who had attracted Schumann's fascinated interest at a ball. It was for her that he wrote this work, which he dedicated to her. Schumann enjoyed musical anagrams: that is, taking the letters of somebody's name and translating the letters into musical tones that could be used as a melodic theme. The name Abegg lent itself readily for such a game, since each of the letters could be represented by a tone in the scale. Once he had transformed the girl's name into a musical theme, he used it for a melody, which then received several variations. With this, his first opus; Schumann already proved himself a pioneer.

Once he had surrendered his ambition to be a concert pianist, Schumann deflected his enormous drive and energies into composition. His next three opuses—all for piano—appeared in 1832: *Papillons* (*Butterflies*), op. 2, which must not be confused with a later and more celebrated piece of the same name that appears within the larger work *Carnaval; Études after Caprices by Paganini*, op. 3; and *Six Intermezzi*, op. 4.

Papillons—like so much Romantic music—was inspired by literature, in this instance a work by Jean Paul Richter, a distinguished German poet whom Schumann admired. In *Papillons* Schumann used a format that he would henceforth favor greatly and in which he would produce his greatest piano compositions: a large work which, like a mosaic, is formed from numerous small but related pieces. *Papillons* is made up of twelve numbers. It begins and ends with the same affecting melody. Several of the pieces describe a ball, which is why so many of Schumann's melodies are derived from Austrian or German peasant dances. In the finale Schumann quotes the *Grossvatertanz* ("Grandfather Dance"), a German dance tune popular in the seventeenth century.

In the *Caprices* Schumann made a brilliant adaptation of six *Caprices* for solo violin by Niccolò Paganini. (We shall have occasion to talk about these violin *Caprices* in a later chapter.) The *Six Intermezzi* are lyrical pieces in song form.

Schumann continued to write for the piano until 1853. All the while he became increasingly expansive in his structure, his techniques in writing for the piano became ever more exploratory, and the way he assembled his musical materials continually more adroit. The kind of subjects he selected for musical treatment was frequently unusual.

Schumann's first masterwork was the *Études symphoniques* (*Symphonic Études*), études in the form of variations, for piano, op. 13 (1834). This work is a huge one that makes exacting demands on both the technique and the musicianship of the performer. The work begins with a borrowed melody: a tune from a flute composition written by the father of a girl with whom Schumann had recently been briefly in love. The nine variations on this melody are in the style of études, since they explore technical capabilities of the keyboard while frequently changing the melody so radically that it is often not readily recognizable. Now from one element of his original theme, now from another, come wondrous new musical thoughts—at times powerful, at times poetic, at times brilliant. The finale is vigorous march music based on an air Schumann had lifted from an opera by Heinrich Marschner (1795–1861).

With *Carnaval* (*Carnival*), for piano, op. 9 (1835) we come upon another of those huge Schumann compositions pieced together with small numbers, each carrying a programmatic title. The whole work is unified by a central nonmusical theme. The unifying subject in this masterwork is revealed by the title, while a subtitle reads "Little scenes on four notes." The "four notes" are *A-S-C-H*—and thereby hangs a tale. Asch is a Bohemian town that was the birthplace of a girl who at that time was a friend of Schumann's. In German A-flat is represented by *As,* E-flat by *Es,* and B-natural by *H.* And so the four notes Schumann used are A-flat, E-flat, C, and B-natural, the musical equivalent of the letters *A-S-C-H.* He shapes these four notes into three different combinations, one or another of which provides the source material for the music of almost all of the principal motives in this composition. One section, *"Sphinxes"* (which is frequently omitted when *Carnival* is now performed), uses all three combinations.

The titles of each of the twenty-two pieces in *Carnival* indicate what nonmusical program the piece is describing. They are as follows: *"Préambule," "Pierrot," "Arlequin," "Valse noble," "Eusebius," "Florestan," "Coquette," "Réplique," "Sphinxes," "Papillons," "Lettres dansantes," "Chiarina," "Chopin," "Estrella," "Reconnaissance," "Pantalon et Colombine," "Valse Allemande," "Intermezzo Paganini," "Aveu," "Promenade," "Pause,"* and *"Marche des Davidsbundler contre les Philistins."*

An explanation of some of the above titles can provide some interesting facts about Schumann himself, his personal life, his interests, and his activities during the early 1830s.

The fifth and sixth numbers are respectively entitled *"Eusebius"* and *"Florestan."* These are names for imaginary characters Schumann invented to describe two facets of his own personality—his dynamic and passionate nature (Florestan), and his poetic, dreamy one (Eusebius). In *Carnival* these two sections are intended as a self-portrait. Schumann had previously used these two names as pen names for his critical writings in the *Neue Zeitschrift für Musik* (*New Journal of Music*), a music magazine that he and a few of his colleagues had founded in April of 1834 to promote progressive ideas in music, new music, and new composers. Schumann was its first editor; under him, the magazine became one of the most dynamic and penetrating music journals in Europe. It was here that Schumann, with remarkable perceptiveness, called attention to the genius of two then still young and unknown composers—Chopin and Brahms.

The young people who helped Schumann found this journal called themselves *"Davidsbundler"* or "Society of David." This brings us to the title of the finale of *Carnival*. *"Davidsbundler"* was formed to fight against corrupt and false musical standards, against all types of sham in music, and to fight vigorously for often iconoclastic ideas and for the highest ideals. These young musicians considered themselves, like David in the Bible, who had overcome Philistinism; they, too, intended to destroy musical Philistinism wherever it was encountered. In the march with which *Carnival* closes, Schumann forcefully proclaims the victory of his society in their struggle against false values in music and chicanery.

The twelfth and eighteenth parts are musical tributes to Chopin and Paganini, two musicians whom Schumann esteemed most highly. In *"Estrella,"* Schumann speaks of his love for Ernestine von Fricken, the young lady whose home, Asch, provided Schumann with the four notes of the three musical combinations in the *Abegg* Variations. Schumann's anticipation of his delight in being reunited with his beloved, after an absence, is suggested in *"Reconnaissance,"* which comes right after *"Estrella."* *"Chiarina"* is Clara, the daughter of Schumann's teacher, Wieck (*"Chiarina"* being Schumann's pet name for her). In 1835 Clara was only sixteen, but already deeply and completely in love with Schumann. Schumann then regarded her as only a sweet and lovable girl with an enormous talent for the piano; he could hardly have guessed in writing

"*Chiarina*" that before long he would become so emotionally involved with her that his love would create a volcanic eruption in his life.

About the other sections: the opening preamble is a picture of a carnival; "*Pierrot*" and "*Arlequin*" are two clowns popular at European masquerades; in "*Coquette*" Schumann presents a flirtatious girl to whom a young man responds sympathetically in "*Réplique*" ("Reply"); "*Papillons*" is a gossamer-like description of butterflies in flight; "*Pantalon*" and "*Colombine*" are characters from old Italian comedies; "*Valse allemande*" is a German waltz; "*Aveu*" ("Avowal") is a simply stated melody; "*Promenade*" is a slow waltz; and "*Pause*" is concisely written music.

The Fantasy in C major, for piano, op. 17 (1836) is in three extended sections played without pause. The first part, the fantasy, is passionate, though often relieved by moody sections. In commenting on this first part two years after its composition, Schumann wrote to his beloved Clara: "I do not think I ever wrote anything more impassioned. . . It is a profound lament about you. You can understand the Fantasy only if you transport yourself back to the unhappy summer of 1836 when I resigned you." The second part has the character of a brilliant and at times discordant march that calls for extraordinary technical resources on the part of the performer. Clara described this section as a "triumphal pageant of warriors returning from battle." The third part is a gentle nocturne, which is lifted to a climax only to subside once again into a revery.

Schumann wrote two charming sets of compositions for piano in which his childlike nature finds outlet. *Kinderscenen* (*Scenes from Childhood*), op. 15 (1838), is not music for children, but music *about* children. It has thirteen sections, the most famous of which is "*Träumerei*" ("Dreaming"). "*Ritter vom Steckenpferd*" ("The Rocking Horse Knight") is also a great favorite, delightful for its offbeat melody and syncopations.

Album für die Jugend (*Album for the Young*), op. 68, came a decade later. Here Schumann was writing the kind of music that youngsters can easily appreciate and in which they can find their own experiences reflected. There are forty-three numbers in this set. These are the best known: "*Soldatenmarsch*" ("Soldier's March"), "*Wilder Reiter*" ("Wild Horseman"), "*Canonisches Liedchen*" ("Canonic Song"), "*Erinnerung*" ("In Memory"), and "*Kriegslied*" ("War Song"). If "*Canonisches Liedchen*" has a very familiar ring to it, it is because it has the same melody as "Three Blind Mice." "*Erinnerung*" is a touching elegy for

Mendelssohn, written on the day of that composer's death. The most popular piece in the entire set is *"Fröhlicher Landmann"* ("The Happy Farmer"), familiar to just about everybody who has studied the piano.

In 1838 Schumann completed the second and most frequently heard of his three sonatas for the piano: the G minor, op. 22. It has a tempestuous first movement (Florestan once again!), into which the more placid character of Eusebius intrudes. The lyrical second movement is an adaptation of one of Schumann's art songs, written a decade earlier, *"Im Herbste"* ("In Autumn"). The third-movement Scherzo is unusual in that it offers a theme of three phrases, each with a different beat. The finale is an electrifying Presto.

Between the years of 1832 and 1840, when he completed his greatest compositions for the piano, Schumann often suffered severe emotional disturbances, which, at times, threatened to destroy him completely. An imbalanced nervous system and neuroticism brought on fainting spells and melancholia. In the fall of 1833 he tried to commit suicide by jumping out of the window. After that he kept moving from one apartment to another in a feverish search for a setting where he could find tranquillity. A room in a little red cottage, from whose windows he could see the distant woods, seemed to provide the answer in 1836, for he stayed there four years, except for the winter of 1838–39, which he spent in Vienna. But tranquillity had to come from within himself and not from conditions around him, and that inner peace he seemed incapable of finding. According to his diary he had a fear of going mad.

In his relationships with his musician friends he went to extremes. Those times when he participated in their conversations, he would become loud, aggressive, combustible. But most of the time he was completely withdrawn. His delicate, effeminate face would become totally expressionless; a vacant look dimmed his blue eyes. He was looking inward, not outward. At such times he became easily upset by noise, loud conversation, and the thick smoke from cigarettes.

Between 1836 and 1840 his suffering was particularly agonizing, for this was the time of his stormy courtship of Clara Wieck, the girl with whom he was now as hopelessly in love as she with him. What stood in the way of their romance was the ruthless, indomitable will, and malice of Clara's father. Clara was on the eve of celebrity as a concert pianist. Father Wieck would not let anything stand in the way of her career. Besides, having Clara married to an impoverished, high-strung composer was unthinkable. Wieck used every conceivable maneuver to keep the lovers apart—and, for the most part, succeeded. For four years, some brief clandestine meetings between Clara and Robert, and some stealthily exchanged love letters, brought Schumann brief moments of ecstasy. But for the most part he experienced only the black despair of separation, and the tortured fear that Clara would never be his. Finally, Schumann went to the law courts and won the legal right to make Clara his wife. They were married on September 12, 1840.

A few years of wonderful happiness now dispelled the gloom that had formerly surrounded him. Schumann became creatively more productive than ever, venturing into areas of composition he had formerly barely if ever touched: symphonies, chamber music, songs, the piano concerto, the cello concerto, among many other compositions, some of which were still for solo piano.

After having occupied himself primarily with piano music up to 1840, Schumann then took up a different branch of music each year, exhausting for himself its possibilities before turning to a new area a year later. In 1840 his main output was in the field of songs. In 1841, he concentrated on orchestral music. In 1842, he turned to chamber music. The chamber music year brought three string quartets (completed within the period of a few weeks), the piano quintet, and the piano quartet.

In his chamber music, even more than in his works for the piano, he was a lyric poet who projected sensitive moods and delicate effects. His supreme contribution was the Piano Quintet in E-flat major, op. 44, the first major work to combine the piano with the string quartet. This composition opens strongly, but melancholia begins to seep through the first movement, becoming particularly expressive in the elegiac second theme shared by cello and viola. More elegiac still is the second movement, which sounds like a funeral march. Restrained vigor is found in the third-movement scherzo, though a somber mood is injected into the first of the two trios. The energetic finale takes its subjects from the main theme of the first and fourth movements and includes a brilliant fugal episode.

The three string quartets, op. 41, are in A minor, F major, and A major. The third is played most often. This work is novel for the way in which Schumann emphasizes an interval, or two intervals, in each of the four movements. When you listen to the introspective introduction and to the first theme, you will detect the frequent use of the interval of a descending fifth. The fourth is prominent in the agitated theme of the second movement, which is then carried through several variations. In the third movement, the emphasis is on the interval of the seventh, and in the finale, on descending sixths.

The Piano Quartet in E-flat major, op. 47, is a more powerful and optimistic work than the Piano Quintet. There are sweeping climaxes in the first movement, while in the second (a scherzo) an energetic staccato phrase is effectively used as a transition to each of the virile sections. The most appealing movement, however, is the third, whose strong romantic feeling leads us to suspect that it was inspired by his love for his wife. Just at the end of this slow movement there appears a subject that prepares us for the principal theme of the finale.

Though 1842 was basically Schumann's chamber music year, he completed several more such works in the ensuing decade or more. In 1847 he wrote two piano trios (D minor, op. 63, and F major, op. 80), and in 1851, a third one (G minor, op. 110). The best of these is the first, which Schumann wrote as a birthday gift to Clara. With the exception of the finale, this is a work suffused with melancholy. The *Fantasiestücke,* op. 73 (1849), for clarinet (or violin or cello) and piano, and the three lovely *Romances,* op. 94 (1849) for oboe and piano, are the first compositions by a major composer for each of these instruments and piano. Two fiery violin sonatas—the A minor, op. 105, and the D minor, op. 121—both are Schumann's last completed chamber music compositions (1851). Both continually reflect the inner turmoil that was then tearing Schumann apart, and drawing him to the abyss of disaster.

For Schumann had been edging toward disaster as early as 1832, but approaching it in 1844, when he showed signs of lapses of memory. In 1850 he was made the musical director of the city of Düsseldorf, which required him to conduct orchestral concerts. His nervousness was now reaching such epidemic proportions, and his mental disintegration was growing so marked, that he was compelled to give up the post in 1853 at the discreet suggestion of his employers. His mind was beginning to give way. Musical tones rang in his head. He was convinced that the great composers of the past were visiting him to dictate new compositions. One winter evening he tried to commit suicide by plunging into the icy waters of the river Rhine. He had to be placed in an asylum in Endenich, near Bonn, where he spent his last two years. Most of this time he was hardly aware of where he was or what was happening to him. He was continually haunted by fantasies and strange visions. He died in his sleep in the asylum on July 29, 1856. "And thus, with his departure," Clara wrote in her diary that day, "all my happiness is over."

Felix Mendelssohn (1809–47) was Fate's favorite child. Life showered on him all the blessings it could gather. Mendelssohn was born to wealth and culture. From his childhood he was physically attractive. He never lacked for love, recognition, or fame. He never knew the meaning of frustration, disappointments, struggle. He did die young (is it not said that this is the fate for those whom the gods love?)—but not before he had fulfilled himself as a composer, conductor, pianist, the founder of a great conservatory, teacher, husband, and human being. The tranquillity, the aristocratic breeding, the immaculate taste of his best music reflects the good life he led.

His piano music is as distinguished as that for orchestra, for chorus, and for voice. Though he was not a concert pianist, his public appearances being confined to the presentation of his own music, he was an elegant performer with exquisite refinement. His touch was light, his phrasing sensitive, his technique facile, his passage work clear and precise, his pedaling discreet. "His fingers sang over the keyboard," remarked one of his contemporaries. The qualities that went into the makeup of the pianist are those that distinguish the composer for the piano. His fingers sang as his pen raced across the manuscript paper.

He was the true Romantic in his short pictorial or programmatic pieces. The most famous are gathered in a series of eight volumes, all called *Lieder ohne Worte* (*Songs Without Words*), which contain forty-eight pieces (op. 19, 30, 38, 53, 62, 67, 85, and 102), the first volume completed in 1829 and the last in 1845. Mendelssohn invented the term "Song Without Words" for a piano piece that is so lyrical that it is virtually a wordless song. These pieces make no pretense at being anything but what Mendelssohn had intended them to be: small, slight items of no great musical consequence but providing pleasurable listening experiences. Some pieces are descriptive, some sentimental, some atmospheric, some whimsical. Most are in a moderate tempo and traditional in harmonic and tonal language. Many bear titles indicating the subject being interpreted. Only four of these titles were concocted by the composer: the three Venetian "Gondola Songs" and the *"Duetto."* All other titles were invented by publishers.

Surely the most popular piece in this collection is that perennial favorite, "Spring Song" in A major, op. 62 no. 6 (1842) one of the most familiar tonal pictures of the vernal season for the piano. Other delightful and well-known pieces are the "Hunting Song" in A major and the Venetian "Gondola Song" in G minor, in op. 19 (1829); the love song *"Duetto"* in A-flat major in op. 38 (1836); "May Breezes" in G major (1844) and the Venetian "Gondola Song" in A minor (in or about 1843), both in op. 62; the "Spinning Song" in C major in op. 67 (1843); the "Elegy" in D major in op. 85 (1845); and the "Tarantella" in C major in op. 102 (1845).

Mendelssohn had a particularly delicate touch in writing scherzos or scherzo-like music—music that moves gracefully on its toes and seems as if it were written as dance music for elves, spirits of the forests, and other members of fairyland. His supreme achievements in such a style are the third movement (marked Allegro leggierissimo) of his Octet in E-flat major, for strings, op. 20, which he wrote when he was only sixteen; the gossamer music of the Overture to *A Midsummer Night's Dream* for orchestra, op. 21, which came just one year after that; and the orchestral Scherzo in 1842 written as part of the incidental music to *A Midsummer Night's Dream,* op. 61. Mendelssohn also carried this gift for scherzo writing into some of his piano works, most significantly to the *Rondo capriccioso* in E major, op. 14 (about 1824). The fleet, mercurial Capriccioso is, however, preceded by a broadly lyrical Andante.

The deftness of his scherzo writing represents the Romantic facet of Mendelssohn's creativity. But Mendelssohn was also very much of a classicist who favored Baroque and Classical forms and styles. He had always, for example, been a profound admirer of Johann Sebastian Bach, with some of whose works he had become acquainted in his boyhood. It should always be remembered that by no means the least of Mendelssohn's achievements as conductor was to present in 1829 a complete performance of Bach's majestic choral masterwork, the *Passion According to Saint Matthew.* This was the first time this mighty work had been heard since Bach's own time; and this event can well be said to mark the beginnings of a revival of interest in the then much neglected and little-known master. Mendelssohn paid further tribute to Bach in some of his piano music and in several compositions for the organ. For the piano he wrote *Six Preludes and Fugues,* op. 35 (1832–37); for the organ, *Three Preludes and Fugues,* op. 37 (137–39), and six sonatas, op. 65 (1844–45). The last of these sonatas, in D minor, is the first composition to acquire a fixed place in the organ repertory since the works of Bach.

On the whole, Mendelssohn's chamber music is less impressive than that for the piano. His output included the octet, a piano sextet, two string quintets, seven string quartets, three piano quartets, two piano trios, two trios for clarinet, horn, and piano, a violin sonata, two cello sonatas, *Variations concertantes,* and a *Song Without Words* in D major,

both for cello and piano. The String Quartet no. 1 in E-flat major, op.
12 (1829) has a lovely Canzonetta for its second movement, which some
annotators have described as a song of thanksgiving. The Piano Trio no.
1 in D minor, op. 49 (1839) is also distinguished for its slow movement,
which has the structural and lyrical character of one of Mendelssohn's
Songs Without Words.

Robert Schumann was particularly fond of the Sonata in B-flat
major, for cello and piano, op. 45 (1838). Schumann speaks of its
"peace" and "spiritual grace" (descriptive words that might also be used
for the string quartet and piano trio mentioned above). "The sonata,"
wrote Schumann, "is the purest kind of music . . . a sonata as beautiful
and lucid as anything that has ever emerged from the hands of an artist." Mendelssohn's successes mounted throughout his life, from the time
when, as a boy, he, with his beloved sister, Fanny, as well as celebrated
visiting musicians, would perform his compositions in a little auditorium
in the garden of the Mendelssohn house in Berlin. He was idolized in
England as no foreign musician since Haydn, and he was revered in all
parts of Europe.

His fame reposed securely on his compositions, but not exclusively.
Between 1835 and 1847 he conducted the Gewandhaus Orchestra in
Leipzig. Through his musicianship and dedication, this became one of
Europe's foremost symphonic organizations, while at the same time
Mendelssohn ushered in a new age of conducting. In 1843 Mendelssohn
helped found one of Germany's greatest schools of music, the Leipzig
Conservatory.

There was fulfillment in his personal life as well. On March 28,
1837, he married Cécile Jeanrenaud. This was an idyllic union from
which came five children.

The sudden death in 1847 of his sister, Fanny, to whom he had been
so devoted all his life, was a traumatic experience from which Mendelssohn failed to recover. Melancholia was followed by fits. The deteriora-
tion of his nervous system undermined his delicate strength, which had
been severely taxed by too much work. Almost overnight this handsome
young man of thirty-eight seemed old and spent. His death in Leipzig
came less than six months after that of his sister.

*Franz Schubert with two friends at a cafe
in Grinzing, a suburb of Vienna.*

*Opposite, Ludwig van Beethoven,
a miniature painted when
the composer was thirty-three years of age.*

*St. Thomas Church and School in Leipzig
during Mendelssohn's time.*

A page from the Schubert Quartet in D minor,
Der Tod und das Mädchen.
An autograph manuscript.

*Clara Schumann and Joseph Joachim
in concert.*

Prince Albert playing for
Queen Victoria and Felix Mendelssohn.

A page from the Third Sonata
for Piano and Violin by Robert Schumann.
An autograph manuscript.

Lyric Poet
of the Piano

Frédéric Chopin

"Off with your hats, gentlemen—a genius. . . . I bend before Chopin's spontaneous genius, his lofty aims, his mastery."

Thus wrote Schumann in 1831 in the *Neue Zeitschrift für Musik,* which he had founded and of which he was the editor. In 1831 Chopin was twenty-one years old. The composition that had inspired such an outburst of enthusiasm was Chopin's second publication, variations on a melody by Mozart for piano and orchestra. Chopin, then, had only just initiated his career as composer. Schumann's perspicacity in recognizing genius in the raw becomes all the more remarkable when we realize that in 1831 Chopin's extraordinary works in the short forms were still to come.

Schumann's enthusiasm for Chopin had not been exaggerated. Chopin *was* a genius. Though even Schumann could hardly have guessed it with the op. 2, Chopin was destined to become unique among the world's greatest composers.

Unique—because Chopin is the only one who devoted himself almost exclusively to the piano. Of his more than one hundred and seventy compositions, one hundred and sixty-nine are for solo piano. A scattered handful are for piano and orchestra. The others—a piano trio,

a cello sonata, an *Introduction and Polonaise* for cello, a set of variations for flute and piano, some Polish songs—enlisted the services of a
piano. There is then not one Chopin work (except for an insignificant
military march for band) in which the piano is not used. Such concentrated dedication to a single instrument has no parallel among the
world's masters.

Unique—because Chopin is the only major composer the vast bulk
of whose output is made up of miniatures. The exceptions are two sonatas, two concertos, the trio, the cello sonata, and the variations for piano
and orchestra.

Unique, too—because few if any composers in history evaluated
their own weaknesses so accurately as did Chopin. He knew that the
piano was the instrument for which his kind of art was best suited, and
that the shorter forms were the molds best able to contain his type of
material. He refused to make a bid for immortality with operas, or symphonies, or oratorios, or quartets. He recognized that, speaking creatively, he was short-winded; that he was at his best with beautiful musical thoughts and sequences encased in circumscribed structures; that
expansive and involved development within ambitious forms was too
long a route for his limitations. He preferred to travel short distances, in
which nobody could rival his championship.

This remarkable capacity for self-evaluation, combined with an un-
blemished integrity, explains why he, more than any other of the great
composers, maintains such a consistently high level of artistic achieve-
ment throughout all his published works. Almost everything he wrote
(with scattered and negligible exceptions) bears the stamp of his mastery,
making almost all his music vital in the repertory. This can be said of no
other composer, each of whom produced quite a generous quota of
music that has deservedly fallen by the wayside. Chopin wrote and rewrote each of his pieces, constantly revised and changed them, continually subjected them to polishing and refinement. He would work on a
single measure a hundred times and spend weeks on a single page. He
unhesitatingly destroyed what failed to satisfy him completely. Never did
he permit something of his to get published that did not meet his high
standards.

He is the greatest composer the piano has known. Because of what he
accomplished, the techniques of playing and writing for the piano were
advanced immeasurably. Anybody writing piano music since Chopin
had to profit from his music. Chopin introduced new concepts of virtuosity, new piano rhetoric, new subtleties of piano expression. He was so *117*

far ahead of his times that his contemporaries looked upon him as a revolutionary. He had his own way of using harmonic progressions, arpeggios, tonality, and voice leading, that is, the technique of counterpoint. His imagination was bold and daring. So personalized is his music that his voice and his language are always easily identified. It is impossible to find in his writing the traces of the influence of the piano composers preceding him. Chopin's music seems to have come into existence fully realized and to have matured without the benefit of a long period of apprenticeship. Almost from his beginnings we encounter his tendency to decorate his melodic line with exquisite embellishments (not unlike those used for the voice in the *bel canto* of Vincenzo Bellini's operas). He had a magical way of using chromaticisms, of combining chords. His melodic invention was as copious as it was varied. He could speak in romantic whispers under a starlit night. He could reflect the sophistication of the Parisian salon. He could be fiery and electrifying. His style and form were always as aristocratic as his speech. He was the supreme lyric poet of the piano.

The one influence that affected his creativity most strongly was his native land. He had left Poland when he was twenty. But for the remainder of his life he carried Poland faithfully in his heart. Again and again he revealed his patriotism by writing masterpieces in such popular Polish dance forms as the mazurka and the polonaise. Here (and elsewhere, too) he often used not only the kind of tonalities found in Polish folk music but also such a mannerism as repeating a phrase or two until it produced a hypnotic effect, a trait characteristic of Polish folk songs and dances. Chopin never quoted Polish melodies; the musical materials were always his own. But in the mazurkas and polonaises the personality of Poland is predominant.

And what Poland meant to Chopin, this, by reciprocity, Chopin has come to mean to Poland. He is not only Poland's greatest composer. He is its voice, its heartbeat, its soul. His music was enlisted to aid Poland in its struggle for liberation from Russian rule in the nineteenth century. In Chopin's music, Poles found an eloquent substitute for the heritage of which the Russians had deprived them. That lordly Polish pianist-statesman, Ignace Jan Paderewski, lived through those trying times and remembered how Chopin "gave all back to us, mingled with the prayers of broken hearts, the revolt of fettered souls, the pain of slavery, lost freedom's ache, the cursing of tyrants, the exultant songs of victory."

Once again Chopin became the voice of Poland when the Nazis launched their brutal attack on that country in 1939 to start World War II.

While Warsaw was being fiercely attacked from the air and on the ground by immeasurably superior forces, the Polish radio station maintained the spirit of its people by playing over and over again Chopin's *Revolutionary* Étude. When Warsaw fell, the last musical sound to come from the Polish radio before the Nazis seized it were the first eleven notes of Chopin's Polonaise in A major. With Poland under Soviet subjugation after the war, the playing and the hearing of Chopin's music continued to serve the Polish people as the principal way of clinging to their national pride and nurturing their hidden dreams of national freedom.

Frédéric Chopin was the second child, and the first son, of Nicolas Chopin, a French teacher in Poland of Alsatian origin, and Justine, a former lady-in-waiting to a countess. He was born in Zelazowa Wola, not far from Warsaw, on or about March 1, 1810. (Reference books have long noted Chopin's birth as having taken place on February 22, but the discovery of a document in recent years proves this February date to be erroneous.)

Soon after Frédéric's birth, the Chopins moved to Warsaw, where, even as an infant, he revealed unusual fascination for the piano. He would always be found clambering up to the keyboard, delighted when he produced pleasant sounds, bursting into tears at discords. Adalbert Zwyny began teaching Chopin the piano when the child was six. A year later, Chopin published his first composition: a Polonaise in G minor. In the same year he wrote a second polonaise and a march (the latter was performed by a military band). Chopin completed two more polonaises between his eleventh and twelfth years, and his first mazurka when he was fourteen. Meanwhile, when he was seven, he made his first public appearance as pianist. He was so successful that the Polish nobility welcomed him into their palaces and lavished gifts and affection on him.

By now his father was a teacher at a high school, in which Frédéric enrolled when he was thirteen. He now studied harmony and counterpoint with Joseph Elsner, who was destined to be the last music teacher Chopin ever had. Elsner, director of the Warsaw Conservatory, was not only an excellent musician but also an intelligent, perceptive, and responsive human being well able to understand Chopin's sensitive nature and individuality and to appreciate to the full the boy's exceptional ability. Elsner could adapt himself to the needs and demands of his pupil, rather than bend the pupil to his own will, giving Chopin the freedom he needed to express his romantic nature and his personal concepts both as a pianist and as a composer. Under such sympathetic instruction, Chopin thrived, first as Elsner's private pupil, and after that as his pupil at the conservatory.

It seemed as if Chopin's pen was never idle. Between 1825 and 1828 came three rondos, three mazurkas, and two more polonaises, together with his first sonata, his first nocturne, his first three waltzes, some Écossaises, and some variations. The year of 1829 brought three more waltzes, two more polonaises, and four more mazurkas, together with other pieces. Youthful efforts all, but it is remarkable to note that already Chopin was favoring the forms to which he would bring such artistic importance, and already these forms contain some of the little stylistic traits that would identify his mature works.

Let us now define some of these forms. The polonaise and the mazurka were both Polish folk dances. The polonaise was stately, in a grand manner, having originated in the Polish courts. It became popular outside Poland in the eighteenth century. Its music is marked by syncopations, and accents on the half beat. The mazurka is a spirited dance in triple time, in two or four sections, with the accent falling usually on the normally weak second or third beat. Other composers had preceded Chopin in writing polonaises for the piano (including J. S. Bach, Mozart, Beethoven, and Schubert). But none had brought to it such flaming national pride and feelings.

Chopin wrote eleven polonaises in all. The A major, op. 40, no. 1, known as the *Military* (1838), the F-sharp minor, op. 44 (1840–41), and the A-flat major, op. 53, dubbed the *Heroic* (1842), are all martial in character, bringing up the pictures of battle, or armies sweeping to attack. The A-flat major Polonaise and the F-sharp minor both also have a military character. Possibly the most greatly admired of Chopin's polonaises are the two of op. 26 (1834–35). They are opposites in mood and style. The C-sharp minor has regal majesty; the E-flat minor, sometimes called *Serbian* and sometimes *Revolt,* is vigorous and fiery. The *Grande Polonaise brilliante* in E-flat major (1830–31), originally for piano and orchestra, was prefaced by a piece called *Andante spianato* (1834) when they were published as op. 22. (*Spianato* means a smooth, clean style with few changes in dynamics.) The two pieces are played either jointly or separately, more frequently, however, as a piano solo than as compositions for piano and orchestra.

Chopin was the first significant composer to make artistic use of the mazurka as a form for piano music. Here, once again, there stream the currents of love of country. To no other form was he more partial, producing fifty-three of these Polish dances. They traverse a wide range of feelings. Some are solemn, others virile; some are tender, others sensuous; some are ironic, others contemplative. Here, even more than in the polonaises, Chopin was faithful to the idioms of Polish folk dance music, by consistently employing modes, rhythms, and accents of the traditional mazurka. But as no less a critic than Franz Liszt remarked, it was Chopin who brought to the surface all the latent musical possibilities of this folk dance. "Preserving their rhythm, he ennobled their melody, enlarged their proportions; and . . . he wrought into their tissues harmonic lights and shadows as new in themselves as were the subjects to which he adapted them." These Chopin mazurkas are such a rich storehouse of musical treasures that it is difficult to select the most precious examples. The following, however, may well be regarded as representative of Chopin's genius within this Polish dance form: the B-flat major and the F minor, in op. 7 (1830–31); the A minor, op. 17 no. 4 (1832–33); the B-flat minor, op. 24 no. 4 (1834–35); the D major and B minor, op. 33 (1837–38); the C-sharp minor, op. 63 no. 3 (1846); and the A minor, op. 67 no. 4 (1846). The very last two compositions Chopin was destined to write were both mazurkas: the G minor, op. 67 no. 2, and the F minor op. 68, no. 4, in 1849, when he was close to death and too weak even to try them out on the piano.

Chopin was not the first important piano composer to write waltzes and nocturnes. In waltzes, he was preceded by Haydn, Mozart, Beethoven, Schubert, and Schumann. In nocturnes, he followed an Irish-born composer, John Field (1782–1837), who first created this form for piano music and in it wrote eighteen compositions. To his waltz-writing Chopin brought an elegance and a sophistication not found in that of his eminent predecessors, whose waltzes still retain much of the lusty character of their peasant origin, while those of Chopin are products of the Parisian salon. As a piano composition, the nocturne is a slow, romantic piece in which a dreamy ornamented melody moves gracefully over an undulating harmonic background. Though there is much to admire in some of John Field's nocturnes (which are heard all too rarely), they are no match for the overflowing beauty and sensitive moods captured in Chopin's compositions.

Chopin graduated from both academic high school and the conservatory, from the latter in 1829, with highest honors. He was now eager to leave Warsaw, mainly because of an unrequited love for Constantia, a singing student at the Conservatory. Too shy to pursue her and try to gain her love, he lavished his adoration from a distance while suffering in solitude and silence. The truth was that Constantia was totally unaware of Chopin's feelings. To flee from his love frustrations, in the summer of 1829 Chopin visited Vienna, where he gave two successful concerts and found a publisher for his Variations on *"Là ci darem la mano"* from Mozart's *Don Giovanni,* for piano and orchestra (the composition that led Schumann to call him a genius).

He came home, his heart still full of love for Constantia. "Six months have passed," he now wrote, "and not yet have I exchanged a single syllable with her of whom I dream every night." He sublimated his emotions by writing the romantic music of the slow movement of his Piano Concerto no. 2 in F minor, op. 21 (1829). This is really Chopin's *first* piano concerto, but it was the *second* to be published, hence its number. It was followed in 1830 by the Concerto no. 1 in E minor, op. 11. Both concertos are celebrated because they are filled with the touching sentiments and the brilliance of pianistic writing Chopin brought to all his music. Both works boast pages that sing, particularly in the slow movements. That of the Second Concerto is a love song for Constantia; that of the First, a Romanza, intended as a musical description of a lovely moonlit landscape.

Chopin introduced his Second Piano Concerto in Warsaw on March 17, 1830. Constantia, the inspiration of its second movement, did not attend the concert. Chopin's performance of the First Piano Concerto in Warsaw on November 11, 1830, marked his last appearance in that city. By then he had come to the decision to leave Poland. A farewell concert was given in his honor in the city of his birth. From the moment he crossed the Polish border and entered Austria— never again to see his native land—he carried with him memories of Poland, memories that often brought tears to his eyes.

Upon leaving Poland Chopin paid a return visit to Vienna, remaining there for eight months. Once again he gave two successful concerts, but he failed to find a publisher for any of his compositions. While in Vienna, Chopin heard that Poland was rising in revolt against Russian rule. His first impulse was to go home and fight for his country. In the end his mother convinced him that he was too frail to be a soldier. En route to Paris, Chopin came to Stuttgart, where, in July of 1831, he was told that the Russians had recaptured Warsaw and had smothered the revolt. Chopin's emotional turbulence at this disaster found outlet in his music: in the rousing and at times majestic strains of the Étude in C minor, op. 10 no. 12, known as the *Revolutionary* Étude.

This étude is the last in a set of twelve collected in op. 10. Chopin had written his first étude in 1829 when he was still in Poland. At that time he informed a friend, "I have composed a study in my own manner." His own manner, indeed! Up to now études had been intended exclusively as teaching pieces. Those by Carl Czerny, Johann Baptist Cramer, and Muzio Clementi are still valuable to piano students. But nobody would think of playing them at concerts. Chopin, too, used the étude to exhibit the solution to some technical problem in piano playing or to experiment with new compositional resources. But the touch of a genius is remarkable. Chopin's études are compositions of the utmost perfection and purest inspiration. They have become concert music of prime importance.

The *Revolutionary* Étude, of course, is not the only famous piece in op. 10, nor is it the only one to carry a title. Popular, too, is the Étude in E major; the C-sharp minor, known as the *Torrent;* and the G-flat, called the *Black Key* because only black keys are used.

Between 1832 and 1836, Chopin completed a second set of études, op. 25. The best loved is the G-flat major, whose delicacy and fleetness of movement earned for it the sobriquet of *Butterfly.* The Étude in F minor has been named *The Balm.* That in A-flat is called *Aeolian Harp* because its music suggests the weird sounds produced when the wind blew through the strings of an ancient musical instrument. The stormy nature of the A minor Etude was responsible for its name of *Winter Wind.*

Chopin arrived in Paris in September of 1831. He expected to pay only a brief visit to the French capital before proceeding to London. He stayed on in Paris, however, and it became the city where he maintained his permanent residence for the rest of his life. On February 26, 1832, he made his Paris debut as pianist, featuring some of his own music. Some critics thought his playing was too refined for their tastes, and his music too revolutionary. But several powerful musicians, then in Paris, recognized him as a genius; among them were Mendelssohn, Liszt, and Meyerbeer, all of whom used their influence to promote him. It was not long before the most brilliant salons in Paris were open to him. He found well-paying pupils among aristocratic families. He was eagerly sought after by the highborn and the powerful to perform his compositions at exclusive social functions. He was sometimes invited to several salons in a single day. "I move in the highest circles," he told a friend in 1833, "among ambassadors, princes and ministers, and I know not how I got there."

As a man, as well as a musician, he was truly an adornment to any salon. He was tall and thin, always well groomed. His facial contours were soft and feminine. A shock of silky, chestnut-colored hair flowed *123* smoothly from his brow to the back of his neck. With his wan, sunken cheeks and dreamy eyes he had the look of a poet or an ascetic. He had courtly manners, refined speech, and graceful movements and gestures, and he always gave the impression of gentleness. His appealing appearance went a long way in advancing his fame both as pianist and as composer. Before he had been in Paris a few years he was the musical vogue. Publishers now sought him out. His music was everywhere getting enthusiastic responses, its compositional or pianistic innovations (of which there were many) unable to destroy for the Parisian public the magic spell Chopin created in each of his pieces.

In 1831 Chopin wrote the Nocturne in E-flat major, op. 9 no. 2. From this time on he conveyed his most romantic thoughts in the nocturne form. The E-flat major Nocturne, highly typical of Chopin's best such works, is world-famous and has been transcribed for many other solo instruments as well as for orchestra. But it has found a rival for popularity in the no less poetic or sensitive Nocturne in F-sharp major, op. 15 no. 2 (1831). Each is a sentimental song for the piano—lyrical, reflective, sometimes rapturous. For the Nocturne in C-sharp minor, op. 27 no. 1 (1835), Chopin himself provided this unusual verbal explanation: "A calm night in Venice, where after a murder the corpse is thrown into the sea while the moon shines serenely on." This is one of Chopin's more picturesque nocturnes. The G minor, op. 15 no. 3 (1833)—inspired by a performance of *Hamlet*—is one of several that sounds like an improvisation. Among Chopin's later nocturnes the following should be singled out for special attention: the G major, op. 37 no. 2 (1839), which sounds like a barcarolle; the C minor, op. 48 no. 1 (1841), which is more declamatory than lyrical; the F minor, op. 55 no. 1 (1843), whose main melody achieves its effect through repetition; the B major and E major in op. 62 (1846); the E minor, op. 71 no. 1 (1827), and the C-sharp minor with no opus number.

He was now also writing his magnificent waltzes, waltzes meant for listening and not for dancing. In 1831 came the Waltz in E-flat major, op. 18, and the exquisite Waltz in A minor, op. 34 no. 2, followed in 1835 by the Waltz in A-flat major, *L'Adieu* (*Farewell*), op. 69 no. 1. The most famous among Chopin's subsequent waltzes are: the F major, op. 34 no. 3 (1838); the A-flat, op. 42 (1840); the D-flat, op. 64 no. 1 (1847); and the C-sharp minor, op. 64 no. 2 (1847), another of Chopin's compositions to gain enormous circulation through transcriptions. The leaping figures in the F major Waltz led one imaginative, and uniden-

tified, commentator to see in this music the rompings of a cat on a keyboard. The D-flat major Waltz has been dubbed the Minute—not because it takes about a minute to play but because it is so short, the French word for "small" being *minute*.

In 1832 Chopin wrote the first of his four scherzos, the B minor, op. 20. Chopin's scherzos did not carry out the long-held concept of light, fanciful, or whimsical music. Chopin's scherzos are either strongly emotional or powerful. The first opens with two shattering chords followed by a musical torrent. The second scherzo, in B-flat minor, op. 31 (1837), and the fourth in E major, op. 54 (1842), are more subdued, but the third, in C-sharp minor, op. 39 (1839), is music of utter despair.

Chopin also wrote four impromptus (the form first popularized by Schubert) and four ballades (a form that Chopin himself invented). Most famous among the impromptus is the *Fantasie-Impromptu* in C-sharp minor, op. 66 (1834), best known for the tender song that comes midway, preceded by a stormy fantasia section. The Impromptu in A-flat major, op. 29 (1837) alternates quiet and agitated parts. Those who have read *Trilby,* the classic thriller by George du Maurier, may recall that this is the music Svengali used to hypnotize Trilby. Marked also by sharp contrasts is the Impromptu in F-sharp, op. 36 (1839).

The ballade is a composition with such a strong narrative or descriptive character that it seems to be telling a story even though it is absolute music, that is, music without a programmatic aspect. Though Chopin's four ballades are not literally descriptive, they are nevertheless inspired by poems, all the work of one of Poland's greatest writers, Mickiewicz. The four ballades are: G minor, op. 23 (1835), F major, op. 38 (1839), A-flat major, op. 47 (1841), and F minor, op. 52 (1842). The first and third are played most often. The first is vigorous music derived from a poem describing the battle of the Christian Knights against the pagan Lithuanians. The third, more delicate and lyrical, is based on the poem *Undine.*

Chopin loved beautiful things—flowers, perfume, art works—and his well-being demanded that he be surrounded by them. Anything vulgar, uncouth, or uncultivated upset him. He was always in complete control of his emotions, never giving way in word or deed to inner combustions. When upset, he would grow pale, his lips would tighten, and he would speak with carefully chosen phrases.

Physically attractive, phenomenally gifted as a musician, and famous among the social and political elite in Paris, Chopin inevitably made a strong appeal to women. In 1835 he fell in love with Marie Wodzinska, a nineteen-year-old girl whom he would have married had not her father and uncle conspired successfully to break up the romance. It was to Marie that he wrote his *Adieu* waltz, as well as several other compositions.

Hardly had he recovered from his anguish at losing Marie than he became involved with the woman who for the next decade dominated his life. She was a famous writer, whose real name was Aurore Dudevant, but who preferred to adopt the name George Sand. When he first met her, in the fall of 1836, Chopin was repelled—and with good reason. This woman, who chose a man's name, was masculine in many ways: in the way she dressed; in the open way she conducted promiscuous love affairs; and in the fact that she smoked cigars. She was as uncouth in her manners as she was unappealing to the eye. Her frankness on all subjects could be offensive. Chopin's sensibilities were offended at this first meeting. "Is she really a woman?" he inquired contemptuously.

She was five years older than Chopin. Her dynamic personality was in violent opposition to Chopin's sensitivity and delicately attuned nature. He was the introvert, she the extrovert. They seemed worlds apart. Yet some inexplicable force began to draw them to each other. Sand's brilliance of mind, writing talent, and fame (for she was a highly successful author), and strength of character all began to make an impression on Chopin. He found himself seeking out her company and enjoying it.

By 1838 the two became inseparable. Whether Chopin's love was nurtured on his need to lean on somebody stronger than himself or whether he had found a mother substitute are questions for psychologists to probe. No psychologist is needed to explain George Sand's interest in Chopin. He was handsome, he was a genius, he was gentle and charming. She had captured the love of many famous men and Chopin was another she could add to her score of victories, a conquest worth seeking.

They spent the summer of 1838 together in George Sand's château in Nohant. Later the same year, they went off to Palma, on the island of Majorca, near Spain. The summer in Nohant had proved idyllic. The winter in Majorca, however, was a nightmare. The miserable rainy weather not only depressed Chopin but also affected his always delicate health. He was stricken by bronchitis, which the people of Palma insisted was tuberculosis. In dread of contagion, they drove Chopin and Sand from Palma to a fifteenth-century monastery in Valdemosa, on the same island. The building's stone walls made the rooms damp and cold. Chopin's health went from bad to worse. He suffered hemorrhages. He was even the victim of nightmares and hallucinations. The townspeople, terrified by him, avoided all contact, so that Chopin and George Sand became pariahs. Nobody would work for them. There were times when there was little to eat.

These were hardly conditions suited for creativity. Nevertheless, this morbid period was the time when Chopin completed his Preludes, op. 28, a few of which he had written as early as 1836. The prelude is a short form which projects a mood or an emotion. The end of the composition leaves the listener with the feeling that the subject matter has not been fully explored. Having no set structure, the prelude usually consists of just one or two musical ideas that are stated simply and directly and avoid extended elaborations. Each prelude is a little poem in music. In the gloom of many of these preludes we find clues of the physical and mental torments suffered by Chopin in Majorca. "Many of them," George Sand has written, "call up to the mind's eye visions of dead monks and the souls of their funeral chants, which obsessed him [Chopin]. Others are suave and melancholy. . . . Others are dreary and sad and wringing the heart while charming the ear."

The Prelude in D-flat major is called *Raindrop* because an insistent rhythm in the left hand behind the melody sounds almost like the tapping of raindrops on a window or roof. Morbid and tortured are the Preludes in A minor and G minor; the C minor is solemn. These are among the best in op. 28, as are the C major, G major, E minor, B minor, and B-flat minor.

Chopin had to be carried away from Majorca on a stretcher. He was brought back to Nohant, where he slowly recovered. On October 11, 1839, he was back in his Paris lodgings, both his strength and his spirits revitalized. During the next few years he divided his year between Paris and Nohant. He gave some concerts and revealed that as a performer he was still in his prime. After a concert in Paris on April 26, 1841, Liszt said, "His exquisite repute has been untouched by any attack. . . . All mouths were full of the same praise." And after his appearance on February 21, 1842, the *Gazette musicale* reported: "The keyboard becomes as it were transformed, turning almost into a new instrument, as it obeys the fevered impulse of a tender and passionate genius." Most of the time, however, he was composing. Among the new works not yet mentioned are his second and third piano sonatas, a tarantella, a berceuse, and a barcarolle.

Whenever Chopin's *Funeral March* is discussed—and surely it is the most frequently played funeral music ever written!—the piece being spoken of is the third movement of his Piano Sonata no. 2 in B-flat minor, op. 35 (1839). This identification is sometimes hard to remember, since the march is so often heard in arrangements for either band or orchestra. This slow movement was written before the other three movements of the sonata. Chopin's infallible artistic intuition made him realize that the sonata could become a unified concept with the inclusion of a large funeral march, since the rest of the movements are filled with emotional upheavals and somber feelings.

Chopin is the master of long, sustained melodies; it is these that provide the main interest in the sonata. He is less facile and inventive in integrating his material, working it out logically and forcefully. All this criticism holds true for the Sonata no. 3 in B minor, op. 58 (1844), which lacks even the dark mood that had unified the second sonata. There is a wealth of wonderful melodies in the third sonata, particularly in the first movement. But the movements fail to blend into an integrated whole, sounding as if they were four separate compositions.

A tarantella is a highly spirited dance with ever-increasing speed, in 6/8 time, from southern Italy. Tarantism was the name for a form of insanity, or hysteria, or St. Vitus dance believed to have been caused by the bite of a large spider (the *Lycosa tarentula*). Legend has it that these maladies were curable by having the patients dance until they fell limp from exhaustion. The feverishly fast movements of the tarantella, then, is supposed to have been inspired by this legendary cure. Chopin's Tarantelle in A-flat, op. 43 (1841), is the first such significant composition for the piano.

Chopin's sole berceuse and barcarolle appeared respectively in 1843 and 1846. A berceuse is a cradle song; the one by Chopin—in D-flat major, op. 57—is a tender lullaby that ebbs away gently in the closing measures as if suggesting that the child has fallen asleep. A barcarolle is a boat song sung by Venetian gondoliers. Chopin's Barcarolle in F-sharp major, op. 60, has been interpreted as a lament for the vanished splendors of old-time Venice by one writer and as the tender dialogue of two lovers in a gondola by another.

Chopin contributed two works for cello and piano well worth hearing, even though they do not rise to the stature of his piano masterpieces. One is an early composition, Introduction and Polonaise, op. 3 (1829–30). The other, and more significant, is the Sonata in G minor, op. 65 (1846)—the last work of Chopin to be published during his lifetime. This piece is not typical of Chopin, since it is more expansive and exuberant than lyrical or romantic. Some authorities believe that Chopin was here beginning to experiment with a new manner of writing, which he might have developed had he lived.

But there were not many years left to Chopin after 1846. These were years of misery because, beginning with 1846, his relationship with George Sand had become strained, and by the summer of 1847 their separation became permanent. They had sharp quarrels involving George Sand's daughter and a man she wanted to marry. Her mother bitterly opposed the marriage but Chopin sympathized with the couple. George Sand had by now already grown impatient with what she herself described as Chopin's "outbursts of vexations, temper, and jealousy . . . in the presence of all my friends and of the children." In short, George Sand was tired of Chopin. By August 14, 1847, she wrote to a friend: "As for Chopin, I never heard a word about him, and I beg you to tell me how he really is: no more. The rest does not interest me at all, and I have no cause to regret his affection."

Chopin was devastated. He continued to think and speak of her; she was never far from his mind. He was convinced that without her his life had become meaningless. Nevertheless, he kept on writing music, wonderful music, including his last three mazurkas, the barcarolle, and the two nocturnes in op. 62. He even made an appearance as pianist in Paris on February 16, 1848, and later the same year visited England and Scotland. But his spirit was shattered, and so was his health. After returning from England he became a recluse in his Paris apartment. Except for his sister and brother-in-law (who had come from Poland to take care of him) he saw nobody. He was now continually haunted by thoughts and fear of death. He gave his sister instructions to destroy all his unpublished manuscripts.

His death came on October 17, 1849. Those who were at his bedside said that in death his face was radiant. Funeral services were held at the Madeleine Church; during them a part of Mozart's *Requiem* and the funeral march from Chopin's Second Piano Sonata were played. Chopin then was buried at the Père-Lachaise Cemetery in Paris, where, one year later, a monument was erected. During the ceremonies attending the unveiling of that monument some Polish earth was strewn over Chopin's grave.

Felix Mendelssohn

Ignace Paderewski

Pablo Casals

Jascha Heifetz

Yehudi and Hephzibah Menuhin

Andrés Segovia

Wanda Landowska

E. Power Biggs

Glenn
Gould

Lili Kraus

Andre Watts

Isaac Stern, Eugene Istomin, Leonard Rose.

8

Enter the Modern Virtuoso

Niccolò Paganini, Franz Liszt

The role of today's violin virtuoso and the present-day techniques of writing for the violin were both first realized by Niccolò Paganini. He was the greatest violinist the world had known up to his time. Because he invented new methods and effects for the violin he had to write compositions for his concerts in which his innovations could be fully exploited. Both as violinist and as composer his technical gifts were formidable. Nobody could match the speed with which his fingers raced across the fingerboard, or the nimbleness with which his bow sprang so lightly on the strings. His harmonics on a single note or double notes produced flutelike sounds of crystalline clarity (harmonics being produced by touching the fingers lightly on the strings at certain places instead of pressing the fingers down). He could extend his two long, lean bony fingers in intervals up to a tenth in extended passages. He employed double stops (simultaneous playing of two notes) and triple stops (the same, for three notes) with unprecedented brilliance. The way he combined bowed (*arco*) passages simultaneously with left-hand *pizzicati* (plucked strings) was electrifying.

Born in the Italian city of Genoa on October 27, 1782, Paganini was raised by his father to become a prodigy. Once his father began giving him lessons, Niccolò made astonishing progress, and more than ever the father was determined to create a musical phenomenon. In this he was stoutly supported by his wife.

Professional instruction was recruited first from Servetto, then from Costa. When he was eleven he startled the audience at his first public concert with his dazzling display of pyrotechnics—especially in one of his own compositions, variations on a French patriotic tune. He was forthwith hired to play the violin every Sunday at church and was always referred to as "the wonder boy."

Paganini made his first tour as violinist, in the company of his father, in 1797, by appearing in several Italian cities in the Lombardy district. Wherever he played he took audiences by storm, especially when he presented his own technically complicated pieces. His mounting successes gave him the courage and confidence to break loose from the controls imposed on him by a domineering parent. Financially independent, and removed from his father's surveillance, Paganini (now seventeen years old) allowed freedom and success to turn his head. He became involved with women and gambling. His excesses almost ruined him, and taking stock of himself he withdrew temporarily from public life to live with a wealthy Tuscan woman.

Since his patroness played the guitar, Paganini abandoned the violin to work industriously on mastering the plucked string instrument. He also wrote music for it, including twelve sonatas for guitar and violin, op. 2 and 3, and a sonatina. With the piano replacing the guitar, the Sonata in E minor, op. 3 no. 6, has remained a favorite with violinists. The Romanza movement from the Sonatina is sometimes programmed by classical guitarists. Paganini thus became a pioneer in writing serious music for the guitar.

With the guitar enjoying such a great revival of interest in our own times, this might be a convenient point at which to speak a few words about that instrument. It was developed and grew popular in Spain, displacing the older lute as the plucked instrument best suited to accompany song and dance. While it was still regarded basically as an accompanying instrument, Luigi Boccherini—who lived his last years in Spain —became Paganini's successor in writing seriously for the guitar by including it in his chamber music, notably in quintets. A remarkable Spanish virtuoso, Ferdinando Sor (1778–1839), gave such successful guitar recitals in France and England early in the nineteenth century that the instrument achieved a vogue in both countries. Two other guitarists helped advance the appeal of the guitar in the concert hall: the Italian Mauro Giuliani (1781–1828) and the Spaniard Francesco Tárrega (1852–1909). Both Sor and Giuliani wrote concert music for their favored instrument. Sor's best works for solo guitar, or guitar and piano, include Variations on a Theme by Mozart, op. 9, Introduction and Allegro, op. 14, and a sonata, op. 15. Giuliani wrote a fine concerto for guitar and strings, op. 30, which has been recorded. He also wrote a sonata for flute and guitar, op. 85, and numerous other compositions. But, for the most part, recital programs by the guitar comprised transcriptions.

The guitar failed to retain a permanent foothold in the concert hall until the twentieth century. Then it was popularized anew in concerts throughout the world of music by a phenomenal virtuoso Andrés Segovia. After that, other exceptional guitarists kept the classic guitar active in concerts and recordings (among these being Julian Bream and John Williams). It was for these artists that many significant twentieth-century composers wrote original compositions for solo guitar, for guitar and piano, or guitar and orchestra. In America, the guitar was particularly popular as an accompanying instrument for folk singers, balladeers, and later on (in the popular field) as a principal accompanying instrument for rock 'n' roll singers.

Let us now return to Paganini and the violin. Paganini's love affair with the Tuscan noblewoman had run its course by 1804. He left her château, returned to Genoa, and there worked assiduously on redeveloping his violin technique and experimenting with new effects for his instrument. For a while he continued writing compositions in which the guitar was used, for example, the six quartets, op. 4 and 5; but the violin reassumed for him prime importance. In 1805 he returned to the concert stage and had no difficulty in reestablishing his success. One of Napoleon's sisters, the princess of Lucca and Piombo, named him music master, conductor of an opera orchestra, and her personal violinist at her court in 1805. He stayed at this post eight years while receiving frequent leaves of absence to allow him to concertize in Italy.

He was becoming more and more of a showman, both as a violinist and as a composer. For a Piombo lady of high station, with whom he was carrying on a secret love affair, he wrote *Love Scene*, a piece that called for the use of just two strings instead of all four. This stunt so delighted the lady that she asked Paganini to write a work on one string alone. He complied with the Sonata on the G String, to which he gave the title of *Napoleon*. (One of his later compositions, still familiar, was also written solely for the G string—the electrifying Fantasia based on a melody from Rossini's opera *Mosè* in *Egitto*.) Once, while playing one of his compositions for four strings at a concert in Leghorn, a middle string snapped. He continued playing the work on the other three strings by skillfully using the highest compass of the other strings.

Another of his secret practices to endow his playing with increasing brilliance was to tune his instrument a half tone higher than was traditional. This is why some confusion exists as to the key of the first and most famous of his five concertos for the violin, probably written in 1811, and published posthumously as op. 6. Paganini wrote it in the key of E-flat major, but it is now heard in D major. Except for the last movement, which is bravura music, the main appeal of this famous concerto lies in the lovely sentimental, thoroughly Italian melodies. These are found in the second subject of the first movement (played by the soloist in the upper register, and then repeated in a lower one) and in the romantic song in the second movement.

Paganini's employment at the court of the princess of Lucca and Piombo ended in 1813. This was also the year when he began to enjoy the greatest triumphs he had thus far known. A performance in Milan in 1813 caused such a sensation that he had to give thirty-six more concerts in that city. For the next few years Paganini traveled the length and breadth of Italy. It was during this time that he became a legend to be spoken of with awe, and at times with terror.

Paganini's greatest contribution to violin literature are his Twenty-Four Caprices for unaccompanied violin. He wrote them in 1801–07, and they are his only violin compositions he allowed to be published (op. 1). Composers before Paganini had written caprices, which are brief, highly technical pieces of music usually in quick tempo. Pietro Locatelli (1695–1764) published an album of violin music in 1733, *L'Arte del violino* (*The Art of the Violin*) which contained twenty-four caprices. These employed double stops and took advantage of the high compass of the violin, but in comparison to those by Paganini these caprices are primitive. Paganini's encompass the entire range of the instrument's technical possibilities. These compositions have become all-important to violinists everywhere in helping them master their instrument. And to the music lover they are exciting to listen to. So highly did Schumann and Liszt regard Paganini's caprices that they transcribed some of them for the piano, while many eminent twentieth-century violinists (including Fritz Kreisler) have provided them with piano accompaniments.

The following are among Paganini's most striking caprices: no. 5 in a minor; no. 9 in E major, called *La Chasse* (*The Chase*) since double-stop passages sound almost like the call of hunting horns; no. 13 in B-flat major, *Le Rire du diable* (*The Devil's Laugh*) in which one passage sounds like a diabolic chuckle; no. 20 in D major; and, most distinguished of all, no. 24 in A minor. The main melody, with which the Twenty-fourth Caprice opens, was ultimately used as the source for major works by Brahms and Rachmaninoff among other composers.

Paganini's first appearance outside Italy took place in Vienna on March 29, 1828. No concert performer up to then had ever been welcomed so triumphantly. "Never has an artist caused such a great sensation in our walls," reported one Viennese newspaper. "The audience was hypnotized." The demand to hear Paganini was so great that he had to give over twenty concerts.

After Vienna, Paganini toured Bohemia, Poland, Bavaria, Prussia, and the German Rhineland over a three-year period. "Paganini will play his violin!" was the cry preceding him to whatever place he visited. His was a path of glory that extended in 1831 to Paris, which, like every other city, succumbed helplessly to the magic of his playing.

From Paris Paganini went on to London, where his concerts inspired the wildest enthusiasm any concert performer had experienced there and brought him the highest fees in English performing history, totaling the equivalent of about $85,000.

He was back in Italy in the summer of 1832, making his home at Villa Gaiona, an elegant estate near Parma. His health was worsening; nevertheless for the next few years he continued to give performances with no visible sign of diminution either in his capabilities or in his public appeal.

In 1836 he invested a fortune in a fashionable gambling casino in Paris. This venture was a disaster that cost Paganini not only a fortune but also his health. He died in Nice on May 27, 1840.

He had refused to accept the last sacraments of the Church. This—and the persistent rumors that he sprang from the devil—denied him the right to be buried in consecrated ground. Five years after his death (through the untiring efforts of his devoted son Achellino, born to the dancer Antonia Bianchi who was his mistress for a dozen years) Paganini's body was at long last put to its final rest in the burial grounds of a village church adjoining Paganini's house near Parma.

Paganini had left behind a fortune, most of which went to Achellino, whom the law courts legitimatized as his son. Paganini left behind another fortune as well—a tradition of violin playing and the writing of virtuoso music that touched and influenced every violinist that followed him. Much of the repertory for the violin came from nineteenth-century violinist-composers who had profited greatly from the lessons they had learned from Paganini. We need single out only three of these contributors to the Romantic literature for the violin, but, to be sure, there were many others.

Henri Vieuxtemps (1820–81), regarded as the guiding light of a generation of Belgian violinists, was impelled to imitate Paganini by making virtuosity the central interest both in his performances and in his compositions. Vieuxtemps is best represented by his seven violin concertos, the most durable of which are the no. 4 in D minor, op. 31 (1853), and no. 5 in A minor, op. 37 (1858). He also wrote many shorter pieces, among which are concert études, fantasies, variations, a tribute to Paganini (*Hommage à Paganini*), the *Ballade et polonaise,* and the *Fantaisie-Caprice.*

Henri Wieniawski (1835–80) was the most distinguished violin virtuoso to come out of Poland in the nineteenth century. He, too, wrote a still-widely-played concerto for the violin: the Concerto no. 2 in D minor, op. 22 (published in 1870), which boasts a beautiful Romanza as the slow movement. Wieniawski's shorter compositions are basic to the violin repertory, most of them exciting for their technical brilliance. Among them are the *Scherzo tarantella,* in G minor, op. 16. Together with a gift for pyrotechnics, Wieniawski also possessed a pronounced talent for melody, as was proved not only by the Romanza movement of his concerto, but also by the *Légende* (*Legend*), for violin and orchestra, or violin and piano, op. 17. *Souvenir de Moscou* (*Souvenir of Moscow*), op. 6—also either for violin and orchestra or violin and piano—is a series of variations on two Russian folk songs. *Kujawiak* in A minor, op. 3, and *Polonaise brilliante* in D major, op. 4 no. 1 (both for violin and piano) are identifiably Polish. (A Kujawiak is a form of mazurka that gained popularity in the Kujawy district of Poland.)

In his concerts throughout the music world, Pablo de Sarasate (1844–1908) was often described as "the Spanish Paganini." He was a dazzling virtuoso who, up to 1872, devoted most of his programs to his own transcriptions or adaptations of Spanish folk songs and dances, and to his fantasias based on melodies from operas. His principal compositions for violin and piano had much of Paganini's technical wizardry. Among his *Spanish Dances,* the four sets of op. 21, 22, 23, and 26 are particularly famous. In the *Malagueña,* op. 21 no. 1, he used *pizzicati* to imitate the clicking of castanets. Broad, sensuous Spanish melody is here tapped, as well as in the *Habanera,* op. 21 no. 2, and the *Romanza andaluza,* op. 22 no. 1, while Spanish dance rhythms characterize the *Jota Navarra,* op. 22 no. 2.

A malagueña is a Spanish dance whose music sounds like an improvisation; it first became popular in the Spanish city of Malaga. A habanera is a slow dance believed to have originated in Cuba, but which became famous in Spain. A jota is a fast Spanish dance accompanied by the rhythm of castanets.

Brilliant bravura writing is found in Sarasate's *Caprice Basque,* op. 24, the *Carmen* Fantasia, op. 25 (all of whose melodies are taken from Georges Bizet's famous opera *Carmen*), and the *Zapateado,* op. 23 no. 2. (A zapateado is a lively Spanish dance with a vigorous rhythm accentuated by clicking of the dancer's heels.) But if we were to single out any one composition by Sarasate that has won the widest renown, we would have to select his *Zigeunerweisen* (*Gypsy Airs*), op. 20 no. 1. This is a potpourri of haunting gypsy melodies and exciting Spanish dance rhythms. A poignant gypsy song is heard midway in the composition, which ends with a series of dance tunes in which technical fireworks erupt.

Hearing Paganini play the violin in Paris upon his debut in that city on March 9, 1831, was an experience that drove Liszt to become the piano virtuoso of his age, "the Paganini of the piano," as he himself put it. Franz Liszt was then twenty. He had already won considerable successes as a pianist. But Paganini convinced him he had much more to learn. Liszt now entered upon a two-year period of seclusion in which he worked almost in a frenzy to make his hands obey his every command. "Here is a whole fortnight that my mind and fingers have been working like two lost spirits," he wrote at the time. "I practice four to five hours of exercises (thirds, sixths, eighths, tremolos, repetitions of notes, cadenzas and so forth). Ah, provided I don't go mad, you will find an artist in me!"

From this concentrated period of self-study and spartan discipline Liszt emerged a virtuoso in the grand manner, the first of that breed—truly a Paganini of the piano. Then, in further emulation of his idol, he went on to combine his now extraordinary pianism with gaudy showmanship.

Until his death Liszt remained a curious study in contradictions, both as a pianist and as a composer. On the one hand he was a genius;

on the other, a charlatan. He combined high-minded musicianship and ideals with shabby circus-type stunts. More times than once he served music selflessly, courageously, and nobly. Yet this same artist could also place showmanship and stage tricks above artistic principles. He played the world's greatest music with the most penetrating insight and musicianship. Yet he was also ready and willing to offer third-rate music or worse (much of it written by himself) to flaunt his phenomenal command of the keyboard before swooning audiences.

Without a doubt he was one of the greatest pianists of all time. His performances created the same kind of charisma that Paganini's did. This would have satisfied any virtuoso—but not Liszt! Liszt had to resort to all sorts of dramatics, trickery, and byplay to magnetize his audience further. "In concert appearances," says Harold C. Schonberg in *The Great Pianists,* "he would, during the tuttis, talk, gesticulate, beat time, stamp the floor, wiggle around so that the medals and decorations he loved to wear would clink and clank." Like an actor, he used facial contortions, grandiloquent sweeps of hands across the keyboard, the tossing of his long lank hair that he wore to his shoulders. No means appeared too extravagant for him to conquer audiences.

It was Liszt who was the originator of the piano recital, since he was the first to devote an entire program to solo piano music without the help of an orchestra or assisting artists. (He was not one to share the limelight with anybody!) This happened for the first time in Rome in 1839 when a solo concert performed by Liszt was advertised as "a musical soliloquy," and repeated in London in 1840, at which time the word *recital* was first used for a concert. He was also the first, conscious of his impressive profile, to establish the present-day custom of playing the piano in a profile position—concert pianists before Liszt either having faced the audience or having their backs turned to it.

The composer was not far different from the virtuoso. Both wooed the public like popular entertainers, and on other occasions both served their art with humility and grandeur. Many of Liszt's compositions for the piano are among the finest since Chopin, remarkable for their musicianship and for the way they seek out and find new ways to make the keyboard more articulate and expressive.

Liszt's life story reads like a novel whose central character is a colorful, picaresque personality. Liszt's father was a humble employee on the estate of Prince Esterházy, in Raiding, Hungary, where Franz was born on October 22, 1811. Father Liszt, being an excellent amateur musician, soon came to realize that Fate had thrust into his hands a remarkable prodigy. Franz began studying the piano when he was six, and when he was nine he gave concerts in two Hungarian towns. His talent made Prince Esterházy take notice of him. The prince and other noblemen raised the money to send Liszt to Vienna so that the boy might receive that kind of expert instruction his talent deserved.

Liszt arrived in Vienna in 1821. Carl Czerny was so impressed with the boy that he refused to accept any payment for giving him lessons. On December 1, 1822, Liszt made an outstandingly successful debut in Vienna. Liszt's first publication appeared in 1823. It was a variation for the album *Vaterländischer Künstlerverein* (*National Artists' Society*), which consisted of a waltz by the publisher Diabelli to which different composers provided the variations. This is the same waltz for which Beethoven wrote not one but thirty-three variations (op. 120).

In 1823, Liszt left Vienna for Paris. He made his debut as a pianist in Paris on March 7, 1824, and in London on June 21 of the same year. In both cities he was a sensation. In Paris he became the pampered pet of the city's most exclusive salons. In London he gave a command performance for George IV. For the next two years he toured France, Switzerland, and England.

Soon after Liszt's father died in 1827, the young musician experienced a mysterious change of heart that temporarily affected his musical life. He was beginning to be contemptuous of his career as a concert pianist. The number of his public appearances now became few and far between. His personal life had also undergone change. The gilded salons now revolted him. He made a fetish of the simple life. After turning over his small fortune to his mother, he rented a simple apartment in Paris, and supported himself by teaching the piano. He now became the total ascetic to whom the pleasures of the spirit were the only ones of consequence.

It was at this crucial juncture in his life, while he was drifting aimlessly from one interest to another, that he heard Paganini. He now deserted all extramusical activities to return to the piano. As he labored painstakingly to become the Paganini of the piano, a new major influence was brought to bear on his development. In 1832 he heard Chopin play and was made to realize how truly poetic and romantic piano playing could be. Then and there—and for the remainder of his virtuoso career—he would continually try to reconcile Paganini's virtuosity with Chopin's delicacy.

Liszt's return to the concert stage in 1833 marked the beginnings of the realization of his dream to become a virtuoso of virtuosos. But it was only the beginning. The complete fulfillment had to wait two more years because the volatile young musician once again temporarily deserted the concert stage, to become enmeshed in a tempestuous love affair. His beloved—Countess Marie d'Agoult—was a grand lady of high social station and with a trenchant mind. (Under the assumed name of Daniel Stern she pursued a successful career as a writer.) The countess unhesitantly abandoned husband and children to live with Liszt in Geneva. Their affair lasted ten years, during which the countess bore three children. One of them was Cosima, destined to become the wife of the famous conductor-pianist Hans von Bülow whom she in turn deserted to live with and marry the genius she loved—Richard Wagner.

Between 1835 and 1839 Liszt and Countess Marie traveled about in Switzerland and Italy, an experience that saw the writing of Liszt's first important composition, *L'Années de pèlerinage* (*Years of Pilgrimage*). These are three sets (or, as Liszt called them, "three years") of tone pictures for the piano. The first was devoted to his Swiss experiences (1835–36), the second to Italy (1838–39); the third (1867–77) was made up of random pieces on Italian subjects. In the first group of nine pieces, *"Au bord d'une source"* ("At the Edge of a Spring") is most famous. A line by Schiller appears above the music on the score, reading: "In murmuring coolness, the play of young nature begins." We hear the ripple of waters in the crossed hand section with which the piece opens, after which we find described the emotion aroused in a poet at the sight. Two pieces in this set were inspired by Byron's poems: *"Eglogue"* ("Eclogue") and *"Les Cloches de Genève"* ("The Bells of Geneva"), the latter a fine example of romantic landscape painting.

There are seven pieces in the second set or "year." Here the composer was influenced by paintings as well as poetry. *"Sposalizio"* is a gentle, lyrical impression of Raphael's painting *The Marriage of the Virgin;* *"Il Pensoroso"*—with its extraordinary boldness of chromaticism —was inspired by a statue by Michelangelo. All the other five numbers are based on poems, three on sonnets by Petrarch and one (*"Après une lecture du Dante"* or "After Reading Dante") intended by the composer as a *fantasia quasi sonata* ("A fantasy somewhat like a sonata") based on a poem by Victor Hugo. The three Petrarch pieces, which had originated as songs, are of surpassing beauty, and so thoroughly pianistic it is difficult to remember that they were first intended for the voice. *Après une lecture du Dante* is the longest and the most ambitiously conceived number in the three sets. The title is taken from a poem by Hugo, and this music is actually a graphic description of Dante's *Inferno.*

The third set or year is inferior to the other two, though one of its pieces—*"Les Jeux d'eau à la Villa d'Este"* ("The Fountains at Villa d'Este")—anticipates Debussy's Impressionism.

Probably as a gesture of gratitude for the way Paganini had helped him chart his course as pianist, Liszt transcribed for the piano six of Paganini's pieces for solo violin, five of them caprices. He named these transcriptions *Études d'exécution transcendante d'après Paganini* (*Transcendental Études After Paganini*) but they are today popularly known as the *Paganini Études*. One way Liszt here opens new vistas for piano technique is to translate pianistically some of the violin effects found in the caprices, such as harmonics and rapid double-stop and octave passages. Another was to try to simulate on the piano the sounds of hunting horns, fifes, and bells. The last étude is a setting of the celebrated Twenty-fourth Caprice, as ablaze with virtuoso fireworks in the piano as it was in Paganini's original version for the violin. *La Campanella*, in G-sharp minor—the third in the group—is not a caprice but a transcription of the last movement of Paganini's Violin Concerto no. 2.

The affair between Liszt and Countess Marie came to an end in 1839. For the next four years they saw each other intermittently, after which their separation became permanent. Then, in Kiev in 1847, Liszt became fascinated by Princess Carolyne von Sayn-Wittgenstein, who invited him to her palace. He came, he saw, he fell in love—a love that was returned in full measure. They were alike in their mutual love of literature and their intuitive response to religion and mysticism.

This relationship reacted favorably on Liszt the musician. It helped to elevate his artistic standards. At the urging of the princess, he now spent more time than ever on composition; he also began to grope toward new, distant horizons in his creativity. Though he had written nationalistic Hungarian pieces before 1846, he now became more fired than ever with the ambition of creating a national musical art through the writing of the first of nineteen Hungarian Rhapsodies, for solo piano. He did not invent the rhapsody form for the piano, but he was the first to make it both significant and popular. In his hands, the rhapsody became a flexible structure in which a succession of national (or popular) melodies is treated in a rhapsodic manner. Liszt's Hungarian Rhapsodies derive their exciting personality from the way in which dynamics, tempo, and rhythm change continually. Every Liszt rhapsody is characterized by sudden alternations of sensuous, languorous melodies (known as *lassan*) and strong, rapid and dramatic ones (*frissan*).

The Second Hungarian Rhapsody, in C-sharp minor (1847), is one of the two Liszt pieces for the piano with which even the uninitiated to music are undoubtedly familiar. (The other is the *Liebestraum,* or *Love's Dream,* no. 3 in A-flat, a sentimental love song for the piano superimposed on an arpeggio accompaniment. Liszt wrote three such works in 1850, all adapted from his own songs, and all of them in the spirit of a nocturne. The two others are rarely played; the middle one is heard continually.)

The second rhapsody is typical of all Liszt's Hungarian Rhapsodies. It opens with a slow, stately declamation (*lassan*) before a spirited melody (*frissan*) introduces a feeling of excitement. After that, the moods and style change frequently until a climax is reached with a rousing presentation of a *frissan* melody. Once again contrast sets in, this time with the appearance of a new plaintive melody. But the dramatic sweep of the music, which had been temporarily halted, now continues to the end of the composition. This rhapsody is heard more often in Liszt's own orchestral transcription than in its original piano solo form.

Other thrice-familiar rhapsodies are: no. 6 in D-flat; no. 9 in E-flat, *Le Carnaval de Pesth* (*The Carnival in Pesth*); no. 12, in C-sharp minor; no. 14, in F minor, adapted by the composer into the *Hungarian Fantasy,* for piano and orchestra; and no. 15 in A minor, *Rakóczy March,* which must not be confused with an orchestral number of the same name by Berlioz, though it makes use of the same Hungarian melody found in Berlioz. Liszt made orchestral transcriptions of nos. 2, 6, 9, and 12.

By 1847 Liszt was beginning to shut the book on his career as a grand virtuoso. The nobler, the more idealistic Liszt now emerges to the forefront, encouraged and inspired by the princess, who was convinced that Liszt was destined for greater achievements in music than he had thus far attained. When, therefore, the duke of Weimar offered Liszt the post of Kapellmeister in 1848, an office that entailed conducting symphony concerts and operas, Liszt accepted. He realized that he could now dedicate himself to promoting new or long-neglected music and composers. To this task he gave himself completely and courageously, with a total disregard of personal gain or glory. He made Weimar one of the most progressive centers of music-making in the world by performing the then still little-known works of Berlioz, by presenting significant world premieres (including that of Wagner's opera *Lohengrin*), and by reviving forgotten operas by Schubert and Schumann. For him to present the first performance of *Lohengrin* represented a particular gesture of boldness and courage, since at that time Wagner was in disrepute, a political refugee who had fled from Dresden to escape imprisonment because of his involvement in revolutionary activities. Thus, ignoring the demands of his audiences, Liszt never allowed expediency to dictate his artistic policy, the maintenance of which on the highest possible performing level had become a rule with which he never compromised.

The home he shared with the princess attracted not only the cream of Weimar's intellectual life but also visiting musicians come to pay him tribute or to seek his advice, guidance, and help. It was here, for example, that Wagner first found temporary refuge from the Dresden police in 1849. It was here that Hans von Bülow became one of many to study with Liszt and prepare for a fruitful career as a pianist. It was here, too, that in 1853 the young Brahms played for Liszt some of his own early compositions to receive the praise he deserved.

Liszt remained in Weimar thirteen years. In that time he made enemies as well as friends. As the years passed, the bourgeois element in Weimar increasingly resented the new music he forced it to hear. And it was shocked that Liszt was living with a woman who was not his legal wife. When, in 1858, there developed a hostile opposition to his presentation of the world premiere of Peter Cornelius's comic opera *The Barber of Bagdad,* Liszt decided he could no longer perform his duties in Weimar as his conscience demanded. He resigned from his post as Kapellmeister in 1858, but continued to maintain his home in Weimar for another two years.

During those Weimar years Liszt greatly expanded his sphere as composer. He had become interested in the orchestra, and in large forms. In 1849 he completed the first version of one piano concerto and revised another, as well as writing the *Totentanz (Dance of Death),* the latter an extended fantasy for piano and orchestra. In 1848–49 there came the first of his symphonic (or tone) poems, a new orchestral medium that he helped to develop and which, within a flexible form, allowed him to interpret a poem, story, or idea musically; in this field he produced such significant works as *Les Préludes, Mazeppa,* and *Tasso.*

He did not neglect the piano, to which he brought an originality and power of imagination not encountered in his earlier compositions. By 1852 he had completed *Harmonies poétiques et religieuses (Poetic and Religious Harmonies)* in which is found the masterpiece *Funérailles (Obsequies).* This was a threnody (a song of lamentation) written in October of 1849, probably in memory of Chopin, who had then just died. A slow dramatic introduction precedes funeral music, which is followed by a passage (marked *"lagrimoso"*) of unutterable grief. *Funérailles* is the seventh of ten pieces, the third of which—*Bénédiction de Dieu dans la solitude* (*The Blessing of God in Solitude*)—has some of the mysticism encountered in Beethoven's last works. This, too, is Liszt music of the highest order.

The Sonata in B minor (1853) passes from nobility to sublimity. It is in a single movement and in fantasia (rather than sonata) form. Four short melodic ideas are developed along monumental lines. Three of the main ideas are found in the opening section; the fourth comes in the middle slow section. The concluding part is a *prestissimo* wherein all earlier material is given new dimension and emotional impact.

In 1861, Liszt left Weimar to make his home in Rome with Princess Carolyne. He now became more and more obsessed with religion. He would have become a priest had not his unsavory past involvements made this impossible. He did, in 1865, receive the tonsure, symbolic of admission to the clerical state. He managed to take minor orders and Pope Pius IX made him an abbé of the Third Order of St. Francis of Assisi, from which time on he assumed the title of Abbé Liszt and wore a cassock.

He devoted much of his time to teaching (without a fee) a select few piano students, some of whom were destined for greatness by carrying on Liszt's grand tradition of piano playing. His students worshiped him. When he arrived for a lesson, the female pupils would kiss his hand, while the males would stand respectfully until he gave the signal that the lesson was about to begin.

The literature for solo piano in the post-Weimar period includes some of his greatest works. In 1863 there appeared two programmatic Legends. The first is *St. François d'Assise prédicant aux Oiseaux* (*St. Francis' Sermon to the Birds*), suggested by the following passage: "He lifted up his eyes and saw the trees which stood by the wayside filled with a countless multitude of birds; at which he marveled and said to his companions: 'Wait a little for me in the road, and I will go and preach to my little brothers the birds.' " The sermon is in the form of a broad religious melody; from time to time we get from the keyboard the sounds of chirping birds. The second *Legend* is *St. François de Paule marchant sur les Flots* (*St. Francis Walking on the Waves*). This music describes how St. Francis was kept from crossing the Straits of Messina in a boat. The boatman said, "If he is a saint, let him walk on the water." Using a cloak as if it were sails, and his staff as if it were a mast, St. Francis walked over the waters to the opposite shore. The music re-creates the sound of waves as St. Francis performs this miracle. The entire composition is filled with descriptive tone painting.

149

A series of variations on a theme from one of Johann Sebastian Bach's cantatas (the Variations on *Weinen, Klagen, Sorgen, Zagen* in 1862) was followed one year later by two concert favorites, the brilliant études *Waldesrauschen* (*The Rustling of Trees*) and *Gnomenreigen* (*Dance of the Gnomes*). To a much later period (1881–83), and among Liszt's last compositions, belong three of his most original keyboard conceptions: *Nuages gris* (*Gray Clouds*), *Le lugubre gondole* (*The Sad Gondola*), and *Sinistre* (*Sinister*).

One of the great sorrows of Liszt's later years was to see his daughter Cosima desert her husband (Hans von Bülow) and their children in 1865 to set up home with Richard Wagner, whom she subsequently married. Though he himself had led an unconventional life, Liszt could neither forget nor forgive. Being, however, a musician of integrity, he remained forever loyal to Wagner's music and to Wagnerian principles. But for a long time he refused to have any personal dealings with Wagner, nor did he have any contact with his daughter. In 1872, finally, Wagner and Liszt and, to a lesser degree, Liszt and Cosima were reconciled, which made it possible for Liszt to attend the first Wagner festival at the Wagnerian shrine of Bayreuth in 1876.

Liszt was attending the Wagnerian festival at Bayreuth in 1886 when he fell seriously ill. In spite of the warnings of his physician, Liszt insisted on attending a performance of Wagner's *Tristan*. At the end of the performance he was forced to leave the auditorium and go to bed. Pneumonia, followed by a congestion of the lungs, proved fatal. He died in Bayreuth on July 31, 1886. His last thought, apparently, was of Wagner's supreme music drama, for the final word Liszt was heard to mumble was "Tristan."

A page from the Chopin Waltz in F minor.
An autograph manuscript.

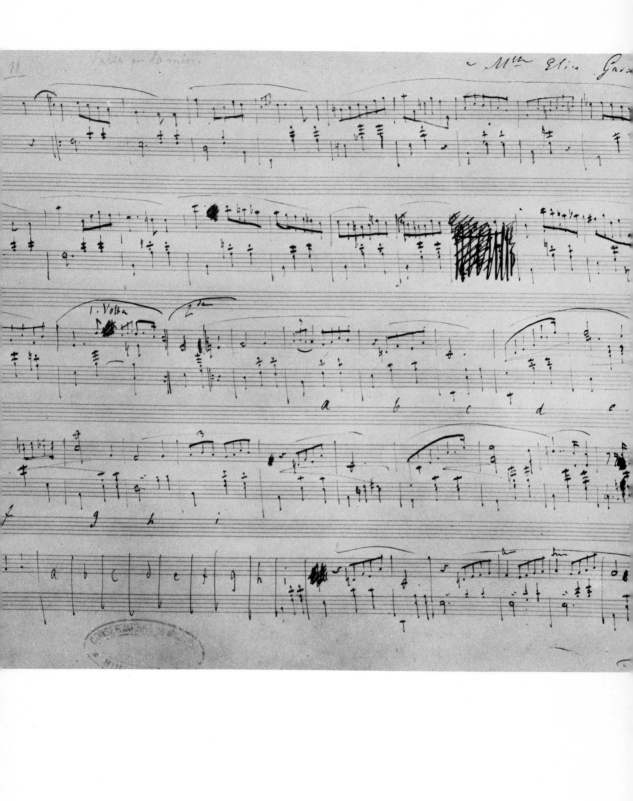

Frédéric Chopin and George Sand,
from a painting by Eugène Delacroix
in the collection of the Louvre.

A caricature of a recital by Franz Liszt.

A caricature of Paganini.

*Niccolò Paganini, a drawing by Ingres
in the collection of the Louvre.*

9

Late Romantics

Johannes Brahms, César Franck

When Brahms was twenty years old he took a walking trip in the Rhineland country of Germany. He was a slender young man, of delicate frame. However, his strong head, with its rich sandy hair, spoke of rugged force.

On arriving in the city of Düsseldorf, on September 30, 1853, he stopped at the home of Robert and Clara Schumann. Though he was a total stranger, he was welcomed warmly. The Schumanns listened attentively as Brahms played for them several of his own compositions. The Schumanns glowed; their enthusiasm overflowed. For already in those early compositions some of Brahms's later strength, and his later skill in fusing Classical structures with Romantic passions, were already evident.

Again and again in their diaries, the Schumanns wrote of their admiration for this young man who bore the stamp of greatness. It did not take Robert Schumann long to use his influence to get Breitkopf and Härtel, a major German publisher, to issue some of Brahms's compositions—Brahms's first publications. Schumann also wrote an article about the young, unknown Brahms, in the *Neue Zeitschrift für Musik,* of which Schumann was editor. This article, which appeared on

October 28, 1853, was the trumpet call to the music world announcing the appearance of a new genius "over whose cradle Graces and Heroes have stood watch." Schumann wrote further: "His name is Johannes Brahms. . . . Even outwardly he bore the mark proclaiming: 'This is the chosen one.' Sitting at the piano he began to disclose wonderful regions to us. We were drawn into even more enchanting spheres. Besides, he is a player of genius who can make of the piano an orchestra of lamenting and loudly jubilant voices. There were sonatas . . . single piano pieces, some of them turbulent in spirit while graceful in form; again, sonatas for violin and piano . . . every work so different from the others that it seemed to stream from its own individual source. And then it was as though rushing like a torrent they were all united by him into a single waterfall, the cascades of which were overarched by a peaceful rainbow. . . . We welcome the champion in him."

And so, once again (as he had previously done with Chopin) Schumann recognized genius in the bud, confident it would sprout into full blossom. As a composer, Brahms was an unknown quantity when Schumann wrote the above report. Brahms would not remain unknown much longer.

His origin was humble; his childhood was filled with misery. The musical endowments with which he was born—in Hamburg, Germany, on May 7, 1833—would have been crushed by the ugliness of his early life were it not for the fact that true genius is indestructible. Brahms, when he was seven, began piano lessons with a local teacher. His progress was so rapid that three years later he was accepted as pupil by Eduard Marxsen, one of Hamburg's most highly esteemed piano teachers. But while he was thus finding an outlet for his musical gifts, and thriving as a music student, Brahms was beset by hardships and trials. His father, an impoverished musician, and his mother, a deformed needleworker, were always quarreling.

To help supplement the all too meager finances of his family, he played the piano in squalid, disreputable saloons and taverns at the waterfront. He also had to give piano lessons, and write hack compositions for a few cents a number. He detested playing popular tunes in taverns, and he was disgusted at his hack assignments. He regretted not being able to give more of his time and energies to developing himself as a pianist and serious composer. In addition, his home life revolted him. All this combined to create such a state of nervous anxiety (as he confided in a letter) that in walking down an avenue he had to stagger from tree to tree for fear of falling down. He might have suffered a nervous breakdown had he not found refuge at the country home of a friend of his family during the summers of 1847 and 1848. Nature and rest helped to soothe his nerves. His mental and physical equilibrium was restored, making him ready to work more earnestly than ever on his career in serious music.

In 1848, in Hamburg, he gave his first piano recital where he introduced one of his own compositions (variations for the piano). At a second public concert, a year later, he performed his piano fantasy based on a waltz. He did not make much of an impression either as pianist or composer. For the time being he gave up appearances as virtuoso to concentrate on composition. Between 1852 and 1854 he wrote several large works, including three sonatas—of which the F minor, op. 5, is the most gifted—and his first chamber music composition, the Piano Trio in B major, op. 8 (1854). Both are brimming over with youthful exuberance, and both also have pages of that serene beauty which would be one of the hallmarks of Brahms's mature works. Thirty-six years after he had written it, Brahms rewrote the piano trio, using most of his early basic material, but bringing to it maturity of thought and full mastery of technique.

In 1853, Brahms was engaged by Eduard Reményi, a Hungarian violinist, as piano accompanist. For several months they toured Germany, where again and again Brahms attracted attention to his exceptional musicianship and pianism. At one of his concerts, Brahms discovered that the piano in the auditorium was a half tone out of tune. He played the entire program by transposing all the music by a semitone at sight. Word of this feat spread rapidly throughout German music circles. Joseph Joachim, one of the foremost violinists of his age, invited Brahms to play for him. Brahms complied with one of his own piano sonatas, among other piano pieces, and then and there completely captured Joachim's friendship. Brahms also visited Liszt at Weimar and gained that master's approval for two of his piano sonatas and a piano scherzo.

The violinist Reményi did not take kindly to the fact that Brahms was continually stealing the limelight from him, both on and off the stage. By the summer of 1853. Brahms was displaced by another accompanist. Brahms now went on a holiday, first to spend some delightful weeks with Joachim in Göttingen, and then on the Rhineland walking trip that brought him to the home of the Schumanns.

For a while, in 1854, Brahms lived in Hanover, working harder than ever on compositions, and enjoying to the full the company of Joachim and other distinguished musicians. One of the latter was Hans von

Bülow, to whom fell the honor of being the first pianist (besides Brahms himself) to present a Brahms composition in public: the first movement of the Sonata no. 1 in C major, op. 1.

In 1854 Brahms brought several new piano compositions to life: the Variations on a Theme by Robert Schumann, op. 9, and four Ballades, op. 10. The Schumann theme came out of Schumann's *Albumblätter*, op. 99 no. 1, and the variations are sixteen miniatures touching many shades of feeling. Schumann was enchanted with this work. "How tender, how original in its masterly expression, how ingenious every one of them," he wrote to Brahms. The Ballade in D minor is based on the Scottish poem "Edward" and like the poem has tragic implications. The Ballade in D major is reflective, and that in B minor, light and whimsical in the distinctive "intermezzo manner" which Brahms employed so often in his later masterworks. The Ballade in B major has a haunting, dreamlike character. Many years later, at the dusk of his career, Brahms wrote still another Ballade, in G minor, op. 118 no. 3 (1893). This is his most celebrated composition in this form, music that opens with a dramatic flourish and proceeds with a light and lovely thought in a contrasting key.

The year of 1854 was a sad one for Brahms. It was the year that Schumann, for whom Brahms had by now formed a deep and all-abiding personal attachment, was struck with insanity and had to be placed in an asylum. Brahms could hardly have suspected that so great a tragedy was to descend on a musician he loved and admired—for when the Schumanns visited Brahms in January of 1854 all seemed well with Robert, and his enthusiastic letter to Brahms about the variations hardly betrays a wandering mind. But just one month after the happy visit of the Schumanns, Brahms received the news about Schumann's mental collapse. His response was immediate. Brahms rushed to Düsseldorf to be with Schumann and help him as best he could. But Schumann was beyond the help of any man. After Schumann was taken to the asylum, Brahms rented an apartment in the house occupied by Clara and her six children so that he might be at hand to give them comfort and assistance. His was the strong shoulder on which Clara leaned most frequently during these, the most trying years of her life. After Schumann's death, the devotion of Brahms and Clara for each other almost passed across the boundary of romantic love. Why they never married, even though this romantic interest lasted until Clara's death, has never been explained.

Between 1856 and 1862 Brahms was much of the time back in his native city of Hamburg, where for about a year he conducted a women's chorus. More deeply than ever he was steeped in the writing of ambitious compositions. His piano Concerto no. 1 in D minor was introduced in Hanover on January 22, 1859, with the composer as soloist, and Joachim conducting. Between 1858 and 1859 Brahms completed two serenades for chamber orchestra. And between 1861 and 1862, Brahms added two masterworks to chamber music literature: his two piano quartets, in G minor, op. 25, and A major, op. 26. He brought these piano quartets with him when, in 1862, he paid his first visit to Vienna, and they were performed at two concerts by Brahms and three members of the Hellmesberger Quartet. "This is Beethoven's heir," said Joseph Hellmesberger, the first violinist, after the second piano quartet had been played. There is something truly Beethovenian in the tragic tones sounded in the first movement of the G minor Quartet. But there is also much of the mature Brahms in both these works: in the light touch with which he writes an intermezzo, which is the second movement of the G minor Quartet; in the elegiac tenderness of this quartet's third movement, written in memory of Schumann; and in the fiery Hungarian spirit which Brahms introduces into the finales of each of these quartets.

At the second of his two Vienna concerts, the one where the second piano quartet was played, Brahms himself introduced his Variations on a Theme by Handel, for piano, op. 24 (1861). How subtle has Brahms's talent become for changing and transfiguring a basic theme, or enlarging some rhythmic or harmonic element of his theme into a new thought! Handel's melody (from the Suite in B-flat, for harpsichord) becomes the spark to light the fires of twenty-five variations, the whole capped by a giant fugue.

Once again, in 1863, Brahms revealed his remarkable skill and imagination in fashioning variations with his Variations on a Theme by Paganini, op. 35. The thirty-five variations are referred to by Brahms as "études." The theme Brahms used was that from Paganini's Twenty-Fourth Caprice, for solo violin. Brahms divided the work into two large sets. Now the two sets are often played together, with some of the weaker sections omitted.

Brahms was the first great composer to write a string sextet for two violins, two violas, and two cellos. His list of compositions include two such works: B-flat major, op. 18 (1860), and G major, op. 36 (1865). Within a basically classical mold, Brahms reveals many of the stylistic mannerisms that distinguish his later masterpieces: the copious supply of idyllic melodies that spring from his deep love of nature; the soaring, sensuous flights of the strings; the romantic moods evoked by the lower strings; the brusque, rustic humor of his scherzo writing. The second, and the greater, of the two sextets is more emotional and romantic than the first, inspired as it was by a young lady with whom Brahms had for a time been deeply in love—Agathe von Siebold, the daughter of a professor at Göttingen University. For a while Brahms considered marrying her. Then (as was to be habitual with him) as he approached matrimony he fled from it. He abruptly broke off his love affair with Agathe, convincing himself that marriage would interfere with his work.

In the first movement of the Sextet in G major, Brahms constructs his second main theme from musical notes representing the letters of his beloved's name: *A-G-A-H* (German for B-natural), and *E* (omitting the letter *T,* for which there is no note). In this movement Brahms speaks not only of his profound emotional involvement with Agathe in passionate passages but, in more poignant ones, of his sorrow in having to reject her. Deep romanticism pervades the pages of the slow movement too (in which Brahms once again exhibits his agility and ingenuity in handling variations). But in the Scherzo and the finale his good humor and exuberant vitality dismiss both romance and pain.

Between these two sextets—in 1864—one of Brahms's supreme achievements in chamber music was made with the justly celebrated Piano Quintet in F minor, op. 34. Brahms first conceived this work as a string quintet (with two cellos), and after that as a sonata for two pianos. Clara Schumann convinced him his material was best suited for the combination of piano and string quartet, with which Brahms immediately agreed. Typically Brahmsian is the brooding opening in the strings over figures in the piano. This is the first of no less than five important themes in a movement that achieves cohesion by the expedient of repeating the cadence (the closing phrase) of a preceding subject in one that follows. The second movement is music of rare loveliness and placidity, creating a mood that is unmistakably Brahmsian from first measure to last. But this is just a temporary transition from the dynamism that had generated most of the preceding movement and which returns in the ensuing Scherzo, where three contrasting themes are discussed. The finale, like the first movement, begins reflectively before Brahms allows the latent strength within him to express itself without inhibition.

Between 1863 and 1864 Brahms led a choir in Vienna and taught the piano privately to several students, with one or two of whom he fell in and out of love. He fell in love with the city of Vienna, too, a romance that motivated his writing sixteen waltzes for piano duet, op. 39

(1865) but which Brahms later adapted for solo piano. These bewitching tunes, influenced markedly by Schubert, capture the infectious spirit of the city.

But Hungary even more than Vienna left its mark on much of Brahms's music (as already we had occasion to note in talking about the finales of Brahms's two piano quartets). During the few months he had toured with Reményi, the violinist introduced Brahms to Hungarian folk songs and dances, which delighted Brahms. Again and again, through the rest of his life, he was impelled to introduce the fiery spirit of Hungarian dance music and the languorous melodies of Hungarian gypsies into major compositions.

This infatuation with Hungarian melodies and rhythms was responsible for Brahms's first two volumes of Hungarian Dances, five dances in each volume. He wrote his first dances in or about 1858 and published the two volumes in 1869. They were also originally written for piano duet, then arranged for solo piano. Here Brahms consciously borrows Hungarian melodies, which he dresses up gaily in the costume of his personal stylistic methods and idioms so that they are as much Brahms as they are Hungarian. But Brahms took special pains to clarify that the melodies were not his own. In the publication he insisted that the phrase "arranged for the piano" be used on the title page. He also refused to allot to either volume an opus number, so that it might not be confused with his original compositions. He presented these dances, as he told his publisher, "as genuine gypsy children which I did not begat but merely brought up with bread and milk." In spite of his every effort to make his position clear in regard to these dances, some critics of his day unjustly accused him of plagiarism. This, however, did not stop them from becoming extraordinarily popular and from helping to spread Brahms's fame throughout the music world. In 1880, he published another two volumes of Hungarian Dances. In all, he wrote twenty-one dances, of which he himself orchestrated three from the first two books (G minor, F major, and E major). Other musicians orchestrated the remainder. The Hungarian Dance no. 5 in F-sharp minor is the one that more than all the others has achieved world recognition—though it became far more popular in various transcriptions than in Brahms's own versions for the keyboard.

Brahms lived mainly in Hamburg up to 1862, while making intermittent visits to Vienna. He hoped to become the musical director of the Hamburg Philharmonic Orchestra, but, despite his rapidly expanding reputation and prestige (which was greatly extended through the success of his choral masterwork, *A German Requiem,* in 1868), the job was never offered him. He decided to desert the city of his birth for Vienna. During the last quarter of a century of his life he occupied a modest three-room apartment in the Karlskirche section not far from the church whose spires he could see from his window.

Now fully confident of his musical powers, now in full command of his technical resources, he ventured upon giant projects, including the writing of major compositions for a large orchestra. The passing years saw him put to paper the Variations on a Theme by Haydn, the four symphonies, three monumental concertos (one for the violin; another—his second such—for the piano; a third for violin and cello).

All the above, with the exception of the Variations on a Theme by Haydn, belong to orchestral literature and therefore do not invade the province of this book. The Variations on a Theme by Haydn is also for large orchestra, but Brahms wrote a second version for two pianos, op. 56b (1873). We do not know whether the two-piano version preceded the orchestral, or vice versa. Both versions are identical in their material. They begin with a hymn, the "Chorale St. Antonii" which Haydn had used in one of his divertimenti. Eight remarkable variations and a finale follow, in which the melody, or elements of the melody, undergo magical changes. Each version, the orchestral and the two-piano one, has its own attraction, but most music lovers are best familiar with the one for orchestra.

The passing years yielded other highly valuable music for the keyboard, all solely for single piano, and all in short forms: capriccios, intermezzi, rhapsodies, and the Romance in F major, op. 118 no. 5 (1893). His first capriccios and intermezzi came in 1878, the last in 1892. A capriccio is a little caprice, a short musical piece in fast tempo that is light in character, slight in structure, and sometimes whimsical. However, the well-known Capriccio in B minor, op. 76 no. 2, 1878) is more romantic and nostalgic than lighthearted. The intermezzo is a form Brahms inherited from Schubert and Schumann. The best by Brahms are those in E-flat and B-flat minor, op. 117 nos. 1 and 2 (1892), and the C major, op. 119 no. 3 (1893). The virile, stormy Brahms appears to best advantage in the three Rhapsodies: B minor and G minor, op. 79 (1879), and E-flat major, op. 119 no. 4 (1893).

In 1873 Brahms turned for the first time to string quartet music with the Quartets in C minor and A minor, op. 51 nos. 1 and 2. A third and last quartet—B-flat major, op. 67—followed in 1876. He was now in fullest maturity as artist, and at the peak of his capabilities. It is then no surprise to find that his only ventures into string quartet music should have resulted in three masterpieces. The first of these quartets, the C minor, is the best integrated, achieving its cohesiveness through the solemnity of mood in most of the four movements (the exception being the trio section of the third), by the use of a recurring motive (an eight-note phrase that opens the work), and by frequently contrasting a rising phrase with a falling one.

The yearning, haunting refrain in the violin that opens the A minor Quartet is the preface to an elegiac movement whose mood deepens into tragedy in the ensuing Andante moderato. But the clouds are dissipated in the third-movement minuet with its Viennese charm and in the finale, where Hungarian rhythms and melodies contribute muscular vigor and sensuousness.

The B-flat major Quartet is cheerful music. A jaunty refrain that sounds like a hunting call gives the work a spirited opening whose vitality persists throughout the movement in rapidly changing rhythms. (This hunting call is the reason why this quartet is named *The Hunt*.)

Brahms's first string quintet (two violins, two violas, and cello)—F major, op. 88 (1882)—is often identified as *Spring,* so ebullient, so effervescent is its overall feeling. Similarly his second and last string quintet—G major, op. 111 (1890)—continually sounds the notes of youthful vigor. And Brahms's last piano trio, in C minor, op. 101 (1886), while bearing no title, might well be named the *Rhythm* Trio, so forceful is the impact of its ever-changing rhythms and meters on the listener.

The larger forms in chamber music did not preoccupy Brahms exclusively. He wrote three sonatas for violin and piano, two for cello and piano, and two for clarinet and piano.

His first violin sonata—G major, op. 78 (1879)—is called *Rain* for two reasons: In it Brahms quotes one of his own songs, *"Regenlied"* ("Rain Song"), op. 59 no. 3 (1871–73); and in the finale, a dashing figure in sixteenth notes sounds like falling raindrops. A motto theme comes and goes throughout the composition: the note *D* repeated three times but heard first in the opening theme of the first movement.

Seven years later came the Sonata no. 2 in A major, op. 100 (1886). This work is called *Thun,* after a Swiss lake at one of whose resorts Brahms wrote most of the composition. The main theme of the first movement has three notes similiar to those that begin the "Prize Song" in Wagner's opera *Die Meistersinger.* The second movement, though marked Andante tranquillo, is a compromise between a slow movement and a scherzo. A deeply felt melody is prominent in the slow part, while a swift-moving section usurps the place of a scherzo. This movement ends in the scherzo mood, which is carried into the buoyant finale.

Brahms's last violin sonata (op. 108) was completed in 1888. Brahms was partial to the tonality of D minor whenever he was emotionally stirred, and that is the key of this sonata, which overflows with poignant feelings. This is one of the rare sonatas by Brahms in four movements, the third being a scherzo. Brahms's tendency to interject Hungarian-type melodies and rhythms leads him to open the fiery finale with a gypsylike tune in double stops.

Brahms's two cello sonatas are separated by twenty years. One would expect that the first—E minor, op. 38 (1865)—would have the incandescent fire of his earlier works, but this is not the case. The first sonata is essentially more pastoral than the second in F major, op. 99 (1886), which is performed more often. This second sonata is in four movements, the noblest being the second, where the cello is given leeway to sing a rapturous melody. The third movement is different from other Brahms scherzos in that it has strength, instead of deftness, and a broad design. The finale is one of the shortest such Brahms ever wrote, and one of the most relaxed.

The springtime and summer of Brahms's life were now ended. The long shadows of autumn had already begun to dim his sun and sky. Often the cold blasts of wind warned that winter was not far off.

As he grew older, Brahms's chamber music substitutes quiet revery and introspection, resignation and contemplation for his former rhythmic strength, sensuousness, and exuberance. This is particularly true of the compositions calling for a clarinet: the Trio in A minor, for clarinet, cello, and piano, op. 114 (1891); the wondrous Quintet in B minor, for clarinet and string quartet, op. 115 (1891); and the two sonatas for clarinet and piano, in F minor and E-flat major, op. 120 (1894). In each, the solemn voice of the clarinet serves well to project the soft gray hues that color these chamber music works, and particularly in the Clarinet Quintet, which is the greatest such work since Mozart, and one of the saddest to come from Brahms.

The death of Clara Schumann in 1896 was a crushing blow to Brahms. He became an old man upon whom were the marks of imminent death. "His appearance was pitiful," was the way his friend and biographer, Max Kalbeck, described him during this period. "His body was shrunken, and his Olympian head fell forward."

A cold contracted at Clara's burial in Bonn aggravated Brahms's long-standing illness (cancer of the liver). His end was at hand. Brahms died in Vienna on April 3, 1897, less than one year after Clara had been buried. It was almost as if Brahms could not bear to be too far away from the only woman to whom he had remained completely dedicated in his love and devotion for the greater part of his life.

The Romantic movement in French music began with Hector Berlioz (1803–69), a flamboyant personality who favored large forms, huge forces, and programmatic music. In striking contrast to him stands one of the major figures in French Romantic music: César Franck. He, too, sometimes wrote large works, including a famous symphony (in D minor), the *Variations symphoniques* for piano and orchestra, and major compositions for chorus. He, too, sometimes wrote programmatically— orchestral tone poems. But his genius expressed itself no less felicitously in absolute music for small chamber music groups, for the piano, and for the organ. In such more modest media he was the foremost French composer of his time.

He was a humble, modest, simple, serene, intensely religious man, never given to dramatic behavior or outbursts of temperament, never seeking personal glory. He had good reason to be bitter if he were capable of self-pity. He had conceived one masterwork after another, yet, until close to his life's end, his music was ignored or slighted. His fame rested exclusively on his ability at playing the organ. Yet he never complained. He knew the full value of his music (as did a handful of disciples who regarded him as their "master," who paid him homage, and who were inspired by him in their own compositions). But he knew that, as a composer, *his* time would surely come—after his death if not in his own lifetime. As it turned out, though recognition came shamefully late, it did come in time for Franck to enjoy its blessing.

Franck came from Belgium, the city of Liège, where he was born on December 10, 1822. Entered into the Liège Conservatory when he was eight, the boy was directed by an ambitious father toward becoming a piano virtuoso. It seemed that this ambition would be realized when Franck, aged eleven, won first prize in piano and shortly thereafter made successful appearances as a piano prodigy.

Between 1837 and 1842, Franck attended the Paris Conservatory. There he captured prizes in fugue, piano, organ, and counterpoint. By this time composing had become for him an interest that replaced his former enthusiasm for playing the piano. Soon after entering the conservatory he wrote a piano concerto, which he himself (aged fifteen) introduced in Paris.

He left the conservatory without graduating because his father was impatient for him to invade the concert platform. In 1843 he proudly held his first publication in hand, a set of three piano trios. In 1846 Franck's first mature and ambitious composition—the oratorio *Ruth,* for solo voices, chorus, and orchestra—was heard at the conservatory by an audience that included Liszt and Meyerbeer, both of whom were impressed. But there was no money in composition. Having married an actress (Mademoiselle Desmousseux) in 1848, Franck was compelled to fill numerous humble jobs to make financial ends meet, teaching and serving as assistant organist at Notre-Dame-de-Lorette Church in Paris. But even while performing his various menial duties by day, musical ideas kept pressing on his consciousness all the time so that he had to steal away in a corner and scribble them down on paper.

In 1851, Franck became principal organist at the church Saint-Jean-Saint-François in the Marais district of Paris. Seven years after that, he assumed the post he would occupy for the remainder of his years, that of principal organist at Sainte-Clotilde. It was there that his fame as organist swelled to such dimensions that this church was packed every Sunday with music lovers come to hear him play. Some crowded the open spaces in or near Franck's organ loft, listening to him with admiration that bordered on rapture. Franz Liszt was one of them. After listening to Franck in 1866 he whispered with awe that it had seemed to him that Johann Sebastian Bach was playing!

Giant compositions occupied Franck: an opera, which was never performed; a large symphonic poem for orchestra and voices, *Rédemption,* (1871–72), a failure when performed in 1873; an oratorio, *Les Béatitudes* (1869–79), which was received so unfavorably when Franck played parts of it for prominent musicians that it failed to receive a public performance during his lifetime; his first tone poems for orchestra; and his first important compositions for the organ, the *Six Pieces* (1860–62), which comprised a fantasie, a "grand symphonic piece," a prelude, fugue and variations, a pastorale, a *"Prière"* ("Prayer") and a finale (op. 16 through 21). The shadow of Johann Sebastian Bach hovers continually over this music, as it does over the *Forty-four Little Pieces* for organ (or harmonium) completed in 1863, and the *Three Pieces* ("Fantaisie," "Cantabile" and *Pièce héroïque"*) in 1878.

In 1879 Franck erected a landmark in French chamber music with the Piano Quintet in F minor, his first return to chamber music writing in some twenty-six years. Because the quintet was written at a time when Franck was in love with one of his pupils, the music is so consistently passionate in feeling that some of Franck's contemporaries denounced it as erotic! It was in this composition that Franck introduced a technique with which he became identified and which is encountered in many of his later works: the cyclic method. This technique calls for the repetition of a principal melodic subject from an earlier movement in later ones to achieve integration. The melody repeated in the quintet is the sensitive subject presented initially by the first violin in the opening movement, and then repeated in the climax of the second movement, and extensively worked upon in the coda of the third-movement finale.

One of Franck's lifelong ambitions was to bring about a renaissance of piano music, a field that he felt had become sadly neglected by composers since the time of Couperin and Rameau. With this goal in view, Franck wrote a symphonic poem for piano and orchestra, *Les Djinns* (1884), and the *Variations symphoniques,* for piano and orchestra, in 1885. He also turned to solo piano, completing two masterpieces between 1884 and 1887: the Prelude, Chorale, and Fugue and the Prelude, Aria, and Finale.

For all the loftiness of his music, Franck seemed incapable of finding the understanding and appreciation he so well deserved—outside the small and intimate circle of his pupils and disciples. When pianist Marie Poitevin presented the premiere of Prelude, Chorale, and Fugue in 1885, Camille Saint-Saëns (then already one of France's most influential and highly revered musicians) wrote: "The chorale is not a chorale, and the fugue is not a fugue." To counteract the lack of interest in their beloved master, his pupils and friends arranged an all-Franck concert in Paris on January 30, 1887. The first part was conducted by Jules Pasdeloup, the second by Franck himself. The part led by Pasdeloup was performed shamefully; at one point, in the *Variations symphoniques,* the conductor made a false start and threw the performance into pandemonium. When Franck ascended the platform to lead the second half, he was hissed. With his customary stoicism he ignored this abuse and went on with the concert as if nothing had happened. There was no question that this concert failed completely to accomplish what Franck's followers hoped it would: throw the limelight of recognition on a great composer.

The Sonata in A major for violin and piano (possibly the greatest violin sonata to come from France) was also shabbily received, when

169

first heard in Brussels in the year of its composition (1886). For almost thirty years Franck had yearned to write a violin sonata. Hearing a performance by the great Belgian virtuoso, Eugène Ysaye, stirred him into action. Franck wrote his sonata for Ysaye. Fate, however, seemed capable of devising more than one way to victimize Franck. The sonata's premiere took place at a concert given in a room of the Modern Museum in Brussels. No lighting was allowed in the museum, and by the time the sonata began the afternoon light was growing dim. In the darkness, the performers were unable to read the music. It seemed that the concert would have to end then and there when Ysaye's bow was heard rapping on his music stand and his voice ordered the pianist to get along with the playing. They performed the sonata from memory in the dark auditorium. This mishap was hardly calculated to put the audience in the proper frame of mind to listen to a composition that was long, subtle in its construction, and complex in the evolution of its material.

The sonata is in cyclic form. The first movement (in sonata form, but with no development of its two themes) serves as a kind of a preface to the remaining three movements. In this opening part, the violin is heard in a three-note motive, which, in one form or another, is the nucleus of the first theme of each succeeding movement. The development of the sonata really begins with the second-movement Allegro. The secondary theme of the ensuing movement, as well as the three-note motive of the first one, are given full treatment in the finale, which opens with an appealing canonic presentation of its first theme.

And still failure continued to dog Franck's footsteps! The first performance of his now greatly admired and frequently played D minor Symphony, on February 17, 1889, was a fiasco. Franck remained sublimely unperturbed. The scathing criticisms leveled at him by several prominent French musicians did not even scratch the surface of his sensibilities. He came home beaming with the happiness of one who knew with finality he had written a masterpiece.

Then when it seemed that he was doomed to perpetual failure as composer, success arrived—none too soon, for the hour in Franck's life was late. On April 19, 1890, there took place the premiere of Franck's last chamber music composition, the String Quartet in D major (1889). The work aroused immense enthusiasm, so much so that it had to be performed again only one month later. The great French writer Marcel Proust requested that it be performed privately at his home. On few compositions had its composer expended such dedication and effort. It took him a long time to begin to work on it, so sacred did he regard its writing. For months he kept filling pages with musical materials that might serve him. It took him over half a year to write just the opening movement, which is not very long. Putting the finale on paper in its final form proved a Herculean effort. When the string quartet was completed, Franck was satisfied.

One of Franck's most dedicated disciples (and his first biographer), Vincent d'Indy, described the first movement of this quartet as a "sonata form inscribed with a *Lied* (art song)," because the opening section sounds like an extended song. This "song" is again heard in the coda of the first movement and is suggested in the winged Scherzo that follows. The glory of the quartet is the five-section slow movement, whose mysticism reminds us of the slow movements of Beethoven's last string quartets. The finale first recalls for us the first-movement "song" before presenting the basic themes of the other movements in accordance with Franck's cyclic method. The quartet ends on a note of sublimity as the exalted slow movement is quoted.

Franck's last composition was his Three Chorales, for organ (1890)—surely an appropriate swan song for a supreme organist, and a deeply religious man. This is the greatest of Franck's compositions for the organ. "Before I die," Franck said, "I am going to write organ chorales just as Bach did, but with quite a different plan." To Bach's sublimity, Franck adds his own brand of religious spirituality and his own method—that method being to treat the chorale in the form of variations. In the first chorale (E major), the melody is ornamented and enlarged, while passing through frequent changes of tonality. The second (B minor) is a noble passacaglia. The last (A minor) opens dramatically before the chorale theme is treated in the style of a toccata.

Here is how Vincent d'Indy described Franck: "César Franck was short, with a fine forehead and a vivacious honest expression, although his eyes were almost concealed under his bushy eyebrows. His nose was rather large and his chin receded below a wide and extraordinarily expressive mouth. His face was round and thick, gray side whiskers added to its width. . . . Anyone who happened to meet this man in the street, invariably in a hurry, invariably absent-minded, and making grimaces, running rather than walking, dressed in an overcoat a size too large for him and in trousers a size too short, would never have suspected the transformation that took place when, placed at the piano, he explained or commented upon some fine composition."

One evening in May of 1890 Franck visited a friend. Deep in thought, as was habitual with him, and completely oblivious of the world outside his inner self, he did not notice a horse-drawn bus as he crossed the street. The vehicle hit him in the chest. Franck regarded the accident lightly. Once he had recovered his equilibrium, he continued on his way. But this accident resulted in a gradual weaking of his strength. When, a few months later, he caught cold, it brought on a fatal pleurisy. Sick as he was, he left his bed to play his Three Chorales in his organ loft at Sainte Clotilde, almost as a farewell gesture to his beloved instrument. He died soon after that, on November 8, 1890. Typical of this man was the fact that his final thoughts expressed concern for the precious friends he was leaving. Among his last words were: "My children, my poor children."

10

The Flowering of Musical Nationalism

Antonín Dvořák, Edvard Grieg,
Isaac Albéniz, Béla Bartók

In the second half of the nineteenth century, nationalism became a significant facet of the Romantic movement in music. Nationalism achieved full momentum in Russia with a group of five composers who came to be known as the "Mighty Five" or the "Russian Five" (Balakirev, Borodin, César Cui, Mussorgsky, and Rimsky-Korsakov). Their principal works have a pronounced Russian identity, since they drew their subject matter from their country's history, culture, geography, and legends and utilized idioms lifted from native folk songs, folk dances, and church music. The main channels through which their creativity flowed were operas and orchestral music. Two piano works, however, deserve attention: Balakirev's *Islamey* (1868), a free development of three Caucasian folk melodies, and Mussorgsky's *Pictures at an Exhibition* (1874). The latter, inspired by a public showing of paintings, drawings, and designs by the composer's artist friend, Victor Hartmann, is invariably thought of as an orchestral work because of Maurice Ravel's brilliant and frequently played orchestration. But Mussorgsky wrote this work for the piano, a version also remarkably vivid and apt in representing in tones ten of Hartmann's art works.

In other lands composers arose as musical spokesmen for the intense patriotism and the pride in their country's heritage that was spreading all over Europe. The father of Bohemian musical nationalism was Bedřich Smetana (1824–84). His comic opera *The Bartered Bride* (1866) and his orchestral tone poem, *The Moldau,* or *Vltava* (1874), are the most celebrated such works to come from that country. Smetana first became fired with the spirit of nationalism when, as an unknown composer, he became involved in political activity in 1848 by joining a movement stirring in Bohemia to free that country from political oppression by Austria (Bohemia then being a part of the Austro-Hungarian Empire). Smetana stood in the forefront of those intellectuals promoting Bohemian culture. He became the most influential musician advancing Bohemian music. Among his many nationalistic compositions are several for the piano, including two books of polkas, *Memories of Bohemia* (1861), and a series of fourteen *Bohemian Dances* (1878). He wrote two nostalgic pieces for violin and piano, *From the Home Country* (1878). Outstanding among his chamber music works is the String Quartet no. 1 in E minor (1876), a tonal autobiography appropriately named *From My Life*. As the composer himself explained, he depicted in his first movement "the love of art in my youth." In the second movement, whose principal theme is in the rhythm of a polka, he remembered "the joyful days of my youth when I composed dance music." The slow third movement recalls "the bliss of my first love for the girl who afterwards became my faithful wife." The finale is alive with the vigor and color of Bohemian songs and dance rhythms as the composer speaks of his joy in discovering he could "treat the national elements in music." This gaiety, however, is suddenly shattered in the coda. At the time Smetana wrote this quartet he was deaf. A high E in the first violin over tremolos in the other strings tells us of Smetana's tragic infirmity.

The cause of Bohemian nationalism was carried on and furthered by Antonín Dvořák (1841–1904), who, for twelve years, had played in the orchestra of the National Opera conducted for the final years of Dvořák's engagement by Smetana. This long professional and personal affiliation with Smetana led Dvořák away from composers he had been imitating in his early compositions (mostly Wagner, Beethoven, and Liszt) to develop his own style molded after national Bohemian patterns. In 1874 he wrote his first real folk opera, and had an earlier opera produced that year at the National Theater. In 1875, 1876, and 1877, he received the Austrian State Prize for his works in a national style. He was also writing Bohemian music for the piano: *Dumka,* op. 35

(1876)—a "dumka" being a traditional Slavic folk ballad, often of a melancholy character; *Two Furiants,* op. 42 (1878)—fiery Bohemian dances in ¾ time marked by changing accents—and *Dumka and Furiant,* op. 12 (1884). World fame came with the first series of Slavonic Dances, op. 46 (1878) for piano duet (since become famous in orchestral adaptations).

Here is how Dvořák came to write these popular Dances. In 1876, his *Moravian Duets* for soprano, contralto, and piano, op. 32 were among the works he submitted to win first prize from the Austrian State Commission. Brahms, a member of the committee voting for Dvořák, took such a personal interest in the young Bohemian composer that he induced his own publisher (Simrock) not only to publish the *Duets* but also to commission Dvořák to write a new composition. Since Simrock had profited greatly from Brahms's Hungarian Dances, for piano duet, he came up with the idea of having Dvořák produce a Bohemian equivalent of these Hungarian Dances. Dvořák complied with eight Slavonic Dances, published in 1878. With consummate artistry and a wide range of emotion and mood, Dvořák adapted Slavonic folk dances into artistic creations that contained both the heart and soul of these people. Each dance is a gem, but if the more iridescent ones are to be chosen we would have to select the following: C major (no. 1); E minor (no. 2); A-flat major (no. 6); and G minor (no. 8). The first is vigorous, the second elegiac, the sixth fiery, and the eighth frolicsome. Dvořák wrote and had published a second set of eight Slavonic Dances, op. 72 (1886), the best of which are the tender E minor (no. 2) and the A minor (no. 7).

Bohemian folk song (which was less sentimental and sensuous than the Hungarian, and far more atmospheric) stimulated Dvořák into writing ten Legends, for piano duet, op. 59 (1881). A "legend" is a convenient nomenclature adopted by Dvořák and others for a composition that, without having a program, seems to be picturing a mood or setting. Dvořák's Legends are generally mood pictures and dances usually in a three-part structure. Dvořák himself orchestrated all ten Legends.

Each of the pieces in the six piano duets collectively entitled *From the Bohemian Forest,* op. 68 (1884) carries a descriptive title. These pieces are "In the Spinning Room," "On the Dark Lake," "Witches' Sabbath," "On the Watch," "Silent Woods," and "In Troubled Times."

Whenever we speak of Dvořák's Humoresque (that semiclassic favorite the world over) we are referring to the G-flat major, become so famous in transcriptions. But Dvořák wrote not one but eleven Humoresques, all for piano solo, eight of which are collected in op. 101 (1894). They are among Dvořák's last creations for the keyboard. When Schumann had conceived the form of the "Humoreske" (or "Humoresque") he intended it to be a short whimsical or humorous piece of music. But those by Dvořák are much more sober. It is only in Fritz Kreisler's transcription for violin and piano that the familiar G-flat major Humoresque is light and airy; as Dvořák wrote it for the piano it is in a much slower tempo and in a graver mood.

Now a world-famous composer, Dvořák was invited to come to the United States in 1892 to fill the post of director of the then newly founded National Conservatory in New York. He remained in America about three years. In that time he became fascinated with the folk music of the new world—the songs and dances of both the American Negro and the American Indian. He used idioms and styles from both these folk sources in several compositions, such as his most distinguished symphony, the *Symphony from the New World* and his Cello Concerto in B minor, both of which were inspired by the plangent melodies of Negro spirituals. American-Indian song and dance material (to which Dvořák was introduced when some Iroquois Indians performed for him) provided the physiognomy for Dvořák's principal melodies and rhythms in his String Quartet in F major, op. 96 (the *American*), the String Quintet in E-flat major, op. 97, and the Sonatina in G major, for violin and piano, op. 100—all of them completed in 1893. The last of these works, the sonatina, is today remembered almost exclusively for its slow movement, the Larghetto, a haunting refrain, which has been published separately under the new title of *Indian Lament*.

In 1895 Dvořák returned to his native land, where his sixtieth birthday brought on a national celebration. From 1901 until he died three years later he was the director of the Prague Conservatory. Arterial degeneration brought on Dvořák's death in Prague. His funeral was officially declared throughout Bohemia as a national day of mourning.

The greatest composer of Norway—Edvard Grieg (1843–1907)—was the musical voice of his country and its people. Through his compositions, the world outside Norway came to know the spirit and the soul of that picturesque Scandinavian country. But Grieg had started out not as a Norwegian musical nationalist but as a German Romanticist, having received much of his musical training at the Leipzig Conservatory, from which he was graduated with honors in 1862. Then, in 1864, he became a friend of Rikard Nordraak, an ardent Norwegian patriot who had written Norway's national anthem. Nordraak convinced Grieg to become a *Norwegian* composer, by tapping the veins of his country's folk songs and dances. Grieg's first composition in a national style was *Humoresques*, op. 6 (1865), for piano, which he dedicated to Nordraak.

The sudden death of Nordraak in 1866 (he was only twenty-three) was a crushing blow to Grieg. When he finally recovered from the shock, Grieg was determined to bring his friend's national ideals in music to full fruition. In every way he could, Grieg henceforth dedicated his energies to advancing the cause of Norwegian music and musicians—as a composer, conductor, pianist, founder of a music school, and promoter of concerts.

Between 1867 and 1901 Grieg combined sixty-six pieces for the piano in ten volumes with the overall title of *Lyric Pieces*. To each number Grieg fixed an identifying title. These pieces are in turn atmospheric, subjective, pictorial, imaginative, realistic. Several provide insights into Norwegian customs, people, ceremonies, dances, and so forth—for example, "Norwegian Peasant March" (Book V, op. 54), and "Wedding Day at Troldhaugen" and "Peasants' Song" (Book VIII, op. 65). The best of the less national compositions include the following: "Butterfly," "Erotik," and "To the Spring" (Book III, op. 43); "Shepherd Boy," "Nocturne," and "March of the Dwarfs" (Book V, op. 54); and "At the Cradle" (Book IX, op. 68). Grieg orchestrated four of these for his Lyric Suite, op. 54: "Shepherd Boy," "Norwegian Peasant March," "Nocturne," and "March of the Dwarfs."

The *Lyric Pieces* is Grieg's greatest work for the piano, but it finds a formidable rival in his Ballade in G minor, op. 24 (1875). This work is in the form of a theme and variations. The theme is a subdued, gentle Norwegian folk song. Fourteen variations follow.

The sprightly Norwegian Dance no. 2 in A minor (one of Grieg's most popular short pieces) belongs in a series of four such dances for piano duet written in 1881 (op. 35). In few of his works did he make so effective and authentic a use of Norwegian folk dance material as here. Grieg orchestrated all four dances besides arranging them for solo piano.

The *Holberg* Suite, for piano, op. 40 (1884)—like the Norwegian Dance no. 2—is more familiar in the composer's version for string orchestra than in its original one for piano. Holberg was one of the immortals of Danish literature. When the bicentenary of his birth was celebrated in Scandinavia, Grieg wrote this suite in his honor. Since Holberg had lived in the seventeenth century, Grieg reverted to the classic suite of that period by using old dance forms in three of the five movements: a Sarabande, Gavotte, and Rigaudon. The suite begins with a Prelude, *177* continues with a Sarabande, while an "Air" separates the Gavotte and the Rigaudon. But the harmonic writing within these old-time forms is always recognizably Grieg and in the Air the melody is identifiably Norwegian.

Before most of the above piano works came into being, and before Grieg had arrived at full recognition as his country's leading composer, he had received heart-warming encouragement from the great Franz Liszt. Liszt came upon Grieg's Sonata no. 1 in F major, for violin and piano, op. 8 (1865), and was delighted with it. He sent Grieg an enthusiastic endorsement: "It evidences a powerful, logically creative, ingenious, and excellent constructive talent for composition, which needs only to follow its natural development to attain high rank." Grieg visited Liszt soon after that, bringing him some more of his manuscripts, which Liszt played at sight. Liszt saw to it that one of his pupils give the premiere of the first Grieg Violin Sonata.

On June 11, 1867, Grieg married his cousin, Nina Hagerup, with whom he had long been in love, and for whom he wrote his greatest song, "I Love You." His joy in marrying his beloved found an outlet in a second violin sonata—in G major, op. 13—which he completed just one month after his marriage. This sonata is in a Norwegian style, whereas his first violin sonata had been basically in a German-Romantic vein though Norwegian tendencies are present. The slow movement is a haunting folk-type song, and the finale is enlivened by the rhythms and melody of a typical Norwegian folk dance.

Grieg wrote just one more violin sonata after that—the C minor, op. 45 (1887). It is the best of the three, more original in its subject matter, more ingenious in its construction, more poetic in concept than the other two. It begins strongly, with a powerful melody in the violin accompanied by chords in the piano, but a more mellow subject follows; the movement, however, ends with an arresting presto. The second movement is for the most part introspective, its main melody once again sounding as if it were a Norwegian folk song. Spirited rhythms and vitality end the sonata on a note of triumph.

The Sonata in A minor, op. 36 (1883), is Grieg's only composition for cello and piano. It ranks with the Third Violin Sonata among Grieg's masterworks for a solo instrument and piano, rich as it is in melodic content and inventive in the way in which the melodies are elaborated. The beautiful Andante, whose enchanting melody begins in the piano for eight measures before being continued by the cello, is among the best slow movements Grieg ever wrote.

Grieg completed only one surviving string quartet—G minor, op. 27 (1878). Here he adopts a motto theme (heard in the introduction to the first movement), which becomes the first measure of the main subject of the movement and after that appears in various transformations throughout all the four movements. This motto theme comes from one of Grieg's songs, "Minstrels" (op. 25 no. 1, 1876). The hauntingly beautiful Romance (second movement) and the atmospheric Intermezzo movement that follows find Grieg at the height of his creative powers.

From 1885 till the end of his life Grieg lived in Troldhaugen, a villa six miles from Bergen, Norway. It was surrounded by forests and mountains and overlooked a fjord. Grieg was now a world figure. Troldhaugen became the destination of musicians come from all over the world to pay him honor. Today it stands as a shrine to Grieg's memory.

Isaac Albéniz (1860–1909) has won recognition as Spain's first important national composer exclusively for his compositions for the piano. His masterwork is *Iberia,* a suite of twelve piano pieces (1906–09) collected in four volumes. This is a series of pictures of Spanish scenes, haunts, and episodes that form a colorful panorama of Spain captured in Spanish melodies and Spanish dance rhythms. These are some of the more fascinating numbers in the suite: from the first book, *"El Puerto,"* a graphic re-creation of a fiesta in a Spanish resort, and *"El Corpus en Sevilla"* (or *"Fête-Dieu à Séville"*), describing a religious ceremony in the streets of Seville; from the second book, *"Triaña,"* in which a gypsy song and dance evoke for us the picture of a haunt outside Seville; and from the third book, *"El Albaicín,"* where a languorous gypsy melody catches some of the excitement of the gypsy quarter of Granada.

Albéniz wrote a good many other piano compositions, large and small, which have won wide favor with performers and audiences because of the exciting exotic appeal of their Spanish subjects and idioms. The best are "Córdoba" from *Cantos de España,* op. 232; "Granada" and "Sevillañas" from *Suite Española; "Jota aragonesa",* op. 164 no. 1; the two Malagueñas, op. 71 no. 6 and op. 165 no. 3; *"Navarra,"* the composer's last composition, which had to be finished by his friend Déodat de Sévérac; "Seguidillas" from *Castilla;* and possibly the best-known tango to come from Spain, the D major, op. 165 no. 2.

With Albéniz we cross the threshold into the twentieth century. Musical nationalism continued to be a powerful force among composers in Spain and many other European countries. It was musical nationalism that lifted Hungary's leading twentieth-century composer—Béla Bartók (1881–1945)—from mediocrity to greatness.

Bartók's first composition was a waltz for the piano, written when he was nine; his first public appearance as pianist came when he was eleven. His piano study took place with private teachers until 1899, when he entered the Royal Academy of Music in Budapest. His ambition then was to become a virtuoso. For four years he specialized in the piano. But during this time he heard Richard Strauss's tone poem *Thus Spake Zarathustra,* which made such an impression on him that then and there he decided that more than anything else he wanted to be a composer. He then wrote some songs, an orchestral scherzo, and, in 1903, *Kossuth,* a tone poem in the style of Strauss.

In 1904 Bartók discovered Hungarian folk music for the first time. It happened by chance when, on a visit to a Hungarian resort, he overheard a chambermaid singing one of the native songs of that region. He soon learned that other districts of Hungary also had folk music of their own. In 1905 Bartók traveled throughout Hungary to seek out these native melodies, the first of many such expeditions he would take in the ensuing years. Thus he came upon a wonderful library of folk music far different from any he had ever heard and completely unknown outside the respective regions. These songs were not the sentimental, sensuous songs and dances that Liszt, Brahms, and Sarasate had assumed to be the *real* Hungarian folk art. Authentic Hungarian folk music held an esoteric character because of its employment of the old modes, known to us mainly through their ecclesiastical use. In its complex rhythms and changing tonalities it possessed an almost savage power. Its melodies were declamatory rather than lyrical. Its harmonies were usually discordant.

In 1906 Bartók published a volume of these folk songs. During his intensive researches in the ensuing eight years he managed to collect over six thousand songs. "The outcome of these studies," he later confessed, "was a decisive influence in my work." In his compositions he no longer imitated Richard Strauss, Liszt, or Brahms as he had previously done. Now his goal was to develop a Hungarian musical art assimilating the stylistic elements of Hungarian folk music. Thus he succeeded in arriving at a style not only authentically Hungarian but also unmistakably Bartókian.

In 1907 Bartók was appointed teacher of the piano at the Royal Academy of Music in Budapest. He held this post for nearly thirty years.

He fell in love with one of his pupils, Márta Ziegler, whom he married in 1909 when she was only sixteen.

The evolution of Bartók's style through the years can be followed in his six string quartets, the greatest single contribution to string quartet writing made by any one composer in the twentieth century. To the String Quartet no. 1, op. 7 (1909), there still cling Romantic influences. It took Bartók almost a decade to write his Second String Quartet, op. 17 (1917). By this time he had learned how to use the materials he had uncovered in Hungarian folk music and how to adapt them to his own artistic needs and personality. With this quartet, Bartók begins to achieve dynamism through discords and rhythmic dexterity.

A decade passed before two more string quartets appeared, nos. 3 and 4 (1927–28). Bartók's writing now becomes even more iconoclastic. He dispenses with any basic tonality, allowing his brusque, terse thoughts to move as they will to whatever key. He becomes increasingly discordant, and the power he unleashes through rhythmic means is like an atomic blast. New instrumental effects are introduced to heighten the tension. (He also deserted the practice of using opus numbers.) Then with his String Quartets no. 5 (1934) and no. 6 (1939), Bartók begins to simplify his writing, to make it more lyrical, more consistently tonal, with occasional excursions into emotional expression. There are even suggestions of humor in the sixth quartet. What we have in these last two quartets is a compromise between Bartók's early Romantic tendencies with his later iconoclastic ways—a compromise he would continue to make in other compositions, and especially during his last years.

None of the Bartók quartets, not even the last two, are easy to listen to or comprehend at first or second hearing. Only familiarity brings appreciation. Young people will find much to appreciate, however, even at a casual acquaintance, with the 153 pieces for the piano upon which Bartók labored between 1926 and 1939, and which he wrote expressly for youngsters. He called this monumental endeavor *Mikrokosmos* (which means "little world"), and his intent was to teach young people what authentic Hungarian, Bulgarian, Romanian, and Transylvanian folk music is like, and how to master certain techniques, including modern ones. All these pieces have titles, so that it is easy to know the lesson Bartók is presenting in each instance. Specific technical problems are posed and solved in "Dotted Notes," "Syncopation," "Parallel Motion," "Contrary Motion," "Chromatic," "Minor Sixths in Parallel Motion," "Broken Chords," and so on. Some of the pieces introduce the young pianist to old church modes. Others provide characteristic examples of East European folk songs and dances, as in "In Hungarian Style," "In Transylvanian Style," and "Hungarian Dance." There are still other pieces that are either descriptive or programmatic: "Buzzing" and "Dragon's Dance."

Bartók wrote two sonatas for violin and piano that have been published, the first in 1921 and the second in 1922. Both give the feeling of improvisation (a characteristic of so many Hungarian folk songs). In both the melodic material has declamatory austerity; both make use of percussive effects. The second is the one violinists prefer. It has two movements. There is little interchange of material between violin and piano—each instrument going its own way independently. In the second sonata Bartók imitates the playing of Hungarian village fiddlers.

When Bartók left Hungary in the early part of World War II, for what became permanent exile, he was a world figure in music—though much more so for his concertos, orchestral music, and stage works than for his chamber music or music for the piano. He established residence in a New York City apartment. Those were sad years for Bartók. He was deathly sick, suffering as he was from leukemia. He was without funds. The little he could earn in America was just about enough to keep him and his family from outright poverty, though insufficient to pay for his medical needs. He was in a strange land, listening to a strange language, surrounded by a strange culture and way of life. He felt as if the foundations upon which he had built his career had crumbled. The greatest pain of all was the fact that, in spite of his immense prestige, so few of his compositions were getting American performances.

Among others who helped him, the eminent violinist Yehudi Menuhin asked Bartók to write for him a work for solo violin. The Sonata for Solo Violin was completed in 1944 and was Bartók's last solo instrumental composition. Here Bartók synthesizes his own modern style with the Baroque structures of the chaconne (first movement) and the fugue (second movement). The three-part third movement is one of Bartók's most lyrical pages. The fourth movement is a presto. In these last years, and in his last compositions, Bartók was growing increasingly free in giving voice to his emotions. There is an outpouring of joyous feeling in the sonata, intensified through the use of quarter tones, which makes it difficult to remember Bartók's state when he wrote this music.

His last words before his death on September 26, 1945, were: "The trouble is that I have to go with so much still to say."

Johannes Brahms.

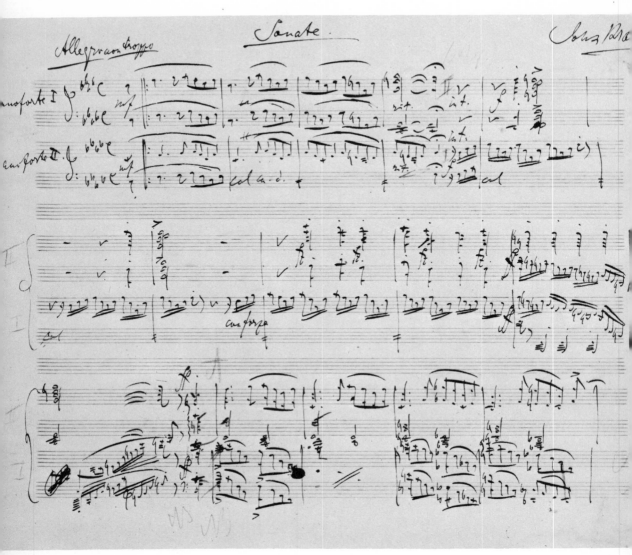

A page from the Brahms Sonata for Two Pianos.
An autograph manuscript.

The Joseph Joachim Quartet.

César Franck at the organ of Sainte-Clotilde.

Isaac Albéniz.

Antonín Dvořák. A drawing by Hugo Boettinger.

II

Russians and Soviets

Peter Ilitch Tchaikovsky, Sergei Rachmaninoff,

Alexander Scriabin, Serge Prokofiev,

Dmitri Shostakovich

The "Russian Five," which dedicated itself to musical nationalism, looked upon Peter Ilitch Tchaikovsky (1840–93) with condescension and at times disdain. To the Russian Five, Tchaikovsky—whom we now look upon as Russia's greatest composer—was more interested in making music a receptacle for his overcharged emotions and self-pity than for the expression of Russian subjects and ideals. The nationalist group accused Tchaikovsky of allying himself with French and German music in his polished-styled and neatly sculptured forms. That Tchaikovsky's music was often nurtured on Russian literature, poetry, and history, and that Tchaikovsky sometimes quoted Russian folk songs or molded his own melodies after folk patterns did not prevent the Russian Five from regarding Tchaikovsky as a musical renegade.

This accusation holds true for Tchaikovsky's chamber and piano music, for the works in which Tchaikovsky is most Russian are his operas, ballets, and compositions for orchestra and for the voice. Most of his other work seems as if it came out of a European salon and not from the Russian scene. These other works are filled with sentimentalized European-type melodies and harmonies. This is music with the breeding and gentility of European nobility (whereas the nationalistic works of the Five had a good deal of the unkempt, uncouth appearance of a Russian peasant). Since neither his chamber nor his piano music is truly representative of Tchaikovsky's genius, they will be touched upon only briefly here. They are, however, too popular to be altogether ignored.

All that most music lovers know of Tchaikovsky's String Quartet in D major, op. 11 (1871) is its second movement: the Andante cantabile, whose two main melodies have a sad sweetness. It is said that the first and more famous of these two melodies (played by muted strings) was something Tchaikovsky heard a carpenter sing under his window; the second melody, equally lyrical, however, is of Tchaikovsky's own invention.

Tchaikovsky's best chamber music work is the Piano Trio in A minor, op. 50 (1882), in memory of Nicholas Rubinstein, a distinguished Russian teacher and pianist who died in 1881. The first movement is an elegy. Tchaikovsky intended the second movement to represent different episodes in Rubinstein's life, each episode symbolized by a different musical form. He used a theme and variations, each variation being in a different structure (mazurka, waltz, fugue, scherzo, and so forth). In the finale, technically belonging to part two, but in reality a separate movement, Tchaikovsky builds material from the first two movements into tempestuous climaxes. The work ends with a dirge-like march recapturing the elegiac mood of the first movement.

Tchaikovsky's piano music contains some happy examples of his gift for melody. *Souvenir de Hapsal,* op. 2 (1865–67) is a three-movement suite whose last movement is one of Tchaikovsky's best-known tunes, the *Chant sans paroles* ("Song Without Words"). Still another beloved "Song Without Words" for piano is found in the album *Twelve Pieces of Moderate Difficulty,* op. 40 (1876–78). The tenderness that makes these pieces so appealing can also be found in the no less popular Romance in F minor, op. 5 (1868), believed to have been inspired by a love affair with a singer. Romantic, too, is the Nocturne in C-sharp minor, op. 19 no. 4 (1873), while—by contrast—the Humoresque, op. 10 no. 2 (1871) is delightfully capricious, and the *Valse sentimentale,* op. 51 no. 6 (1882) suave and elegant.

One of Tchaikovsky's most interesting piano works is *The Months,* op. 37b (1876), a suite where the composer describes each month of the year musically, beginning with January. The best movements are "Barcarolle" (June), "Harvest" (August), "Autumn Song" (October), and "In the Troika" (November). Tchaikovsky also wrote a thoroughly charming suite of twenty-four pieces for young people—the *Children's Album,* op. 39 (1878).

Sentiment is the strong suit for two of Tchaikovsky's best-known works for the violin: the *Sérénade mélancolique,* for violin and orchestra (also for violin and piano), op. 26 (1875), and the *"Mélodie"* from *Souvenir d'un lieu cher* (*Memory of a Beloved Place*), op. 42 no. 3 (1878).

The most distinguished solo instrumental music by a Russian Romantic did not come from any member of the Five, nor from Tchaikovsky, but from Sergei Rachmaninoff. Rachmaninoff used Tchaikovsky as his model and inspiration. Like the best of Tchaikovsky, Rachmaninoff's works were indigenously Russian, while the influence of European music cannot be discounted. Throughout his life Rachmaninoff remained true to the Romantic traditions of Tchaikovsky. The new idioms with which other composers were electrifying audiences did not interest him at all. Rachmaninoff refused to leave the nineteenth-century, though physically he belonged to the twentieth.

He was born in Oneg, in the district of Novgorod, on April 1, 1873. After receiving some preliminary piano lessons, he was given a scholarship for the Saint Petersburg Conservatory when he was nine. Strange to say, in view of his pronounced musical talent and his seemingly infallible musical instincts, he proved to be a shiftless student who neglected practicing the piano or working on his exercises in theory, often even failing to attend classes so that he might indulge his love for swimming, boating, and taking long solitary walks.

To shake him out of his irresponsible habits, his family decided to send him to Moscow in 1885. For his first three years there he studied the piano at the Moscow Conservatory with Sverev, a hard taskmaster who brooked no nonsense from his pupils. Discipline helped bring about a radical change in Rachmaninoff's response to music study. He now applied himself industriously to his lessons. In 1888 he became a pupil of Siloti in piano, and of Taneyev and Arensky in composition, at the conservatory. During the next seven years his extraordinary musical gifts came fully to the surface. Tchaikovsky himself praised Rachmaninoff's *Song Without Words,* for piano, when the young man played it at an examination. While still attending the conservatory Rachmaninoff also wrote his first piano concerto, in F-sharp minor (1891), and *Two Pieces* for cello and piano and *Five Fantasy Pieces* for piano both in 1892. All three were published (op. 1, 2, and 3 respectively), and the concerto was performed by its composer at a conservatory concert. Rachmaninoff's *191* first opera, *Aleko,* was completed in seventeen days as a graduating exercise, winning the Gold Medal for composition, and getting performed at the Bolshoi Theater in Moscow in 1893. When Tchaikovsky heard this opera he was most enthusiastic.

Tchaikovsky died in 1893, a tragedy that affected Rachmaninoff deeply. As a child, Rachmaninoff's love for music had first been aroused by listening to Tchaikovsky's work. Much of his own writing had been markedly influenced by Tchaikovsky. On two occasions, singled out in the preceding paragraph, Tchaikovsky had personally encouraged Rachmaninoff with praise. The master's death, then, was a personal loss. To sublimate his grief, Rachmaninoff wrote his best chamber music work, the *Trio élégiaque* in D minor, op. 9, finished just five weeks after Tchaikovsky's death and written in his memory. This work is tragic in content and mood.

In the *Five Fantasy Pieces* for piano, op. 3, will be found a sprightly little item, *"Polichinelle,"* describing a buffoon. But what gives this group even greater interest is the fact that it also contains a composition with which Rachmaninoff's name is invariably linked: the world-famous Prelude in C-sharp minor. The piece begins with solemn chords, now loud, now soft. They sound like tolling bells. A restless subject then becomes the root of an agitated section, after which the opening theme returns. This prelude achieved such fame soon after its publication that it made Rachmaninoff a household name even outside Russia and brought a fortune to its publisher. Unfortunately, Rachmaninoff never profited from this phenomenal success since he had sold this piece outright for a pittance. In fact, the sustained popularity of this prelude cost him considerable anguish, since he felt it threw into a shade other of his works which he esteemed far more highly.

During the next few years Rachmaninoff enhanced his reputation as a composer for the piano with *Seven Salon Pieces,* op. 10 (1893–94), whose best number is the Humoresque in G major. This was followed by six delightful *Moments musicaux,* op. 16 (1896).

Fame, then, and the high esteem of outstanding musicians, came early to Rachmaninoff—too early, perhaps, for it softened him and made him incapable of absorbing the adverse blows that were soon to come. The premiere of his first symphony in 1897 was a fiasco (due for the most part to an execrable performance). Rachmaninoff was convinced he had written a very bad work. He rushed out of the auditorium as if from a scene of crime, wandering about the streets in a daze. The shock of failure proved traumatic. "My dream of a brilliant career lay shattered," he later recalled. "My hopes and confidences were destroyed."

For a few years he was so overwhelmed by despair that at times he went through the motions of living as if in a stupor. He was incapable of working. Finally he had to seek the help of a Dr. Dahl, a physician specializing in autosuggestion. Daily treatments eventually revitalized Rachmaninoff and restored his self-confidence. He returned to composition in 1901 by creating a masterpiece that was an instantaneous success and has since become one of the most frequently heard piano concertos of the twentieth century: the Concerto no. 2 in C minor, op. 18.

Life now began to assume a normal, busy course. Rachmaninoff married his cousin (and long-time sweetheart), Natalie Satina, a half year after the premiere of his concerto. He began concertizing as pianist, soon attaining a phenomenal box-office success as well as a formidable reputation as an interpreter of piano literature.

The year of 1903 found Rachmaninoff creating the Variations on a Theme of Chopin, op. 22. The theme is Chopin's Prelude in C minor (op. 28 no. 20). Since Rachmaninoff was paying tribute to Chopin, he used several variations to simulate the forms for which Chopin became celebrated (nocturne, étude, mazurka); in other variations, he suggested the suave, facile virtuosity that distinguished Chopin the performer.

In 1903 Rachmaninoff also brought into being ten new preludes for piano (op. 23), and in 1910, thirteen more (op. 32). Chopin had established the prelude as a composition expressing a mood or a passing emotion. Rachmaninoff filled his preludes with theatricalism; in his hands they became miniature dramas, tempting annotators to provide programmatic interpretations the composer had never intended. Second in universal fame to the Prelude in C-sharp minor is the G minor in op. 23. With a tempo marking of *"alla marcia"* ("in the style of a march"), this prelude opens with martial music to whose strains, it seems, soldiers are off to the wars. The later poignant melodic section appears to represent the yearnings of soldiers for home and family. Rachmaninoff, however, has disavowed any such, or any other, program for this prelude, insisting that it be accepted as absolute music.

From 1904 to 1906 he was conductor of operas at the Bolshoi Theater. All this time he was writing music: some wonderful songs; the melodious Sonata in C minor for cello and piano, op. 19 (1901); and several important pieces for the piano. By 1906, Rachmaninoff was one of Russia's most celebrated musicians, famous in three fields— composition, playing the piano, and conducting. He was in great demand in fashionable salons and at parties in the palaces of nobility. His home in Moscow overflowed with distinguished visitors. Convinced that his social obligations were usurping the time he needed for creativity, he resigned as conductor in 1906. At the end of 1906 he entered a period of comparative seclusion in Dresden, Germany, where he absorbed himself in two major compositions: the Second Symphony in E minor and the orchestral tone poem *The Isle of the Dead*.

With these works completed and successfully introduced, Rachmaninoff embarked on an extensive concert tour as pianist in 1909. This was the time when he made his debut in the United States—in Northampton, Massachusetts, on November 4, 1909. Before the end of the month he appeared in New York City, where he presented the world premiere of his Piano Concerto no. 3, which he wrote in Russia soon after his return from Dresden.

Back in Russia, Rachmaninoff concocted a new piano form in 1911, the *Étude-Tableau*. This is a two-part or three-part piece in which a picture or scene is graphically re-created in brilliant virtuoso music. He completed six of these, published as op. 33. Nine more were written in 1916–17 (op. 39). In each instance Rachmaninoff had a specific image in mind when he put his music on paper, but for a long time he refused to divulge what that image was—once again preferring to have his compositions accepted as absolute music. However, when five of these were orchestrated by Ottorino Respighi in 1931, Rachmaninoff was persuaded to reveal the picture or scene he was portraying in each. Thus we learned that the *Étude-Tableau* in E-flat major, in op. 33, represents a fair; the A minor (no. 1) in op. 39, sea gulls flying over a body of water; the C minor, in op. 39, a funeral procession; the D major, in op. 39, an oriental parade; and the A minor (no. 6) in op. 39, the story of Little Red Riding-Hood. Rachmaninoff, however, was never persuaded to disclose the programmatic intent of his other *Études-Tableaux*.

When Russia was torn apart by revolution in 1917, Rachmaninoff bitterly opposed the excesses of the revolutionists. He knew he could stay in his native land no longer. In December of that year he fled to Sweden, before settling in Switzerland, where, for the next seventeen years, he made his home in a villa on the banks of Lake Lucerne. From time to time he toured Europe and America both as pianist and conductor. In Switzerland he wrote his last important work for solo piano, the Variations on a Theme of Corelli, op. 42 (1931), using the familiar "La Folia" melody found in Corelli's Violin Sonata in D minor.

After 1935, Rachmaninoff transferred his permanent residence from

Switzerland to America, while maintaining only a summer retreat in
Switzerland. He acquired a house in Beverly Hills, California, and just
before his death became an American citizen. He was terribly homesick
for Russia, which he stoutly refused even to visit since it was under
Communist rule. He embarked on what was advertized as his last extensive tour of the United States early in 1943. That tour was never completed. A month later he collapsed in New Orleans. On March 28,
1943, he died at his home in Beverly Hills.

As a composer of piano music, Alexander Scriabin started out to imitate Chopin. He then developed into a mystic who sought to express religious and mystical concepts in his music. With this aim in mind, he invented his own harmonic system and worked out a thoroughly
individualized style and structure. His later piano compositions are like
none written before him—or since.

He was a strange man, neurotic to the point of almost being a psy-
chopath. Being alone was such torture that even when he composed he
had to have people near him. Yet when in the company of others he
became so moody and introspective that, as one of his friends remarked,
there was "a gap of some millions of miles between himself and those to
whom he was talking." A helpless hypochondriac, he was continually
haunted by fears of drafts and sicknesses, or else he was convinced he
was the victim of sicknesses that did not exist. He continually took medi-
cines for real or for imaginary ailments and lent an attentive ear to any
quack cure suggested to him. The horror of germs made him wear
gloves all the time. The fear of losing his hair compelled him to avoid
wearing a hat even in icy weather.

He had strange ideas. He went beyond egotism and vanity to con-
sider himself somewhat of a superman, or (to use his own words) "the
apotheosis of creation." He said he represented "the aim of all aims, the
end of all ends." He was obsessed with the mission of creating a new art
that combined music, poetry, drama, dance, colors, and perfumes with a
new language consisting merely of sounds, exclamations, and sighs. He
called his art the "Mystery" and planned a globular theater at the side of
a lake in India where it could be performed. He was convinced that his
"Mystery" would represent a new religion, that its audience would become worshipers transported into a "supreme final ecstasy." He was confident that his "Mystery" would be the last will and testament of a dying
civilization, and the means through which a new and greater one would
come into being. When World War I broke out, Scriabin was overjoyed. *195*

This holocaust, he felt, would bring about the conditions in which his "Mystery" could become the force creating a new world on the ruins of the old, a world in which he would be received as a Messiah.

He spent the last decade of his life dreaming and planning his "Mystery." All he managed to get down on paper were some musical sketches for a preamble. Then death smothered his impossible dream.

But if there was more than a touch of madness to him as man, there was almost more than just a touch of genius to the musician. He wrote five major orchestral works, three embodying metaphysical, cosmic, or intellectual ideas (the symphony *The Divine Poem,* and *The Poem of Ecstasy* and *Prometheus*). In the last he combined musical sounds with colors flashed on a screen, produced by a color keyboard of his own invention. For all of its confused and involved extramusical pretensions, each of these works contains many a page of grandiose music.

But it was with his piano music, even more than with his orchestral works, that Scriabin won a place with the elite in Russian Romantic music. From those earlier pieces in which Chopin's presence is ever detected, to the later ones when his writing was influenced by his bent for mysticism, his best piano compositions are the musical revelations of an individualist who felt deeply, thought profoundly, and wrote eloquently.

He had a strange childhood. Born in Moscow on January 6, 1872, he was just an infant when his mother died. Since his father, a consul, was often traveling to far-off places, Scriabin was raised by his grandmother and aunt. They were so solicitous about his well-being that they did not permit him to go out into the street alone until he was fourteen. Playing with other children was also not allowed. Worrying and fretting all the time that he might get sick or be hurt, the two women hovered over him to shield him from any possible harm. They were largely responsible for making the child into a lonely introvert, a social misfit, a hypochondriac, and a neurotic.

Music was a passion to which he reacted with characteristic excesses of emotion. He received his first piano lessons from his aunt, then went on to master the instrument as best he could without formal instruction. Since he was allowed to develop in any way he wished, he spent all his time improvising. He was infatuated with the piano. He would kiss it daily as if it were a human being. When it had to be tuned he became as overwrought as if somebody he loved dearly were being operated upon.

At ten, he entered the Military School of Moscow, remaining there until 1889. While there he studied piano privately with Conus and Sverev. He later combined piano study with lessons in composition from Taneyev. Between 1888 and 1892 he attended the Moscow Conservatory, where his teachers included Arensky and Safonov, as well as Taneyev. Scriabin worked so industriously to develop his piano technique that he developed a paralysis of the right hand. In spite of this, he was graduated from his piano class with a gold medal. When he failed his examinations in composition, he left the Conservatory without a composition diploma. But this failure did not keep him from writing music—numerous piano pieces in the style of Chopin that one Moscow publisher (Jurgenson) thought good enough to accept. Scriabin's first opus was a waltz; his second, three pieces (an étude, an impromptu, and a prelude); his third, ten mazurkas.

A more influential and powerful publisher—Belaieff—became his sponsor after Scriabin had given a successful piano recital in 1894 in Moscow, where he presented some of his own compositions. After this concert, Belaieff made Scriabin an offer to publish everything he wrote and to subsidize his career as a pianist. With such backing Scriabin made his first European concert tour in 1896–97. Despite Scriabin's success as a performer, Belaieff was convinced that this young musician should devote himself more assiduously to composition. To allow him to do so, he provided Scriabin with a generous annuity, the financial independence that enabled Scriabin to complete his Piano Concerto in F-sharp minor, which he himself introduced in Odessa in 1897. Scriabin was also in a position, in 1897, to marry a young pianist, Vera Isakovitch. She sometimes gave joint recitals with him, and, when she appeared in solo performances, she usually devoted her programs to her husband's music. When Belaieff died late in 1903, and Scriabin's subsidy passed away with him, the composer was supported by one of his friends.

By 1905 Scriabin had fallen in love with another woman, Tatiana Schloezer, an attractive young pianist who had studied with him for a time at the Moscow Conservatory where Scriabin had taught between 1898 and 1903. In 1906 Scriabin toured the United States as pianist-composer, where he was soon joined by his mistress, Tatiana. The morals of some Americans were outraged when the newspapers revealed that Scriabin and Tatiana were not legally man and wife. The ensuing scandal compelled Scriabin to terminate his tour abruptly and return as quickly as possible to Russia.

There, in 1908, he found a new patron in the person of Serge Koussevitzky, then virtually at the dawn of his brilliant career as conductor. Having married a wealthy woman, Koussevitzky had the means to advance his own career as conductor and at the same time to found a publishing house sponsoring new Russian composers. Scriabin's music, Koussevitzky realized, could be a powerful addition to the publishing lists. Koussevitzky therefore became not only Scriabin's publisher but also his benefactor by endowing him with a bountiful yearly income. From this time on, Koussevitzky proved indefatigable in promoting Scriabin's career and music. When, in 1910, Koussevitzky and his orchestra toured the cities along the Volga, he had Scriabin perform the Piano Concerto in F-sharp minor eleven times. It was not long, however, until Koussevitzky and Scriabin became involved in ugly disagreements and clashes of temperament. Koussevitzky withdrew his subsidy and refused to have any further personal dealings with Scriabin. He never, however, permitted his ill feelings for Scriabin to interfere with his indefatigable efforts to make Scriabin's music better known. It was Koussevitzky who gave the world premiere of Scriabin's *Prometheus,* in 1911.

Scriabin was now delving ever more deeply into mysticism, in which he first became interested early in the twentieth century. At that time he joined a philosophical club engaged in discussions of mystical insight, divine revelations, and religious thought. This growing involvement in mystic concepts convinced Scriabin that music must be more than just a pleasant aural experience and a feast of beautiful sounds. It must become a "transformer of life," a force capable of making life "a kingdom of God on earth" (to quote his own phrases). He became conscious of the power of his creative ego, glorifying himself almost to the point of self-deification. In his own estimation he was the Superman to make music express superhuman ideas. He devised the "Mystery chord," made up of intervals of the fourth (say, C, F-sharp, B-flat, E, A, D). The "Mystery chord" and his tonal probings into nonmusical concepts are encountered in the Sonata no. 5 in F-sharp major, op. 53 (1908)—a one-movement sonata, just as all of Scriabin's sonatas are, beginning with the fourth, in F-sharp major, op. 30 (1903).

In the Sonata no. 5, Scriabin's musical message is expressed in the following lines printed in the published score:

> *I call you to life, O mysterious forces,*
> *Submerged in depths, obscure!*
> *O thou creative spirit, timid of life,*
> *To you I bring courage!*

As he progressed from one composition to another in the
last crop of his eighty-five preludes and twenty-six études, and

in his last six piano sonatas, his forms became more and more nebulous, his style ever more esoteric, and his musical thought more involved. He abandoned his former windswept melodies for episodic themes with unusual intervals. Earlier romantic and poetic moods were replaced by strange, elusive feelings. His tonality became as vague as his progressions became unconventional. There are times when his musical ideas do not seem to travel in a logical sequence. His musical organism throbs with quivering nerves.

By the time he had arrived at his last three Études in 1913 (B-flat major, C-sharp major, and G major in op. 65), his last five preludes (op. 74 in 1914), and his last sonata, in C major, op. 70 (1917), both structure and technique had become so complicated and the content so obscure that it is often difficult to follow his train of thought. But his major preoccupation, beginning in or about 1905, was dreaming about and planning his overall "Mystery"—that super-art, that new religion, that last supreme testament of a dying civilization.

On March 20 and 26, 1914, Scriabin gave piano recitals in London. A year after returning to Moscow he was stricken by a fatal gangrene brought on by a neglected carbuncle of the upper lip. He died in Moscow on April 27, 1915. His Gargantuan project—the "Mystery"—died stillborn with him.

When the Czarist regime was overthrown in Russia in 1917 to be replaced by a proletarian society, Russian music slowly began swerving toward a new direction: away from the fervent nationalism of the Russian Five and the emotionalism of Tchaikovsky and Rachmaninoff; away from the mysticism of Scriabin. Music now became the servant of the new political and social ideologies of a people's regime. Proletarian music had come into existence, slanted for the masses, reflecting their experiences, interests, ideals, and beliefs.

The two most distinguished composers to represent this new proletarian approach to music—music of the Soviet Union—are Serge Prokofiev (1891–1953) and Dmitri Shostakovich (1906–   ). Both are famous for their symphonies, concertos, ballets, and operas. But both also found the more intimate media equally gratifying to their immense gifts.

Serge Prokofiev was a child prodigy who composed his first piece of music (a *Galop Hindu,* for piano) when he was five, wrote an opera at nine, and by the time he was twelve had completed a symphony (for piano four hands), a set of twelve piano pieces, and two more operas. *199*

He was graduated from the Saint Petersburg Conservatory with highest honors in 1914. Already he had written his Piano Sonata no. 2 in D minor, op. 14 (1912), his first two piano concertos, and his first mature opera. The First Piano Concerto in D-flat major, op. 10 (1911) shocked some of the more conservative professors at the conservatory. Nevertheless it captured the Rubinstein Prize there. Two of his shorter pieces of this period are, however, better known to us: Toccata, op. 11, and *Sarcasms*, op. 17, both written between 1912 and 1914. The former is a brilliant virtuoso piece based on repeated notes; the latter allows Prokofiev to indulge in bristling sarcastic statements.

During World War I he was exempt from military duty and devoted himself to works large and small in which full artistic maturity began to show. In 1917 he wrote for the piano Sonatas nos. 3 and 4, respectively in A minor (op. 28) and C minor (op. 29). The third sonata is marked by electrifying bravura writing and colorful sonorities.

In 1918 Prokofiev made his first tour of the United States, his first solo piano recital taking place in New York on November 20, 1918, in a program including his own compositions. "He is blond, slender, modest as a musician," wrote Richard Aldrich in *The New York Times*, "and his impassability contrasted with the volcanic eruptions he produced." Aldrich and the other critics liked Prokofiev's piano playing, but turned sharply away from Prokofiev's music. Aldrich said of the finale of the Sonata no. 2 in D minor, op. 14 (1912), that it "evoked visions of a charge of Mammoths on some vast immemorial Asiatic plateau," while considering the entire work as "rather negligible." Another distinguished New York music critic, James Gibbons Huneker, described all of Prokofiev's music on the program (including *Suggestion diabolique*) as "Russian chaos."

Prokofiev stayed in the United States two years. He had no intention of ever returning to Russia, being antagonistic to the new proletarian regime. After spending some time in Paris he returned to the United States a second time. Two of his important new works were introduced in America: the Piano Concerto no. 3 in C minor and the opera *The Love for Three Oranges,* both premiered in Chicago in December, 1921. Prokofiev then returned to Paris and settled permanently there. During the next few years he made concert appearances throughout Europe and America. In 1927 he paid his first return visit to his native country for tremendously successful concert appearances.

During the time he lived in Paris, Prokofiev became an international figure by virtue of his symphonies, ballets, piano concertos, piano music, and his first string quartet. The last—the String Quartet in B minor, op. 50 (1930)—was one of the most human and emotional compositions he had thus far written. His customary wit and whimsy, or muscular power and virtuosity, were replaced by both depths of feeling and a beatific calm.

In 1933 Prokofiev decided to return to the land of his birth. The prodigal son had come home, and he was welcomed with wide-open arms. Forthwith he was accepted as one of the most important musicians in the Soviet Union. Though he continued to produce large works with the most serious artistic intent in his individualistic manner, he dedicated a good deal of his creative efforts toward music for the masses—notably music for the movies and that for children. In 1935 he wrote *Pieces for Children,* op. 65, twelve easy pieces that are serviceable as teaching material and at the same time musically valid. In 1941, the composer orchestrated seven of these numbers and offered this work for concert presentation under the new title of *Summer Day.*

When the Soviet Union was invaded by the Nazis in 1941, Prokofiev directed his creativity toward the writing of military marches and anti-Fascist songs to help the war effort. But the war also inspired him to write some of his most epic compositions, including his Symphony no. 5 in B-flat major, a monumental opera, *War and Peace,* based on the novel by Tolstoi, and three piano sonatas. The Sonata no. 6 in A major, op. 82, the Sonata no. 7 in B-flat major, op. 83, and the Sonata no. 8 in B-flat major, op. 84, are referred to as "war sonatas," because each suggests the turbulence and tensions of the times. Prokofiev's last piano sonata—no. 9 in C major, op. 103 (1947)—is a much more modest effort. The overwhelming emotions that the war had aroused in the composer had, in peacetime, become subdued and restrained; the large dimensions of the "war sonatas" had been reduced to modest proportions.

During the war, Prokofiev had also completed his String Quartet no. 2 in F major, op. 92 (1941), and his Sonata no. 2 for Violin and Piano in D major, op. 94-bis (1944). The melodic material of the quartet was influenced by Caucasian folk music (one of the few works by Prokofiev to utilize authentic folk material).

Prokofiev's so-called Sonata no. 1 in F minor for Violin and Piano, op. 80, was completed about two years *after* the Second Sonata. Prokofiev designated his op. 80 as the first because he had begun writing it before he worked on the second. In the First Sonata he aimed to emulate a Handel sonata, but in modern terms. This is why this work has such a Classic character but with an infusion of Romantic feeling.

After the war, most of the principal composers in the Soviet Union were subjected to a violent attack by the Central Committee of the Communist Party, which denounced them for their overindulgence in modernistic idioms and cerebral styles. Prokofiev was by no means exempt from criticism. He promised to follow the new music policy of the committee, and in time he was able to reinstate himself to his former exalted station in Soviet music. In 1951 he once again was awarded the Stalin Prize (the first had come after his Piano Sonata no. 7). By that time he had become an invalid due to a stroke. He died of a cerebral hemorrhage in Moscow on March 5, 1953 (on the same day as Stalin's death).

All of Dmitri Shostakovich's best music has a recognizable identity. He is partial to wit or whimsy in his scherzos, to broad majestic statements in his slow movements, and to irresistible motor energy in his finales. He likes to open a composition forcefully, then to alternate sensitive and stormy passages. He enjoys contrasting high and low registers of wind instruments. He is partial to strong rhythmic patterns and explosive *brio* passages. He exploits unusual instrumental effects.

Shostakovich is Prokofiev's junior by fifteen years. Prokofiev had been a cosmopolitan before he settled down to be a Soviet composer. Until his middle years Shostakovich knew no society other than a Soviet one. This led him to a kind of provincialism that made him far more flexible than Prokofiev in conforming to whatever standards in music government officials chose to impose upon him at any given time. He was also better able to withstand and recover from attacks by the authorities, which he suffered not once but several times.

Fame came to him early. He was not yet twenty when, for his graduation exercise in composition at the Leningrad (formerly Saint Petersburg) Conservatory, he wrote his Symphony no. 1. It traveled the international circuit, beginning with its premiere in Leningrad in 1926 up to its American premiere in 1928. It made Shostakovich one of the luminaries of Soviet music.

This success came as no surprise to those who had known him. From his childhood on, when he studied the piano with his mother, he had demonstrated the most remarkable musical capabilities, which he continued to develop during his seven years of attendance at the Leningrad Conservatory. As a conservatory student, he had one of his compositions published, the *Three Fantastic Dances,* op. 5, for piano (1922).

After the phenomenal success of his first symphony, Shostakovich entered upon a one-year period of self-reevaluation during which he wrote no music. Now that he was famous he came to the conclusion that henceforth he must write major compositions that would speak loud and clear for and to a Communist society. He returned to his work desk in 1927. During the next decade he produced symphonies, operas, and ballets that made him one of the foremost musical spokesmen for the Soviet system.

But he also wrote a good deal of piano and chamber music that had no political or social implications. The year of 1933 saw the completion of Twenty-four Preludes, for piano, op. 34, which were influenced partly by Chopin, partly by Rachmaninoff, and partly by Scriabin, in establishing a mood or expressing an emotion. The tenth, in C-sharp minor, and the fourteenth, in E-flat minor, represent the cream of this crop for their expressive lyricism and depth of feeling. (The former was transcribed for violin and piano by Jascha Heifetz; the latter, for orchestra, by Leopold Stokowski.) Between 1950 and 1951 Shostakovich wrote another series of twenty-four preludes (op. 87), this time with each prelude joined by a fugue in the same key in the manner of Bach's *Well-Tempered Clavier.*

Though his success had become solidified with these and other successes, Shostakovich was suddenly victimized by a violent attack by Soviet authorities, centered on his opera *Lady Macbeth of Mzensk,* to which Premier Stalin took exception.

But then, as later, Shostakovich proved as resilient as a rubber ball. However hard the ball is squeezed it rebounds to its original shape when the pressure is released. Shostakovich sprang back to government and public favor with his Symphony no. 5, op. 47, which had a formidable success in 1937 and later became acknowledged as Shostakovich's best symphony (though the first never lost its popularity). In 1940 Shostakovich received the Stalin Prize for the first time for his Piano Quintet in G minor, op. 57.

What distinguishes this quintet from most other Shostakovich works is its human equation. This is the element that gives Shostakovich's best chamber music compositions their distinction. In this quintet, as in many of his subsequent quartets, the showman in Shostakovich (so often evident in his symphonies, operas, and ballets) is suppressed as the composer seeks to express himself simply and honestly. In his chamber music he makes no effort to preach dogmas, promote ideologies, or use a political message. He speaks for himself rather than for his country and people; he makes chamber music a sounding board for his most personal feelings. That is why he chose a chamber music medium whenever he wanted to write elegies for personal friends (the Piano Trio in E minor, op. 67, in 1944, and the String Quartet no. 11, in 1966).

For his award-winning piano quintet Shostakovich used an unusual structure. It opens with a Prelude and Fugue (Shostakovich modernism within a Bach-like structure). A Scherzo then permits the lighter side of Shostakovich's nature to emerge. In the concluding Intermezzo and Finale, Shostakovich seemed to have kept in mind a circus, for he quotes the familiar Russian melody that introduced clowns in Russian circuses.

Shostakovich's first string quartet—in C major, op. 49—appeared in 1938. The World War II year of 1944 produced his second quartet, in A major, op. 69, an important work where, once again, as in the piano quintet, unusual movement markings are used: Overture, Recitative, Romance, and Waltz. The last movement (whose main melody is in the style of Tchaikovsky) is a theme and variations. Among Shostakovich's best string quartets after that are the following: no. 4 in D major, op. 83 (1949); no. 8 in C minor, op. 110 (1960), which was orchestrated by Rudolf Barshai and retitled *Chamber Symphony;* no. 10, op. 118 (1964); and the frequently elegiac and deeply moving String Quartet no. 11 (1966), whose unusual movement markings are Introduction, Scherzo, Recitative, Study, Humoresque, Elegy, and Conclusion.

During the years of World War II Shostakovich was hailed as a hero, for once the Soviet Union was invaded by the Nazi army Shostakovich was inspired to write stirring music suitable for wartime consumption. The most publicized of these compositions was his Symphony no. 7 in C major, the *Leningrad,* in 1942, inspired by the stalwart resistance and the indomitable spirit of the Russian people during the Nazi siege of Leningrad. This symphony, heard and acclaimed all over the free world during the war years, brought Shostakovich his second Stalin Prize.

After the war, Shostakovich continued to be remarkably productive and wrote works that met with such great favor that in 1950 a third Stalin Prize was given him. On his sixtieth birthday he was given the title of Hero of Socialist Labor, the highest tribute the Soviet government could bestow on him.

12

Twentieth-Century France

Erik Satie, Claude Debussy,

Maurice Ravel

An eccentric musician by the name of Erik Satie represented one of several rebellions in French music against the excesses of Romanticism.

When Satie was alive many distinguished French musicians like Debussy, Ravel, and Milhaud regarded him highly. But many others refused to take him seriously, regarding him as a clown, a charlatan, a poseur, a ridiculous pixie. It was easy to laugh at him, because both as a man and as composer he was peculiar. In appearance he cut a strange figure with his bowler hat, a pince-nez, pointed beard, and the quizzical expression of eyes and face. He often dressed from head to foot in gray velvet. Out of one of his pockets stuck a large clay pipe. From another there bulged the outline of a hammer, which he always carried with him for protection.

His habits were outlandish. He never used a public conveyance, insisting on walking even when his destination was miles away. He always carried an umbrella, even in perfect weather. He spent large periods of his time in cafés, where he did much of his composing. In the company of acquaintances or strangers he made enemies effortlessly with his sharp tongue and combustible temper. His apartment in Montmartre, the Bohemian section of Paris, and during his last years, in the Parisian suburb of Arceuil, was the last word in Spartan simplicity: a bed, a chair, a table, and so old, battered, and unplayable a piano that he had to use one at a friend's house to try out his compositions.

He was also a curiosity as a composer. Here was a musician of seemingly high standards who did not resent earning his living by playing popular tunes in a Montmartre cabaret, and who did not hesitate to write popular songs for cabaret performers or even to introduce popular styles in his serious works. Here was a composer whose piano pieces bore such quixotic titles as "The Dreamy Fish," "Flabby Preludes for a Dog," "Sketches to Make You Run Away," and "Three Pieces in the Shape of a Pear." Here was a composer who interpolated into his music whimsical verbal comments, such as advising the performer (at one point in the music) to put his hands in his pockets, or suggesting (at one phrase) that the music be played "dry as a cuckoo, light as an egg," or that it should sound like "a nightingale with a toothache." When he quoted Chopin's *Funeral March* he identified it as a Schubert mazurka (Schubert never wrote a mazurka!). Satie reduced the practice of appending verbal explanations to compositions (a practice with many Romantics) to absurdity by adding absurd comments, as, for example: "This is the case of the lobsters; the hunters descend to the bottom of the water they run. The sound of a horn is heard at the bottom of the sea. The lobster is tracked. The lobster weeps."

Yet this man, for all his shenanigans—and often *because* of his shenanigans—represented the first important break with Romanticism in French music. He made this break by ridiculing the exalted aim and lofty pretensions of the Romantics through laughter and mockery. He arrived at a new set of values for music. No longer was music to serve as an outlet for a composer's emotions or ideals. Music must derive its interest from *sound,* from *structure,* from the logic of musical thought. In carrying out this aim Satie devised new idioms, new processes, new techniques. What he finally accomplished was nothing short of a revolution, whose importance was first generally recognized only after his death. Darius Milhaud, one of France's highly esteemed twentieth-century composers, regards Satie's piano pieces as the cradle of modern French music. The distinguished American composer Virgil Thomson maintains that the three "S's" of modern music are Satie, Schoenberg, and Stravinsky, and in that order of importance.

Satie was born in Honfleur, near the harbor town of Le Havre, France, on May 17, 1866. A local organist began teaching him the piano when Satie was still a child. He instilled in Satie a love for old church music (especially Gregorian chants written in the old modes) that he never outgrew. After additional study of piano and harmony, Satie entered the Paris Conservatory in 1879. His teachers were puzzled by his passion for medieval plainchants and were thoroughly upset by his infatuation with new idioms and techniques. With no exchange of either sympathy or understanding passing between pupil and teachers, Satie decided to abandon the conservatory after several years, preferring to go his own individual way in completing his musical education.

The pixie in him surfaced in his very first publication: *Valse-Ballet et Fantaisie Valse* (1885), to which he fixed the opus number of 62. This fellow, then, was an individualist from his beginnings; he would remain so till his end.

His first important piano pieces, written between 1886 and 1890, had unusual (though not yet whimsical) titles and were inspired by unusual subjects. In *Ogives* (1886)—"ogives" being a term in Gothic art meaning "pointed arches"—Satie tried to imitate through music the arched curve designs popular during the Gothic era (from the thirteenth to the sixteenth century). Medieval music, with its modal harmonies, had always interested Satie; this interest had led him to study Gothic art. The exotic character of *Ogives* came from his use of medieval modes. There is thus some religious feeling in these pieces, which Satie continued to carry over into his *Sarabandes* (1887), in which he combined the stately Baroque dance form with discordant chords and progressions. *Gymnopédies* (1887) was his attempt to suggest musically a "gymnopedia," an ancient religious Spartan festival where gods were worshiped with songs and dances. Satie had decided to use this subject for a musical composition after being impressed with some designs on a Greek vase. These three *Gymnopédies* are all in slow ¾ tempo, the melody and harmonies built from the old Aeolian mode, and all the melodies of a classic serenity. But the harmonies are even more discordant and the progressions more unconventional than they had been in his earlier pieces. Experimentation characterized *Gnossiennes* (1890), where for the first time Satie dispenses with bar lines separating one measure from another to achieve greater fluidity of musical movement. The pieces have no basic tonality and the cadences are in modal harmonies, both helping to contribute a nebulous atmosphere to the music. And for the first time Satie indulges in whimsical comments. In one of the parts of *Gnossiennes* he suggests that the music be played "in a fashion to achieve a pit or a hole"; in another he instructs the pianist to "open" his head.

207

From 1897 on, Satie allowed the pixie in him full freedom of expression. He now began to use bizarre titles for his piano pieces and to interject outlandish verbal indications. He made a mockery of those Romantics who liked to use picturesque, euphuistic titles, and to translate into music elaborate nonmusical subjects. In 1897 Satie wrote *Pièces froides* (*Cold Pieces*), following it with a large repertory of piano music including the *Trois morceaux en forme de poire* (*Three Pieces in the Shape of a Pear*) for piano duet in 1903, *Trois préludes flasques* (*Three Flabby Preludes*) in 1912, *Embryons desséchés* (*Dessicated Embryos*) (1913), and *Avant-dernières pensées* (*Next to Last Thoughts*) (1915).

The titles are silly; the verbal comments within the pages of the music make little sense. But the music itself has highly serious artistic value. By employing modest forms, a concise style, economy of means, and a single approach, Satie parted company with the Romantics once and for all. At the same time he was achieving nobility of musical content, power of invention, and classic beauty.

Even while attracting notoriety for his unconventional compositions, and even though he was now already middle-aged (thirty-nine years old), Satie suddenly decided, in 1905, to return to the schoolroom and begin his theoretical studies anew. He wanted to broaden his creativity, and he sensed that to do so he had to develop his technique further. And so, for the next three years, he diligently attended the classes of Vincent d'Indy and Albert Roussel at the Schola Cantorum with pupils who were half his age. Satie worked as hard at his exercises as if he were a youngster with a career still ahead of him.

After completing his studies, Satie kept on writing piano pieces (some of those mentioned earlier in this chapter came after 1908); nor did he desert the lonely path of experimentation he had formerly struck for himself. He now ventured on several ambitious works, including ballets. The most celebrated of these was *Parade* (1916), a satirical "realistic ballet" about a touring company of entertainers who performed in Parisian streets and at fairs. Based on a concept by Jean Cocteau, with choreography by Léonide Massine and stage and costume designs by Pablo Picasso, *Parade* caused a furore when introduced in Paris in 1917 —so novel was it in every department. In his score Satie used American ragtime, French music hall tunes, and the sounds of sirens, lottery wheels, revolvers, and clicking typewriters. Another of his ambitious works was a large symphonic drama for four sopranos and orchestra based on three dialogues of Plato—*Socrate* (1918).

Erik Satie died in a Paris hospital on July 1, 1925. By then French music had undergone a major metamorphosis. Romanticism was, for the most part, in discard, replaced by Impressionism and modernism. Nobody had been more influential in bringing about this change than Satie.

Claude Debussy (1862–1918), the father of musical Impressionism, first met Satie at a Paris café in 1891. Satie's anti-Romantic ideas and technical innovations impressed the then still young and unknown Debussy, for they came at a time when Debussy himself had long been groping for a new kind of music with fresh idioms. As a student at the Paris Conservatory from 1873 to 1883, Debussy had shocked his fellow students and teachers with the ways he continually broke textbook rules of harmony and counterpoint and improvisations. He called these experiments "feasts for the ear." His first compositions, some songs, were bold in their harmonic and melodic writing for that time.

In 1884 Debussy captured the Prix de Rome with a cantata, *L'Enfant prodigue*. From Rome he dispatched to the authorities of the Paris Conservatory compositions that defied accepted procedures. The academicians in Paris shook their heads with dismay at his audacities. Massenet (the composer of the famous operas *Manon* and *Thaïs*) said of him, "He is an enigma."

Debussy did not complete the three-year period in Rome prescribed by the award. Instead he returned to Paris in the spring of 1887 to work out his own ideas of composition without outside interference. He completed the cantata *La Damoiselle élue* and some music for the piano. Among the latter were the Arabesques in E major and G major (1888). An "arabesque" is a composition with an ornamented melody and repeated graceful patterns. The *Petite Suite* (*Little Suite*) for piano duet followed in 1889, and the gentle *Rêverie* (*Reverie*) in 1890. All these pieces still cling to the apron strings of French Romanticism in spite of harmonic innovations.

At last, in 1891, he met Satie, whose impact upon him was like a whirlwind's. Later on, when his own style was finally developed, Debussy made highly effective use of some of Satie's technical innovations. But however much he admired Satie and however much he would profit from Satie's ideas and methods, Debussy soon came to realize that Satie's kind of music was not *his* own kind at all. Wit, irony, whimsy, caricature, popularism—all of which were so basic to Satie—were alien to Debussy's nature and temperament. His personality demanded music that were more sensitive, delicate, refined, atmospheric, and subtle. He came to the conclusion that he would have to formulate a new musical aesthetic with new laws and new values.

He found that aesthetic in Impressionism, about which he learned from his personal contacts and conversations with a group of then avant-garde painters, among whom were Cézanne, Manet, Degas, and Renoir. These painters rebelled against the photographic realism (on the one hand) and the sentimental Romanticism (on the other) that dominated so much of French painting at that time. The rebels created a new art form in which the artist's main concern was to carry to the canvas the impressions or feelings that their subject matter aroused in them. To convey such impressions and feelings these young artists became concerned with light and shade, nuances of color, design, and subtle effects.

As a member of a group that met regularly at cafés, Debussy became acquainted not only with the work of these Impressionist painters but also with their theories and artistic values, which were elaborately discussed. Debussy now came to the conclusion that if he were to accomplish anything as a composer it would be by emulating these painters, by doing in music what they were executing in painting. Away with romantic concepts of emotion in music! Away with music burdened by explicit programs! Debussy would seek out subtle sensations, delicate images, exquisite nuances, subdued colors and hues, refined sounds, sensitive moods. Like the Impressionist painters, he would be far more interested in the effect that his subjects had upon him than with the subjects themselves.

Debussy's first fully realized Impressionist masterwork was the String Quartet in G minor, op. 10, introduced in Paris in the year of its composition (1893). Though Debussy adopted the traditional four-movement structure, there was nothing traditional about the way this music sounded. The four strings continually spun a gossamer texture. The colors shimmered and glowed. A new kind of melody and harmony, built from the whole-tone scale, projected a rarefied atmosphere. The music frequently spoke in eloquent whispers, as in the opening melody for muted strings of the slow third movement where emotion is heightened through understatement. A motto theme first heard in the beginning of the first movement, then appearing transformed in the second-movement scherzo, and after that given considerable attention in the finale, served as a unifying factor for the whole work.

In this quartet, some of Debussy's Impressionistic techniques have been arrived at. There was, first and foremost, his use of the whole-tone scale. This scale is made up entirely of whole tones, in which the octave is divided into six equal parts—as, for example, C–D–E–F sharp–G sharp–A sharp–C. Debussy did not invent this scale. But he was the first to use it extensively, to make it the means of achieving his suggestive, nebulous kind of music through Impressionism.

Themes were often made up of fragments, and repeated phrases became so-called melodies. Individual chords introduced color and nuance without concern for their harmonic relationship to other chords. Debussy allowed his unusual chords and chord formations to move about freely and discordantly, unconcerned with a tonal center or a consonant point of rest. Formal cadences were avoided. The beat was hidden. Sometimes bar lines were dispensed with to give rhythm and melody an uninterrupted flow. Occasionally, exoticism was introduced through the use of old church modes. All this represented the method and means by which Debussy was able to evoke a world of dreams and shadows, of evanescent moods and elusive suggestions. "He was," the French critic Henri Prunières wrote of Debussy, "the incomparable painter of mystery, silence, and the infinite, of the passing cloud, the sunlit shimmer of the waves—subtleties which none before him had been capable of suggesting."

Debussy wrote works for orchestra beginning with that incomparable Impressionist prelude, *L'Après-midi d'un faune* (*The Afternoon of a Faun*) in 1894. He was responsible for some of the most exquisite songs in the French repertory. He wrote the greatest of all Impressionist operas: *Pelléas et Mélisande* (1902). And he fashioned a glorious treasury of piano music.

Estampes (*Etchings*), in 1903, is a series of three piano portraits: "*Pagodes*" ("Pagodas"), "*Soirée dans Grenade*" ("Evenings in Granada"), and "*Jardins sous la pluie*" ("Gardens in the Rain"). The first is exotic, utilizing an oriental scale to depict a far-Eastern sacred tower. In the second we seem to hear a strumming mandolin and the languorous song of a Spanish serenade in culling the image of the famous Spanish city at dusk. In the third, Debussy quotes two French folk songs.

L'Isle joyeuse (*The Joyous Island*), in 1904, was inspired by a painting by Watteau. The piano sonorities (which simulate orchestral timbres) and the ever-changing rhythms contribute to much of its musical interest.

The most widely played of the numbers from the *Suite bergamasque* —composed in 1890 but not published until 1905—is "*Clair de lune*" ("Moonlight"), one of the most appealing and pictorial representations in music of subdued colors and mood of a moonlit night. In writing the entire suite, Debussy attempted to re-create the Baroque suite form and the delicacy of Couperin's harpsichord music. This is why the other movements are Prelude, Minuet, and Passepied.

Between 1905 and 1907 came two sets of *Images* for the piano. (Debussy also wrote another series of *Images* for orchestra.) Each has three numbers. The finest in the first is *"Reflets dans l'eau"* ("Reflections in the Water"), concerning which the composer said he had used "the newest discoveries in harmonic chemistry." The figures and outlines distorted by reflecting waters are magically suggested by nebulous-sounding chords. The other two numbers in this set are *"Hommage à Rameau"* ("Homage to Rameau") and *"Mouvement"* ("Movement").

In the second set, *"Cloches à travers les feuilles"* ("Bells Through the Leaves") sound the echoes of tolling bells filtered through the maze of forest leaves. *"Poissons d'or"* ("Goldfish") was suggested to the composer after he had seen oriental lacquer on which goldfish in a stream were painted. Between these two favorites is *"Et la lune descend sur le temple qui fut"* ("And the Moon Descends on the Temple Which Used To Be"), a title conceived not by Debussy but by one of his friends after its composition.

Children's Corner (1908) is among the cherished musical works for and about children. Debussy wrote it for his five-year-old daughter, whom he playfully nicknamed "Chouchou." Debussy used an English title not only for the suite as a whole but also for its movements, since he had in mind an English governess playing games with a French child. The six movements re-create six such games or pastimes.

La Plus que lente (1910), literally translated as "more than slow," is a gentle take-off on sentimental waltzes. At that time Paris was humming and dancing to a popular waltz entitled *La Valse lente* (*The Slow Waltz*). Debussy poked fun at this musical trifle in another of his all too rare escapes into humor.

In all his piano writing, thus far, Debussy had been exploring new resonances and colors for the instrument through his personal way of using chords, dynamics, touch, and pedaling. These experiments carried him to the quintessence of his Impressionist art: the twenty-four preludes for the piano, the first twelve in 1910, the next dozen, three years later. In each of these short, free-form, and somewhat improvisatory pieces Debussy requires just a mere melodic motive or a rhythmic phrase or an unusual chord as the basic source of a perfectly realized mood picture.

Debussy placed his titles not at the beginning of his composition but at the end to minimize their importance, as if they were afterthoughts.

The first book is better than the second, but each is filled with iridescent jewels, cut and polished by a master craftsman. Exquisite in every detail, for example is the very popular *"La Fille aux cheveux de lin"* ("The Girl with the Flaxen Hair"), one of Debussy's most exquisitely wrought melodies grown as famous in transcriptions as in its original piano version. Wide in their appeal are also *"La Cathédrale engloutie"* ("The Sunken Cathedral") and *"Minstrels"* from the same first book.

In the second book, four preludes are of prime interest. *"La Puerta del vino"* is an evocation of the famous gate of the Alhambra palace in Granada. Spain is identified by Spanish-type melodies and rhythms. *"Bruyères"* is the French word for "heaths"; the music suggests a pastoral scene. *"Ondine"* is music with a vague atmosphere describing the famous water nymph of legend of that name. And *"Feux d'artifice"* ("Fireworks") depicts the brilliant outburst of a firework display celebrating probably the French national holiday of Bastille Day, since the strains of the *"Marseillaise,"* the French national anthem, are introduced.

In two books of études embracing six pieces each (1915), both dedicated to Chopin, Debussy offers various technical exercises to help develop piano technique and Debussy's impressionistic methods. But for the most part these études have greater value as teaching pieces than as compositions for concert presentation.

En Blanc et Noir ("In Black and White"), also in 1915, are three pieces for two pianos, the musical equivalents of pictures in black and white. For each composition Debussy provides an explanatory motto. For the first, a waltz, he lifts a line from the libretto of Gounod's opera *Romeo and Juliet:* "He who keeps his place and does not join in the ring silently confesses to some disgrace." The second, an elegy for a French soldier killed during World War I, bears a quotation from a ballad by François Villon, and the music quotes the famous Lutheran hymn *"Ein' feste Burg."* For the third, a scherzo, Debussy quotes a line from Charles, Duke of Orleans: "Winter, you are nothing but a villain." The last is the most programmatic of these three pieces. It describes an old château stricken by a raging storm as an old castellan is recounting a legend. When the storm ends, the setting once again becomes peaceful.

Debussy's last compositions were three sonatas: one for the cello and piano, another for flute, viola, and harp (both in 1915), and one for violin and piano, in 1917. The best is that for the violin and piano. But none finds Debussy in top form as to creative imagination and perfection of Impressionistic writing, though all reveal a masterful workmanship and some highly ingratiating material.

Debussy was under a severe handicap when he wrote these sonatas. The war (World War I) had placed a strain on the daily lives of all French civilians, and Debussy had been no exception. His financial resources had become so depleted that often he did not have the price of fuel or food. The war, however, was not his only problem. He was suffering from cancer. In 1917 he attended the premiere of his violin sonata in Paris, then played the piano part of the same work at a concert in southern France later the same year. He was never again to play in public. By 1918 the boom of German guns could be heard in Paris. A German invasion of the French capital appeared imminent. This added to Debussy's mental and physical sufferings. He collapsed, and on March 25, 1918, he died—eight days after he had applied for membership in the renowned French Académie des Beaux-Arts.

His death passed unnoticed because Paris was too deeply involved in the war and the possibility of invasion. When his hearse passed through the streets on the way to the cemetery only a straggling handful followed it. "The sky was overcast," is how one of the mourners described the funeral. "In the distance was a rumbling. . . . In the wide avenues only military trucks. . . . People on the pavements pressed ahead hurriedly. . . . Children in the gutter stared at us. . . . Shopkeepers . . . glanced at the streamers on the wreaths saying, 'It seems that it was some musician.' There was but one oration."

Maurice Ravel (1875–1937) was the foremost musical Impressionist following Debussy. Ravel fashioned Impressionism to his own image and not to that of Debussy (the reason why he is described as a "post-Impressionist").

As men, Ravel and Debussy were opposites. Debussy looked and dressed like a Bohemian. He was flabby. He looked like a Mongol with his swarthy complexion, black hair and beard, and prominent cheekbones. Ravel was slight and slender. His face was delicately molded. His eyes were soft and dreamy. He always dressed with meticulous good taste. He was the debonair sophisticate—whereas Debussy always seemed somewhat unkempt.

Debussy loved many women through the years; he lived for several years with one of them; after that he was twice married, the second

time to a woman who had deserted her husband and children. His life
was continually enmeshed in amatory complications. Ravel was more
discreet. He never married. In his personal life Ravel liked order and
discipline, whereas Debussy seemed to thrive on chaos.

As composers, they were both Impressionists. Both liked to use exotic scales and both occasionally favored similar subjects for musical
treatment. But here the similarity ends. Ravel never used the whole-tone
scale, for example, avoided Debussy's type of chords, and was stricter
than Debussy in adhering to basic tonalities. Ravel was partial to clearly
outlined and symmetrically conceived structures, where those of Debussy
were nebulous. Ravel was in his element in wit, satire, and fantasy, none
of which were Debussy's strong points. In short, Ravel proved that there
was another way of writing Impressionistic music besides Debussy's.

Ravel was brought as an infant to Paris from his native town of Ci-
boure, in the Basque region of France. In 1889 he entered the Paris
Conservatory. There, like Debussy, he was the rebel in flouting rules set
down by teachers—although one, Gabriel Fauré, not only tolerated
Ravel's heresies but encouraged them. Like Debussy, too, Ravel was at
first greatly influenced by Satie. But in his earliest compositions his own
personality surged to the fore. His first composition to be published was
Menuet antique for solo piano (1895). His first to be performed in public was *Les Sites auriculaires,* for two pianos, composed in 1896 and
performed two years later.

His fame came early, arriving with two of his best-known piano
pieces: *Pavane pour une Infante défunte* (*Pavane for a Dead Infanta*) in
1899, and *Jeux d'eau* (*Fountain*) in 1901. The pavane is a slow, stately
court dance of Italian origin; an infanta is a Spanish princess. Ravel's
composition is a simple but touching elegy, but not without a dash of
sentimentality. It had a whirlwind success both as a piano composition
and in the composer's orchestral version. *Jeux d'eau* is the more remarkable of these two compositions, particularly in the way Ravel uses the
upper register of the piano and in his resonances and sonorities. "This
piece," the composer explained, "was inspired by the sound of water and
the music of fountains, cascades, and streams." The composition is made
up of two motives. Scale passages, arpeggios, and sensitive chords are
used with immense skill and imagination in reproducing the play and
ripple of waters.

Both pieces scored a giant success when introduced in Paris in 1902.
Another masterpiece, this time for string quartet, brought the composer
another triumph. Ravel's String Quartet in F major (1903), with Debus-

sy's quartet, is the most renowned chamber music composition in the Impressionist style. Its premiere in Paris in 1904 led Debussy to write to Ravel: "In the name of the gods of music and of my own, do not change one thing in your Quartet!" Like Debussy's, this quartet has four movements, but it is far more lyrical than the Debussy quartet and has less of a tendency to be obscure and vague. Ravel comes closest to approximating Debussy's exquisite sensibility in the slow third movement. The first movement is in the sonata form. The second is a delightful scherzo that opens with a theme for plucked strings, after which a broad melodic passage is played by the strings with the bow. The finale has youthful excitement. The quartet is unified by having all the themes of the four movements based on a germinal motive.

Despite his successes, and acceptance in reputable quarters and that with Debussy he stood at the head of the Impressionist movement, Ravel was three times turned down by the Paris Conservatory for the Prix de Rome—an honor that had not been denied to Debussy. These rejections and the refusal to let him compete a fourth time caused such an outburst of protest from his admirers that the director of the Paris Conservatory had to resign to make way for Gabriel Fauré (who forthwith instituted major reforms in the conduct of the school). But by the time this happened, Ravel was beyond the age when he could receive the Prix de Rome. Ravel apparently never forgot this hurt. From then on, he looked upon any form of public recognition with disdain to the point of three times rejecting the decoration of Chevalier of the Legion of Honor.

Leaving the conservatory in 1905, Ravel went on further to discredit those stuffy academicians who found him unworthy of the Prix de Rome by writing one masterpiece after another. The year of 1905 was particularly eventful, since it saw the birth of two remarkable piano works: the Sonatina and the suite *Miroirs* (*Mirrors*). The Sonatina is notable for its elegance, precision, grace, tenderness and mastery of structure. It belongs with Ravel's finest works for the piano. Here, too, Ravel employed the technique he had favored in his string quartet, that of building up his thematic material (for three of the movements) from a basic motive. *Miroirs* consists of five pieces, the most celebrated of which is the fourth, *"Alborada del gracioso."*

"Alborada del gracioso" is a tone picture inspired by some external image. This type of inspiration holds true for the other four numbers, of which the second and third are typical. The second is *"Oiseaux tristes"* ("Sad birds") in which, as the composer told us, "I evoke birds lost in

the torpor of a somber forest during the most torrid hours of summertime." The third is *"Une Barque sur l'océan"* ("A Boat on the Ocean"), which presents the sea in ever-changing colors.

Ravel extended his creativity through the writing of major works for the orchestra and for the stage (including his masterwork, the ballet *Daphnis and Chloé,* in 1912). But he never deserted either chamber music or the piano, two media uniquely favorable to the precision of his thought, his meticulous attention to detail, his sense of economy, his instinct for understatement, and the perfection of his structures. These are the most distinguished of his later works for the piano: *Ma Mère l'Oye* (*Mother Goose*), for piano duet but later orchestrated, and *Gaspard de la nuit* (*Gaspard of the Night*) both in 1908; *Valses nobles et sentimentales* (*Noble and Sentimental Waltzes*) in 1911 which Ravel orchestrated a year later, and *Le Tombeau de Couperin* (*The Tomb of Couperin*) in 1917. His chamber music included the septet *Introduction and Allegro,* for harp, flute, clarinet, and string quartet (1906); the Piano Trio in A minor (1914); and *Tzigane,* for violin and piano (also violin and orchestra) in 1924.

Debussy's *Children's Corner* finds its Ravelian counterpart in *Ma Mère l'Oye.* Both composers knew how to write enchantingly for and about children; both compositions were written specifically for children, and both appeared in the same year (1908). Ravel's suite was intended for the two children of one of his friends; this is why he wrote it at first for piano four hands. Lifting five tales from *Mother Goose,* Ravel begins his suite with *"Pavane de la Belle au bois dormant"* ("Pavane for Sleeping Beauty"), delicate music extending for just twenty measures. *"Petit Poucet"* ("Hop o' My Thumb") bears a brief programmatic note reading: "He believed that he could easily find his path by means of bread crumbs, which he had scattered wherever he had passed; but he was very much surprised when he could not find a single crumb; the birds had come and eaten everything up." *"Laideronnette, Impératrice des pagodes"* ("Laideronnette, Empress of the Pagodas") tells us about Laideronnette, who is cursed with ugliness by a wicked princess but who regains her beauty through the love of a dashing prince. *"Les Entretiens de la Belle et le Bête"* ("Conversations of Beauty and the Beast") is a light waltz set against a vigorous rhythm in the bass. The suite ends with *"Le Jardin féerique"* ("The Fairy Garden"), a melody of rare loveliness. Like so many other Ravel compositions for the piano, the suite was orchestrated by the composer and is often heard at symphony concerts.

Gaspard de la nuit consists of three "poems" for the piano in which

217

virtuosity is combined with nocturnal mystery and enchantment. The best number is the first, "Ondine," which, similar to Debussy's piano pieces of the same name, is a tonal picture of a water nymph; the rippling sound of the waters is suggested by gently broken chords.

Valses nobles et sentimentales is made up of seven waltz tunes and an epilogue inspired by Franz Schubert. All are played without interruption. This work is best known in Ravel's orchestration.

Le Tombeau de Couperin—once again a work originally for the piano but four of the sections then orchestrated by the composer—was planned as a memorial to the dead of World War I. Utilizing seventeenth-century forms and dances and simulating Couperin's harpsichord style, Ravel conceived tranquil music in a classic spirit. The composition begins with a prelude, continues with a fugue, and ends with a toccata. In between the fugue and the toccata we find such old dances as the Forlane, Rigaudon, and Minuet.

Two of the four movements of Ravel's Piano Trio in A minor are unusual. The second is designated by the composer as a "Pantoum," a form of Malayan poetry where two independent thoughts are expressed conjointly. The third is a passacaglia, whose special interest lies in the nimble way in which the sounds of the piano are joined with those of the strings. The opening movement and the finale are traditional.

Tzigane is a rhapsody where Ravel imitates stylized Hungarian gypsy music because he wrote this composition for a female Hungarian violin virtuoso. As first conceived, this music was intended for violin and *"luthéal"*—the latter being an organlike attachment to the piano. Ravel then rewrote the *"luthéal"* part for the piano, and after that adapted the entire work for violin and orchestra.

Late in 1927, Ravel paid his sole visit to the United States, touring in concerts of his own works. In America he met George Gershwin and was profoundly impressed by Gershwin's music. Ravel was influenced by Gershwin in one of his last compositions, the Concerto for Piano Left Hand and Orchestra (1931).

Ravel lived in the quiet and seclusion of his cherished villa in Montfort l'Amaury, in the Ile de France region near Paris, after 1921. There he was stricken by a fatal brain condition. He died in a hospital in Paris on December 28, 1937 following an unsuccessful operation.

Sergei Rachmaninoff.

Peter Ilitch Tchaikovsky.

Alexander Scriabin.

Maurice Ravel.
Drawing by Roger Wild.

Claude Debussy at the piano,
playing for a group of friends.

Other Crosscurrents
in Twentieth-Century Music

Arnold Schoenberg, Alban Berg,

Anton Webern, Igor Stravinsky,

Paul Hindemith

Impressionism was just the first of several movements in twentieth-century music rejecting Romanticism and helping to launch a new course. Two other major movements have been Expressionism and Neo-Classicism, both producing copious literature for the piano and in chamber music.

Though they are worlds apart as to style and technique, Expressionism and Neo-Classicism meet on common ground in their mutual interest in objectivity: the removal of human relationships and deeply felt emotion from music. No extramusical implications must exist. The interest of music should lie in its sounds, in the logic of its structure, in the development of musical thought. In Neo-Classicism this removal of emotion and extramusical interest is brought about mainly through a return to classical forms and traditions of the past. In Expressionism—which, on the other hand, is music not of the past but of the future—it is achieved through abstraction: the concentration on a single quality or aspect of an object while ignoring all other qualities and aspects. The Expressionist composer looks inward, not outward, and explores the subconscious.

Whether in painting (where this term originated) or in music, Expressionism strips art of all but the barest essentials. An Expressionistic composition has to be the last word in brevity, its content so reduced to basics that it becomes the ultimate in compression and concentration. A few tones may serve as a melody; the harmonic writing is spare. No basic tonality exists (atonality). Discords do not find relief in consonance. What had once been flesh, muscle, and tissues covering the bare bones becomes in Expressionism just the skeleton, with all the flesh and tissues removed.

Arnold Schoenberg (1874–1951), a Viennese-born composer, was carried into the mainstream of Expressionism through the paintings of one of the earliest and most important Austrian Expressionist painters, Oskar Kokoschka. Those paintings were removed from all sense of reality. Figures and shapes were distorted. Only line arrangements and designs were stressed. Studying those paintings, Schoenberg became determined to do for music what Kokoschka had realized in painting. He would break all ties with past concepts.

The reason why Kokoschka made such a profound impression on Schoenberg is because at that very time Schoenberg was questioning his own values as a composer and was dissatisfied. Up to then, his compositions had been thoroughly Romantic, carrying over into instrumental music the grandiloquence, sensuousness, and dramatics of Wagner's style. Schoenberg's first string quartet in D major (1897)—which preceded the one now officially designated as String Quartet no. 1 by seven years—was supercharged in emotion, besides being highly traditional in structure. From there, Schoenberg went on to write works just as deeply rooted in the Romantic traditions of Wagner: *Verklärte Nacht* (*Transfigured Night*), op. 4 (1899), a sextet that in 1917 became celebrated in Schoenberg's adaptation for string orchestra; the *Gurre-Lieder* (*Songs of Gurre*), in 1901, a Gargantuan cantata for five solo voices, three male choruses, an eight-part mixed chorus, and an orchestra of one hundred and forty instruments; and the String Quartet no. 1 in D minor, op. 7 (1904–05). He had gone as far as he could with the Romantic style—and he knew it. Reaction set in, and as so often happens with reaction it carried Schoenberg to the opposite extreme. The paintings of Kokoschka revealed to Schoenberg the nature his reaction should take: Expressionism.

His personal revolution began in the finale of the String Quartet no. 2 in F-sharp minor, with soprano voice, op. 10 (1907–08). The three earlier movements adhered basically to its key signature, but in the finale

Schoenberg embarked for the first time on atonality—the first complete piece of music ever to be written this way.

Atonality and abstraction, dissonance and total objectivity continued to fascinate Schoenberg more and more in his works for the stage, for orchestra, or for speaking voice and instruments in the 1910s. In the early 1920s, Schoenberg implemented his Expressionist methods by adopting the twelve-tone system (dodecaphony). He did not invent it, any more than Debussy had invented the whole-tone scale. But just as Debussy made the whole-tone scale an all-important device for Impressionist music in general and his own in particular, and brought this scale to world prominence, so Schoenberg developed, perfected, and circularized the deployment of the twelve-tone system as the principal technique of the Expressionist school.

The twelve-tone system is a rigid formula that made it possible for a composer to construct music according to set laws in the same way a building is erected from an architect's blueprints. Schoenberg saw the twelve-tone system as the method by which he could totally obliterate self in the shaping of music. It is unnecessary to enter here into a detailed analysis of this complicated system, but a few essentials must be explained. The twelve-tone system is based on a "row" of the twelve tones of the chromatic scale. This row is prepared before a composer begins to work on a piece of music. One inflexible rule prevails in the construction of this row: no note can be repeated until all the other eleven notes have been used. This rule was imposed to make each tone as important as any other within a thematic scheme, thus obliterating the old concept of melody in which certain tones were repeated in a pattern. This twelve-tone row—and some clearly defined variants—become the source from which a composition springs thematically, harmonically, contrapuntally.

The first time Schoenberg used the twelve-tone system was in the last piece (a waltz) in *Five Pieces* (*Klavierstücke*) for piano, op. 23 (1923). The first composition he wrote entirely in this system was the Suite for Piano, op. 25 (1924). In the String Quartet no. 3, op. 30 (1926)—the first such Schoenberg composition in which a key signature is completely dispensed with—Schoenberg uses the twelve-tone system within a traditional four-movement structure. The sounds are consistently discordant, the thematic material epigrammatic, and the development of the musical thought progresses with a mathematical exactitude in each of the movements. The music of both the piano suite and the string quartet is an intellectual experience.

In time, Schoenberg brought to his twelve-tone writing greater and more varied musical interest. Indeed, he even succeeded in making it a medium for an expressivity absent from his earlier twelve-tone works. We first encounter this development in the String Quartet no. 4 op. 37 (1936), especially in the third-movement Largo. In time Schoenberg was able to make a compromise between the strict logic of his twelve-tone system and human and dramatic values. But this happened in his late years, after he had come to the United States (in the fall of 1933) to find permanent refuge from Nazism, which had risen to power in Germany that year. Convinced that Nazism would menace all Europe, and most assuredly his beloved Austria, Schoenberg came to America to establish his home in the Brentwood district of Los Angeles. Schoenberg tried his best to assume the posture of an American. He became a citizen in 1941. He preferred to speak in broken English than in his native tongue. He signed his letters and manuscripts "Schoenberg" and not "Schön-berg" as had been his custom in Europe.

Schoenberg was a superstitious man. He had a particular dread for the number thirteen. He was convinced that the misfortunes that had dogged his career—the disapproval of public and critics from which he had suffered so bitterly for many years—came about because he had been born on the thirteenth day of the month. When he was seventy-six he lapsed into a period of depression because the numbers seven and six add up to thirteen. He insisted that if he could only pass that fateful year he would survive much longer—but he doubted that this would happen. As he expected he died before he reached age seventy-seven—at his home in Brentwood, in Los Angeles. And he died thirteen minutes before midnight on July 13!

The human and emotional quality that entered Schoenberg's writing late in his life had been arrived at before him by one of his most dedicated pupils and disciples, Alban Berg (1885–1935), who is most famous for his atonal opera *Wozzeck* (1921). Berg has come to be identified as the "Romanticist" of the "Schoenberg school," which sounds like a contradiction, since the "Schoenberg school" represented a negation of Romanticism. Berg's best chamber music work is the *Lyrische Suite* (*Lyric Suite*), for string quartet (1926). It is subjective and melodic from a modern point of view, even though it is atonal, but with some of its movements in the twelve-tone system. To the tempo marking of each movement Berg appended a descriptive word to pinpoint its emotional content: the first movement is Allegretto gioviale ("jovial"); the second,

Andante amoroso ("loving"); the third, Allegro misterioso ("mysterious"); the fourth, Adagio appassionato ("passionate"); the fifth, Presto delirando ("delirious"); and the sixth, Largo desolato ("desolate"). Cohesion between movements is realized by using some motive or phrase from a preceding one in the motive or phrase that follows. The second movement has moments in the style of a Viennese waltz, the fourth movement is the most melodious, and the sixth (where Berg quotes from Wagner's *Tristan and Isolde*) is discordant in its expression of utter desolation.

Schoenberg's goal as an Expressionist to achieve brevity and compression was surpassed by another of his devoted pupil-disciples, Anton Webern (1883–1945). Some of Webern's motives consist of a few tones, sometimes even of a single tone! Some of his compositions are so short they take less than a minute to play. He distributed the tones of his chords to different instruments, sometimes just one tone to each, in order to arrive at the barest of harmonic statements. Sometimes each single tone assumes a different color by such various string methods as pizzicato, harmonics, playing on the bridge—so that each individual timbre stands out prominently. He never repeated a motive, or developed it, but followed it with a new one, insisting that "once started, the theme expresses all it has to say and must be followed by something fresh."

Some of these methods, uniquely Webern's, are to be found in his Six Bagatelles, for string quartet, op. 9 (1913), which are atonal and not twelve-tonal. This music has a concentration and economy without precedent. The six bagatelles combined have fifty-eight measures in all: the first piece has ten measures; the second and fourth have eight measures; the third and sixth, nine measures; and the fifth, thirteen measures. "A whole novel is expressed in a single sigh," Schoenberg once said of these Bagatelles. "They are melodies in one breath," is the way a noted Austrian critic, Erwin Stein, put it. "The composer says only the barest essentials and his expression determines the form of the piece."

"Neo" means "new." Neo-Classicism, then, represents a return to the objectivity of Classicism, which had preceded Romanticism and of which it was the antithesis.

Igor Stravinsky (1882–1971) made his official debut as a Neo-Classicist with a chamber music composition: the Octet, for wind instruments (1923–24). By then he had already become a world-famous composer, though in a far different style. Russian-born and Russian-trained, he first became prominent in Paris with his scores for ballets produced by the Ballets Russes, of which Serge Diaghilev was artistic director as well as founder. Beginning with *L'Oiseau de feu* (*The Firebird*) in 1910, and continuing with *Petrouchka* (1911) and *Le Sacre du printemps* (*The Rite of Spring*) (1913), Stravinsky became an international figure in music as well as the leading exponent of the then avant-garde movement in music. In all these scores, Stravinsky released dynamic forces: harrowing discords and polytonal combinations, orgiastic sonorities and dynamics, an explosion of changing rhythms and meters. This was primitive music of brutal strength within the framework of sophisticated structures and techniques. Stravinsky forthwith became the prophet of a new all-important movement in twentieth-century music (neoprimitivism), and he remained its prophet for a decade. Since the neoprimitive style was best suited for a large orchestral force, Stravinsky produced little of consequence in this idiom either for chamber music or for a solo instrument.

By 1918, Stravinsky felt that he had developed neoprimitivism to its ultimate artistic potentialities. He now felt a compelling need to speak more simply and economically, and to employ as often as possible smaller forces and shorter forms. And so, he slowly broke with his neoprimitive tendencies that had won him international fame and began to drift toward Neo-Classicism.

His changeover from a neoprimitive to a Neo-Classicist caused as much shock and outrage and furore in musical circles as his initial emergence as a neoprimitive composer had done. At the world premiere of his octet in Paris on October 18, 1923, the audience was caught completely by surprise by this music. Aaron Copland, the distinguished American composer (then young and unknown), was in the auditorium when this octet was introduced. He has described the bewilderment of the public at the lean, neat structure, and the pure, refined sounds. That audience could hardly have become aware that in this modest chamber music composition Stravinsky had embarked upon a new career as composer. In that career he reverted to Classical forms and often to contrapuntal textures in his determination to arrive at objectivity and tight-lipped restraint.

Stravinsky remained a dedicated Neo-Classicist up through 1951. His last Neo-Classical work was his only full-length opera, *The Rake's Progress* (1951), where he looked back to the classical operatic style of Handel, Gluck, and Mozart. In that quarter of a century or so he revived the orchestral concerto grosso and adopted such other classical structures as the concerto for solo instrument and orchestra, the symphony, the Mass, the oratorio, and the sonata. In two works for the piano, Stravinsky's Neo-Classic style appears in all its crystalline purity: the Concerto for Two Solo Pianos (1935) and the Sonata for Two Pianos (1944). For other solo instruments he wrote the five-movement *Duo Concertant* for violin and piano (1932) and *Élégie* (*Elegy*), for viola (or violin) solo (1944).

Most of Stravinsky's Neo-Classic works were completed in France, where he became a citizen in 1934. Some of these works also came into being in the United States, to which Stravinsky transferred his family and possessions in 1939 with the outbreak of World War II. Virtually to the end of his life, Stravinsky lived in Hollywood, California, but just before his death he moved to New York. He had become an American citizen in 1945.

In his compositions beginning in 1952, Stravinsky deserted Neo-Classicism to embrace what for him was a totally new idiom and one that for a long time he had held in disdain: the twelve-tone system. One of Stravinsky's earliest experiments with twelve-tone writing was made in 1953—a septet, for violin, viola, cello, clarinet, horn, bassoon, and piano. All three movements suggest that Stravinsky was making a compromise with the Neo-Classicism he had just abandoned and the Expressionist style he was now embracing: in the first movement he employs a fugato passage; the second movement is a passacaglia, and the third, a gigue. Actually, the septet is not in strict twelve-tone style since this technique is used with extreme flexibility. It is more of an atonal work, in which only some of the thematic material is constructed from a twelve-tone row.

In Stravinsky's compositions that followed the septet—the large religious works for voices and orchestra and his orchestral *Variations* (1964)—Stravinsky became a strict conformist to serial rather than twelve-tone music. Serialism is an extension of the twelve-tone system that concerns itself not only with pitch (as had been the case with Schoenberg and Berg) but also with color (in which Webern had pointed the way), rhythm, dynamics, note values, and other elements of music. In other words, besides constructing a twelve-tone row for his basic melodic material, the serial composer also arranges a row of twelve different tone colors, twelve different rhythms, twelve different shades of dynamics, and twelve different note values. In each case none is repeated until the other eleven have been used. This is known as "total organization."

The first musician to evolve the technique of serialism was an American, Milton Babbitt (1916–   ), then instructor in mathematics at Princeton University, but since become professor of music there. In 1946 he wrote a treatise expounding the theory of serialism, the first such. He then put theory into practice by writing *Three Compositions for Piano* (1947) and *Composition for Four Instruments* (1947), both in a serial technique. The latter received a special citation from the New York Music Critics Circle.

But the first composer achieving international renown through serialism was a Frenchman, Pierre Boulez (1925–   ). Since the end of World War II, Boulez has been a leader in the avant-garde movement in music (besides achieving world fame as a conductor). Boulez was convinced that the main problem facing the twentieth-century composer was to free himself completely from Romanticism, and that, to do so, the composer must be thoroughly guided by a controlling, predetermined system. That is why, virtually from his beginnings as a mature composer, he used the twelve-tone system. "Since the discoveries of the Viennese [Schoenberg, Berg, Webern]," he said, "all composition other than twelve tones is useless."

But the twelve-tone system, he soon felt, had to extend to areas other than pitch. Without being at all aware that Milton Babbitt in America was at that time thinking along the very same lines, Boulez wrote his Piano Sonata no. 2 (1948), which, in his own words, was "a total and deliberate break with the universe of classical twelve-tone writing . . . the decisive step towards an integrated serial work." When the Piano Sonata was first played (in Paris) is created horror among Schoenberg's admirers and followers, who felt that by altering Schoenberg's methods Boulez had become a heretic to the cause of twelve-tone music. But the young composers in Europe and America before long looked upon Boulez as their musical prophet and embraced serialism. The composition generally regarded as Boulez's masterpiece in serial style is *Le Marteau sans maître* (*The Hammer Without a Master*) in 1955, a nine-movement work for contralto and six instruments based on three poems by René Char. In four of the movements, the Char poems are sung; the other five movements are instrumental commentaries on the same poems. "I have tried," says Boulez, "to find the deep roots of poetry in music, in the instrumental parts even more than in the vocal sections."

Karlheinz Stockhausen (1928–   ) is a German avant-garde composer who progressed from serialism to electronic music. Between 1952 and 1954 he completed ten piano pieces, *Klavierstücke,* and a chamber music composition, *Kontrapunkte no. 1* (*Counterpoint no. 1*) for ten instruments, in which he employed the fullest resources of serial writing with outstanding skill.

Paul Hindemith was the leading German Neo-Classicist. He used polyphony extensively but without ever abandoning twentieth-century idioms. His technique has come to be known as "linear counterpoint," in which several different melodies move simultaneously (as they do in Bach's polyphonic compositions), but without consideration for harmonic relationships. This leads to dissonance and at times to atonality. Hindemith's music is highly complicated and cerebral. It has to be listened to many times before the originality of his language and the inexorable logic of his musical thought make an impression.

Paul Hindemith was born in Hanau, Germany, on November 16, 1895. He demonstrated exceptional talent for music as a child when he took lessons on the violin and the viola. By the time he was eleven he earned his living playing in coffeehouses and theater orchestras. But he had not ended his musical training, which continued at Hoch's Conservatory in Frankfurt. After serving for a year in the German army during World War I, Hindemith was appointed concertmaster of the orchestra of the Frankfurt Opera. He soon made a name for himself. He founded and played the viola in the Amar-Hindemith String Quartet, which promoted new German music. He helped found an important modern music festival (the Donaueschingen Festival). And he was making his mark as a Neo-Classic composer with the String Quartet no. 2 in F minor, op. 10 (1919) and the Sonata no. 2 in D major, for violin and piano, op. 11 no. 2 (1920), in both of which a linear style is suggested.

He developed his linear technique in 1922 with two string quartets —no. 3 in C major, op. 16, and no. 4, op. 22—and with the *Kleine Kammermusik* (*Little Chamber Music*), op. 24 no. 2, for flute, oboe, clarinet, horn, and bassoon. The five-movement Third String Quartet opens with a fugato in which the voices move independently of any tonal center and where time values and the key signature are dispensed with. The first movement of the Fourth String Quartet is a fugue and double fugue in linear style. This is followed by a slow second movement that is also contrapuntal. A brief march movement is the bridge to a passacaglia with twenty-seven variations, then ending with a fugato.

The *Kleine Kammermusik* is one of Hindemith's most successful chamber music works because its interest is centered not so much on Hindemith's polyphonic skill as on wit. Some of its themes are parodies of the kind of tunes that were popular in Germany soon after World War I.

This excursion from intellectualism to levity was not to be a solitary one for Hindemith, as many of his works in the 1920s proved. After he married Gertrud Rottenberg (the daughter of the conductor of the Frankfurt Opera) in 1924, Hindemith became temporarily infected with a popular movement then in vogue in Germany—*Zeitkunst* ("Contemporary Art"). This favored modern, popular subjects for musical treatment, with the music in a light, breezy style. In this vein Hindemith wrote a jazz opera, *Neues vom Tage* (*News of the Day*) in 1929, whose text and music were farcical to the point of becoming burlesque.

This does not mean that Hindemith had ceased to be a Neo-Classicist, or that he had completely deserted his linear style. Far from it! Extraordinarily prolific, he produced compositions in all forms in the severe, complicated contrapuntal manner with which he was henceforth to be identified and which made him one of the masters of twentieth-century music. For chamber music combinations he produced two trios for violin, viola and cello no. 1, op. 34 (1924), and no. 2 (1934); String Quartet no. 5, op. 32 (1924); *Kammermusik* (*Chamber Music*) no. 2, for piano and twelve instruments, op. 36 no. 1 (1924); and sonatas for various solo instruments (some unaccompanied, some accompanied by piano). His principal works for piano were *Klaviermusik* (*Piano Music*), op. 37 (1927), three sonatas for solo piano (1936), a sonata for two pianos (1942), and *Ludus Tonalis* or *Tonal Play* (1943). *Ludus Tonalis* is a giant venture, an exercise in contrapuntal writing sometimes described as "Hindemith's *Art of the Fugue.*" This work, which requires three-quarters of an hour for performance, begins with a prelude (Praeludium). Twelve fugues follow, each in one of the keys of the chromatic scale. Between each fugue there is an interlude adopting a light form or style, such as pastorale, waltz, march, and cakewalk. This is to introduce a welcome respite from the severities of his often dissonant fugal writing. The entire composition ends with a postlude (Postludium). When *Ludus Tonalis* was introduced in Chicago in 1943, an unidentified critic for the magazine *Modern Music* called it "staggering," adding that "as an instance of contrapuntal skill [it was] probably unequalled since Bach as an investigation of the possibilities of the piano as a virtuoso instrument."

Hindemith also wrote many major compositions for orchestra, for chorus, and some for the stage. One of these brought him into trouble in 1934: *Mathis der Maler* (*Matthias the Painter*), which he wrote both as a symphony and as an opera. The Nazis were then in power in Germany. The new totalitarian regime had no sympathy for Hindemith's kind of music, which it regarded as "degenerate" because it was so discordant and complex; nor could it forget that Hindemith, an Aryan, had married a Jewess. Nevertheless, since Hindemith by now had become one of Germany's most celebrated musicians, he was left unmolested. But when he chose for his symphony and opera the subject of a successful uprising of peasants against the authority of the Church, the Nazis leaders could not sit by quietly any longer. Though the symphony was performed in Berlin, the opera was banned before it could achieve its premiere. Hindemith, now in disgrace with the government, had to leave Germany, to find a new home for himself in the United States.

In America, where he became a citizen in 1946, he joined the music faculty of Yale University, wrote theoretical treatises on music, and completed some of his noblest and most enduring linear compositions. So extraordinarily prolific was he that it is virtually impossible to comment on all the chamber music that came from his busy pen, nor is it necessary to do so, since all these works follow the Hindemith pattern of austere music in a linear style. Among his best chamber music works were numerous sonatas for solo instruments, accompanied and unaccompanied, two more string quartets (1944–45), the *Four Temperaments,* and *A Frog He Went A-Courting,* variations for cello and piano (1946). He also wrote a wind quintet, a septet, and an octet.

After World War II, his native country made overtures to Hindemith to return home. He stoutly refused to do so. However, he did reestablish himself in Europe—in Zürich, Switzerland—where he joined the faculty of its university. Intermittently, he returned to the United States to attend performances of his compositions, the last time being in 1963, when he was present at a four-day Hindemith festival in New York. A world figure, he was showered with honors, including the Bach Prize of the City of Hamburg in 1950, the Sibelius Prize in 1955, the Italian Balzan Prize in 1963, and the New York Music Critics Circle Award in 1953 and 1960.

When he escaped from the supercharged intellectual life of composer-teacher-scholar-theorist, Hindemith did woodwork and cartooning; earlier in life he had such a passion for toy trains that a full train set always cluttered his living quarters. Making practical use of his gift at drawing, he used to send his friends Christmas cards of his own design. When, in 1963, his American friends failed to receive them they knew he must be fatally sick. He was. Hindemith died in Frankfurt, Germany, on December 28, 1963.

14

America's Music

Edward MacDowell, Aaron Copland, Roy Harris,
Samuel Barber, Elliott Carter

In 1960, Edward MacDowell became the first composer of serious intent to be chosen for the Hall of Fame for Great Americans at New York University (the only other composer being Stephen Foster). The one hundred or so distinguished men and women from all over the United States selected MacDowell for this signal honor with good reason. Serious American concert music as we know it today really began with Mac-Dowell. He was the first American composer to gain the admiration and respect of Europe, the first whose name and best compositions (most for the piano) are still cherished.

MacDowell was a Romanticist in the tradition of Mendelssohn and Grieg. Having spent many years in Germany in the last decades of the nineteenth century, and having received there his principal musical training, MacDowell was so saturated with European Romanticism that when he began to compose in earnest in Germany he inevitably involved himself in its Romantic movement. Like so many German Romanticists, MacDowell became an exquisite miniaturist, a prolific creator of cameos. Like so many German Romanticists he had a gift for elegant melodies, which he spun over well-sounding harmonies and built into im-

pressive climaxes. And like so many German Romanticists he drew his
inspiration from landscapes and forests, and from the supernatural world
of gnomes, elves, and witches.

But he was also an *American* Romanticist. He was the first important composer to use native American source material in several of his works: the songs and dances of the American Indian, which he used so ingeniously in his best orchestral work (*Indian Suite,* in 1897) and in such piano pieces as the "Indian Idyl" from the *New England Idyls* (1902); the syncopated rhythms of Negro popular music in "From Uncle Remus" in his most celebrated composition for the piano, the *Woodland Sketches* (1896). He was also American in the way his music evokes for us images of America's natural beauties, to which he was so sensitive: American forests, lakes, ponds, meadow brooks, and so forth.

It speaks volumes for the tolerance and intelligence of MacDowell's parents that they encouraged him to become a professional musician. In the latter half of the nineteenth century, American society looked with condescension, if not contempt, on professional musicians. A boy with artistic aspirations who wanted to make a living through his chosen art was looked upon as the black sheep of the family.

Edward MacDowell's father, a Quaker, was a frustrated artist who had been compelled to turn to business, in which he became successful. He was a man who had a hunger in him that material success could not satisfy. Regardless of the standards of the time, he would never permit a son of his to know such spiritual starvation. The mother was a brilliant, energetic woman who was artistically inclined. Edward MacDowell—born in downtown New York on December 18, 1861—was their third son. When, in childhood, Edward revealed an interest in drawing and painting, the parents eagerly provided him with the materials he needed to express himself. In his eighth year, Edward became a voracious reader. His parents saw to it that he was supplied with good books. (He never lost his boyhood passion for either drawing or reading.) And when, also at eight, Edward expressed a desire to play the piano, they had a young, well-trained musician, Juan Buitrago, live in their house so that Edward could get training regularly and frequently.

After a period of study with "Uncle Buitrago"—and some coaching from Teresa Carreño, then already recognized as the foremost woman piano virtuoso of her time—Edward studied the piano for three years with Paul Desvernine, with whom he made such remarkable progress that his parents decided to send the boy to Europe for further study. In Paris he played the piano for Marmontel, the head of the piano department of the Paris Conservatory. Marmontel embraced the boy and forthwith took him on first as a private pupil, then on a two-year scholarship in his piano class at the Paris Conservatory. In 1878, MacDowell went on to Germany to complete his musical education at conservatories in Stuttgart and Frankfurt.

In 1880, Joachim Raff, director of Hoch's Conservatory in Frankfurt and MacDowell's teacher in composition, urged him to write a serious work for the piano. MacDowell responded with the *First Modern Suite,* op. 10, which convinced Raff of his talent. Up to that time Mac-Dowell had no wish to be a composer, his goal being to become a piano virtuoso. But Raff's praise was not to be taken lightly. MacDowell went on to write other piano works, including the *Second Modern Suite,* for piano, op. 14 (1881). The joy of creation now seized him, compelling him to reevaluate his aims in music. He was determined to make composition his prime endeavor.

One day, in 1882, Raff checked up on MacDowell's progress as composer by inquiring what he was working upon at that time. As it happened, MacDowell had no composition in progress, but was too embarrassed to tell his teacher so. Instead, he stammered that he was deeply involved in a concerto. "Excellent, excellent," Raff replied. "Bring me what you already have written." Somehow MacDowell managed to postpone bringing Raff the concerto in question for several weeks, during which time he worked furiously. When his concerto was finished, Raff was so taken with it that he sent MacDowell to Weimar to play it for the great Liszt. "This young American is going to be someone," was Liszt's verdict. Liszt arranged for MacDowell to play his *First Modern Suite* at a German festival and convinced Breitkopf and Härtel to publish both this and the *Second Modern Suite.*

The Concerto no. 1 in A minor, op. 15, for piano and orchestra was introduced in Zürich in 1882 with MacDowell as soloist. It was warmly received. Encouraged, MacDowell went on to write the *Serenata,* op. 16, in 1883, and in 1884 the *Two Fantastic Pieces,* op. 17 (one of which, ''Witches' Dance,'' is the first of his outstanding miniatures), and *Two Pieces,* op. 18, all for the piano.

In 1884 MacDowell married one of his pupils, Marian Nevins, a young American. For the next four years they occupied a charming cottage in woods skirting Wiesbaden in Germany. They were as one. They took long walks every day in the woods. During vacations, they went on extended walking trips. They shared other pleasures, such as photography, reading poetry aloud to each other, and bicycling. Stimulated by a wife whose faith in his genius was unshakable, MacDowell now became increasingly fertile as composer.

MacDowell's first tone poem for orchestra—*Hamlet and Ophelia,* op. 22—was completed in 1885. This was followed in 1887 by a succession of Grieg-like compositions for the piano among which were the *Four Pieces,* op. 24, *Six Idyls after Goethe,* op. 28, and *Six Poems after Heine,* op. 31, the last of which contains the notable "Scotch Poem."

The MacDowells returned to the United States in 1888 to make their home in Boston. His European successes had made him much in demand in Boston as teacher of the piano, as a performer, and as composer. The American premiere of his First Piano Concerto was given in Boston in April of 1888. In 1889 he himself played the world premiere performance of his Piano Concerto no. 2 in D minor, op. 23, first in New York and soon thereafter in Boston and Paris. This is the first concerto by an American still being played occasionally. It is a thoroughly delightful work, charming in its lyricism, appealing in its romantic spirit, and with a third-movement Scherzo that possesses Mendelssohnian grace.

MacDowell devoted his winters to Boston, except for a brief period immediately following Christmas, when he embarked on limited concert tours as pianist. Most of his summers were spent in Maine. To avoid looking like an artist, he went out of his way to appear dapper. His mustache was always neatly curled, and for a time he sported a goatee. His clothes were well tailored in the latest fashion.

Those Boston years saw the writing of some of his best piano music. It included sonatas. The first, in G minor, the *Tragic,* op. 45 (1893), was called by James Gibbons Huneker, the distinguished critic of that time, "the most marked contribution to solo sonata literature since Brahms' F minor Sonata." The Sonata no. 2 in G minor, *Eroica,* op. 50 (1895), was based on the legends of King Arthur, his wife Guinevere, and the Round Table. MacDowell wrote two more sonatas several years later inspired by old myths and sagas: the Sonata no. 3 in D minor, *Norse,* op. 57 (1900), tapping the same mythological source Wagner had used for his cycle of music dramas *The Ring of the Nibelungs;* and the best of the four sonatas, that in E minor, the *Celtic,* op. 59 (1901), derived from Irish folk tales.

MacDowell's masterwork for the piano, the *Woodland Sketches,* is a suite of ten pieces, op. 51 (1896). These are true nature poems in music, each picture projected romantically without descending either to banality or sentimentality. The best known are "To a Wild Rose" and "To a Water Lily." It is surely amusing that the one piece with which MacDowell's name is inextricably associated—"To a Wild Rose"—was considered by the composer so substandard that when he finished it he crumpled up the manuscript and threw it away in his wastebasket. It was found there by his wife, who insisted that he use it in his suite.

When, in 1896, Columbia University in New York established a department of music, MacDowell was invited to become its head. Mac-Dowell left Boston for New York, where he hurled his Herculean energies and idealism into the exacting task of building a music department of the highest standards. He had come to his appointment with the high hopes of creating an altogether new standard in America for music education. But his hopes were stillborn. During his first two years he had to teach all the music courses, a duty that proved an ordeal because so many of his students were indifferent or unresponsive. Then and later he became enmeshed in burdensome administrative duties he abhorred, and though he had been promised total independence, he was continually thwarted by red tape.

Escape from his agonizing frustrations and disenchantment came during the summer when he and his wife could seek refuge in a farm, Hillcrest, in Peterborough, New Hampshire, which he had acquired in 1896. There, first in a music room and later on in a log cabin which his wife had had built for him deep in the woods near a spring, he found the peace and serenity to work on compositions. It was there that he wrote his *Woodland Sketches*. There, too, he wrote his last important piano work, *New England Idyls*, op. 62 (1902).

But in the winter, in New York, things were degenerating for Mac-Dowell. So much bitterness developed between the university and Mac-Dowell, and so hostile an exchange of charges and countercharges, that a scandal exploded, which was fully exploited by the press. Since Mac-Dowell would not surrender his ideals nor compromise his standards, he decided at last, in 1904, that he could stay in the post no longer.

His physical resources and his nervous makeup sorely taxed, he and his wife escaped to the peace and solitude of Hillcrest with the hopes of restoring depleted energies and a ravaged spirit. All he now wanted to do was to write music. But not even Hillcrest could repair the damage of the preceding few years. In 1905 MacDowell suffered mental collapse. He withdrew so deeply into himself that he was oblivious of where he was or with whom. He was like a child again. He sat at a window, gazing out into the horizon. His eyes were glazed, his mind blank. Not his closest friends, not even his beloved wife, could penetrate the darkness into which MacDowell had slipped so silently.

He died not in Hillcrest but in a hotel room in New York, on January 23, 1908. His body was brought back to his farm in Peterborough for burial on a hilltop near his log cabin.

For many years MacDowell had dreamed of building a place in the woods where creative people—freed of the responsibility of earning a living—could do the work they were born to do in pastoral surroundings. He did not live to realize this dream. But after his death, his widow concentrated her every effort to realize her husband's wish, at Hillcrest, the place he loved best. There she founded the MacDowell Colony, where writers, artists, poets, and musicians could work in their separate cabins. Removed from the stresses of the outside world, and with their basic comforts attended to, they could devote themselves completely to their art.

Aaron Copland (1900–   ) occupied, for a number of summers one of those log cabins that Mrs. MacDowell had built for the artists at the MacDowell Colony. There he worked on various of his compositions. Copland, who has come to be known as "the dean of American composers," is one of many Americans who have profited from the vision and the indefatigable efforts of Mrs. MacDowell, who, until her death in 1956, had helped to create the only kind of memorial her husband would have respected and cherished. From 1962 to 1969 Copland served as president of the colony.

Copland began his career as a composer in Brooklyn, New York, where he was born. By the time he was twenty he had completed several short compositions, including a piece for the piano, *The Cat and the Mouse*. At that time Copland was studying harmony with Rubin Goldmark. Since this piece was in the then modern style, and since Goldmark was an ultraconservative musician, Goldmark told his pupil that he just had no criteria with which to judge *that* kind of music. Goldmark always looked upon Copland as a musical renegade.

Only after Copland had studied composition and orchestration for three years in Paris, between 1921 and 1924, did he find in Nadia Boulanger a teacher able and willing to encourage him in his modern ways. Following his return to the United States in 1924, Copland made his

American debut both as composer and as pianist by playing in New York *The Cat and the Mouse,* and a second of his own piano pieces, *Passacaglia* (1922).

Though Copland has become famous for large works for orchestra and his scores for ballets, he has written much important music both for solo piano and for chamber music combinations. Copland has undergone several phases in his growth as composer. He first made his mark with experiments with jazz idioms within serious contexts in a studied effort to realize an American style. In this manner we find the orchestral suite, *Music for the Theater* (1925), and his Piano Concerto (1926). He then deserted jazz for a more abstract kind of music with intellectual appeal, utilizing what was then regarded as the advanced idioms: polytonality, unresolved discords, polyrhythms, and so forth. Among these complex works is the *Piano Variations* (1930), an austere composition whose theme, based on a four-note motto, is followed by twenty variations and a coda. Copland apparently thought highly of this work, for twenty-seven years later he adapted it for orchestra, calling it *Orchestral Variations.*

Copland's best chamber music during this period was a one-movement trio for piano, violin, and cello, *Vitebsk* (1929). Vitebsk is a Russian village with a large Jewish population from which came a Jewish folksong Copland uses in this trio and upon which he embellishes. Copland called this trio a "study on a Jewish theme." This melody is heard in the cello after an introduction with the piano supplying polytonal accompaniment.

In the middle 1930s Copland became convinced he had lost contact with his audiences by writing in such a complicated way. "I felt that it was worth the effort to see if I couldn't say what I had to say in the simplest possible terms," he explained. This is the time when Copland popularized his style by quoting American folk songs and popular tunes of the past, and by writing functional music for the movies, the stage, radio, and for children. The Sonata for Piano (1941) and the Sonata for Violin and Piano (1943) are in this more assimilable style, though neither work resorts to quotations in the way his ballet scores do. Both sonatas have pleasant-sounding melodic ideas and a humanity not to be found in Copland's earlier works.

In his last phase Copland passed back from simplicity to complexity by adopting the twelve-tone system and serialism. The first composition to employ the twelve-tone method was his Quartet for Piano and Strings (1950). In 1957 Copland's *Piano Fantasy* was in a strict twelve-tone technique. Though Copland continued to produce other compositions in either the twelve-tone or serial systems, he also employed other styles. In the Nonet for three violins, three violas, and three cellos (1960) he reverted to the Baroque forms of the concerto grosso and the ricercar, and to contrapuntal writing. In the Duo for flute and piano (1971) he is tonal, melodic, and, in certain passages, dramatic.

Roy Harris (1898–   ) is another striking figure in American music who early in his career found refuge at the MacDowell Colony to work on his music. The descendant of pioneer American stock, Harris did not begin to think seriously about music until after World War I, when he entered a class in harmony at the Southern Branch of the University of California. Then he studied composition privately for two years with Arthur Farwell, whose faith and encouragement were important stimuli to Harris's development. Harris's first composition was an Andante, for orchestra, introduced in Rochester in 1926, then given the same year in New York and in Hollywood, California. His first compositions to be performed, however, were pieces for a string quartet entitled *Impressions of a Rainy Day,* heard in Los Angeles about five weeks before the world premiere of his Andante. Between 1926 and 1929 Harris lived in Paris, where he received advice and direction from Nadia Boulanger without actually being her pupil. There he completed his first mature composition, the Concerto for Piano, Clarinet and String Quartet introduced in Paris in 1927 (the year of its composition). After his return to the United States he produced some more chamber music: a string quartet (1930); *Fantasy,* a sextet for piano, flute, oboe, clarinet, bassoon, and horn (1932); Three Variations on a Theme, for string quartet (1933); and Piano Trio (1934). In all these he showed a marked gift for contrapuntal writing.

By the mid 1930s Harris grew to be one of the most widely publicized, extensively performed, and sought-after composers in America. His first symphony (1933) became the first such American work to be recorded in full. His pen was tireless. One work after another added to his stature. Two chamber music compositions are especially noteworthy, since in both he demonstrated his highly personal way of writing contrapuntally within Baroque structures. The Piano Quintet (1936) opens with a passacaglia and ends with a fugue. Midway comes a cadenza, the high point of which is a serene recitative-like section for string quartet. The String Quartet no. 3 (1937), played without a break, is a series of four preludes and fugues. After that, Harris completed *Soliloquy and*

Dance, for viola and piano (1939), String Quintet (1940), and Sonata for Violin and Piano (1941), all of them predominantly polyphonic.

Since the 1940s Harris has been far more prolific in orchestral and choral music than in chamber music. His chamber music output included a Duo, for cello and piano (1964). Though an excellent pianist himself, and the husband of a concert pianist (Johana Duffy Harris), Roy Harris has contributed only a handful of compositions for solo piano, the most interesting of which is an excursion into musical nationalism with *American Ballads* (1942), an adaptation of several American folk songs.

Samuel Barber (1910–   ) has also made salient contributions to solo instrumental and chamber music. While attending the Curtis Institute of Music in Philadelphia he received the Bearns Prize for a violin sonata in 1928. In 1929 he completed a Serenade, for string quartet, and in 1932 (the year of his graduation from the institute) a sonata for cello and piano. These are apprentice works. But the String Quartet (1936) is representative of his later romantic tendencies and his strong lyricism. Its slow movement (adapted for string orchestra in 1938) is the now famous *Adagio for Strings*. It became the first American composition conducted by Arturo Toscanini with the NBC Symphony. This is deeply moving, elegiac music—so much so that it was played as a memorial to the late President John F. Kennedy over radio and television upon his assassination.

In his later works Barber made a neat compromise between his native Romantic tendencies and twentieth-century idioms. This fusion of Romanticism and modernism characterizes one of his major creations, the Sonata in E-flat minor, for piano, op. 26 (1949), which had been commissioned by the League of Composers, using money donated by two giants of American popular music, Richard Rodgers and Irving Berlin. This is a composition in a large classic design that generates power without sacrificing contemplative beauty and poetic thought.

Some of the most important chamber music in America since the end of World War II has come from Elliott Carter (1908–   ). He was born in New York City and received a Bachelor of Arts degree at Harvard. At Harvard he took graduate courses in music, completing his musical education in Paris with Nadia Boulanger. Among his earlier significant compositions is a Sonata for Piano, introduced in New York in 1947. He came into the limelight of recognition as a major new force in

American music in 1951 with his String Quartet no. 1. Carter here first evolved his own style, compounded of polyrhythms and continual changes of tempo, meter, and key, but nevertheless maintaining a fluid continuity; each of the four instruments has such freedom of musical direction that it seems to be producing its own music without regard to the other instruments. With his String Quartet no. 2 (1959) Carter further developed his personal intricate method with a composition that won him international renown. It was received so rhapsodically when first introduced in New York in 1960 that it captured the Pulitzer Prize in music, the New York Music Critics Circle Award, and the first prize of the International Rostrum of Composers sponsored by UNESCO. To endow each instrument with greater independence Carter instructed the players to sit as far as possible from one another on the stage. But during rehearsals Carter decided that this was not feasible and abandoned his experiment. However, within the quartet, the individuality of each instrument is stressed by having its music adopt an intervallic pattern of its own. In five sections, this quartet is played without interruption. A violin cadenza makes the transition from one part to the next.

Once again, in 1973, the Pulitzer Prize in music went to Carter, and once again it was for a string quartet: the String Quartet no. 3 (1971). The individuality of the instruments again concerned Carter deeply. Instead of combining the four players into a single group in which each is involved with the others in a give-and-take exchange of musical ideas—traditional with string-quartet writing—Carter here splits up the string quartet into two contrasting duos. In a single movement lasting about twenty minutes, this string quartet has Duo II (second violin and viola) play in strict time while Duo I (first violin and cello) indulges in a free rubato style, that is, variations in the tempo. So unorthodox is Carter's technique that when this quartet was rehearsed by the Juilliard String Quartet—for whom the work was written and who gave it its world premiere in 1973—its first violinist remarked: "We had to forget everything we ever learned about playing together and perform in a new way." Complex and austere though this music is, it also has a compelling power as well as intriguing originality which further establish its composer as one of America's foremost creators of string-quartet music.

A major experiment in combining electronic sounds with chamber music was undertaken by Leon Kirchner (1919–   ) with his String Quartet no. 3 (1967). This experiment was successful enough to win him the Pulitzer Prize in music. The electronic sounds come from magnetic tape transmitted through loudspeakers; the live music is produced by a string quartet. Here is how an unidentified critic for *High Fidelity Magazine* described the results after this quartet had been introduced in New York in 1967: "The electronic element is used conservatively—discreet percussive accents and pitched 'woodwind' sounds mingle with the four strings extending the textural range of the piece to almost orchestral proportions. At the work's conclusion, the two stage loudspeakers take over completely, wresting the thematic material from the human players and turning it into a breath-taking contrapuntal display that mere live performers cannot hope to equal. Totally routed, the strings can only answer this outburst with a final pianissimo chord, which sounds a knell of death."

Various other American composers have experimented in combining electronic sounds with those produced by traditional instruments. Donald Erb (1927–   ), for example, wrote *Reconnaissance,* for violin, string bass, piano percussion, and two electronic setups; and Kenneth Gaburo (1927–   ) created *Antiphony I and II,* the first for three string groups and electronic sounds, and the second for piano and electronic sounds. Still other Americans have produced solo or chamber music exclusively through electronic means. Milton Babbitt has been the pioneer in using a synthesizer for musical composition, the synthesizer being a giant electronic machine created by RCA. His *Composition for Synthesizer,* in 1961, was the first major work ever written by means of this instrument. Since then Babbitt, who has been discussed in the preceding chapter, has completed other compositions for the synthesizer, and Charles Wuorinen (1938–   ) captured the Pulitzer Prize of 1969 for *Time's Encomium,* the first time that a work produced by a synthesizer—or, for that matter, an exclusively electronic composition —received this award.

Obviously new vistas have opened up for music in general, and instrumental and chamber music in particular, through electronic devices. What has already been accomplished, however, has only just begun to open up a totally new world for music, a world that American composers will undoubtedly continue to explore fruitfully for years to come.

Igor Stravinsky.

Paul Hindemith.

Edward MacDowell and his wife Marian.

Elliott Carter.

Leon Kirchner recording one of his own compositions.

Circulo armᵒ à 4. voces, con 3ᵃ ✱ 5ᵃ nat. y 8ᵃ y con sus falsas de 2ᵃ 4ᵃ y 6ᵃ La 3 ✱ se puede mudar en 3♭.

LA PASTORIL

ACADEMIA MUSICAL DE LOS INSTRUMENTOS, QUE EXPLICA PABLO MINGU
sus Tratados, los quales enseñan el nuevo estilo de tañerlos por musica, y cifra con per

Glossary

Accelerando   Quickening of tempo.

Accompaniment   The part of a musical composition that assumes a supporting role.

Accompanist   Performer of an accompaniment (usually on the piano).

Action   Mechanism of piano, organ, or harp in which the fingers control the sound of strings or pipe.

Ad Libitum, or A Piacere   Term designating that the tempo, expression, and sometimes even the instrumental medium is left to the discretion of the performer; also that a passage may be omitted.

Alberti Bass   A broken-chord accompaniment in the music of the classical keyboard.

Alla Breve   An indication that the speed of a composition is doubled so that four-to-a-bar becomes two-to-a-bar.

Alto Clef   A clef used for viola music with the middle C on the third (middle) line of the staff.

Animato   Spirited.

Appoggiatura   A grace note, embellishment, or ornament.

Glossary **Arco** Following a plucked-string (pizzicato) passage, an indication in string music that the bow is to be used.

Arpeggio Consecutive playing of ascending or descending notes of a chord.

Assonance Agreement of sounds.

Atonality Absence of key center; music without basic tonality. See discussion in Chapter 13.

Attaca Indication at end of movement that the next movement is to be played without pause.

Bagatelle A brief musical composition for the piano of light content.

Ballade A composition with a strong narrative character but without a specific program, usually for the piano.

Bar, or Measure Section of music marked off by bar lines.

Barcarolle A boat song of Venetian gondoliers adapted from vocal to piano music.

Baroque An era in music between the late sixteenth and early eighteenth centuries. See discussion in Introduction and Chapters 1 and 2.

Basso Continuo *See* Figured Bass.

Berceuse Cradle song adapted from vocal to instrumental music.

Binary Form A two-part form, such as a movement in a sonata, consisting of two principal sections or two contrasting themes.

Bitonality Simultaneous use of two different keys.

Bow A wooden implement with horsehair used in the right hand by string players to create vibration of strings. Originally it was shaped like a bow used in archery; hence its name.

Bowing Way in which bow is applied to strings, or manner in which a string passage is to be played.

Bravura Ornamental passage requiring technical skill for execution; a virtuoso style.

Bridge Wooden support for strings of an instrument terminating one end of the vibrations of the strings.

Bridge Passage Transitional section from one main theme to another or from one movement to another.

Broken Chords Arpeggios.

Broken Octaves Successive alternation of higher and lower tones of a series of octaves.

Cadence Ending of phrase, section, or movement.

254 **Canon** Style in contrapuntal music in which the melodic theme is

given by one instrument, then taken over in strict imitation by one or more other instruments.

Cantilena   An air, or melody.

Canzona   Instrumental composition of the sixteenth century in contrapuntal style and in several sections.

Canzonetta   A short song, sometimes used as a movement of a large instrumental work.

Capriccio   Caprice. A composition consisting of a medley of popular melodies; also used for short piano pieces of a light character.

Capriccioso   Free, playful style.

Cavatina   A simple solo song in an opera, and also an instrumental composition with a sustained songlike character.

Cello   Contraction of *violoncello (q.v.)*.

Cembalo   Contraction of *clavicembalo;* a harpsichord.

Chamber Music   Music for small combinations of instruments intended for performance in an intimate auditorium. Chamber music embraces sonatas for two or more instruments, trios, quartets, quintets, sextets, octets, nonets.

Chests of Viols   In the sixteenth and seventeenth centuries, a set of viols of varying sizes. These viols were kept in a special chest in some English households. See discussion in Introduction.

Chord   Combination of three or more tones sounded together.

Chromatic   Tones foreign by a semitone to key or chord.

Classical Period   A style epoch beginning roughly in the middle of the eighteenth century and ending in the first decade of the nineteenth. See discussion in Chapters 3 and 4.

Clavecin   French for *harpsichord (q.v.)*.

Clavicembalo   *See* Cembalo.

Clavichord   Small keyboard instrument, precursor to modern piano, popular from sixteenth to eighteenth century. See discussion in Introduction.

Clavier   Literally "keyboard," a term used in Germany before the nineteenth century for any keyboard instrument. See discussion in Introduction.

Clef   Sign preceding each staff to indicate pitch.

Coda   Concluding part of a passage or movement.

Col Legno   Playing with the wood of the bow on the strings of a string instrument, instead of using the usual hair side of the bow.

Compass Range; the area of pitch between the highest and lowest notes of an instrument.

Con Sordino With a mute.

Concert Étude *See* Étude.

Concerto Grosso A composition in which a group of instruments rather than a single instrument is opposed to the main orchestral group.

Consort A sixteenth- and seventeenth-century term designating a set of instruments or several instruments playing together. See discussion in Introduction.

Continuo In performances in the seventeenth and eighteenth centuries, the accompanying figured bass part on a keyboard or a plucked string instrument.

Counterpoint Simultaneous combination of two or more independent melodic lines.

Cross Rhythm Simultaneous use of different rhythms.

Development Working out of thematic material. In the sonata form it represents the middle section, preceded by the exposition and followed by the recapitulation.

Diapason The combination of organ pipes that gives the basic tone of the instrument.

Drone Bass A sustained tone in the bass simulating the drone of a bagpipe.

Duet Composition for two instruments; also composition for two players at one keyboard instrument.

Dynamics Gradations of sound from loud to soft and vice versa.

Elegy A short composition of melancholy character commemorating a dead person.

Ensemble Group of performers or combination of instruments.

Equal Temperament Method of tuning now used in which octave is divided into twelve equal parts. For discussion *see* Chapter 2.

Étude Exercise for solo instrument attempting to solve specific technical problem. Composers have written études with such serious artistic intent that they are more concert than pedagogical pieces. Such compositions are referred to as "concert études."

Exposition First principal section in the sonata form, in which thematic material is presented.

Expression Nuances of dynamics, phrasing, and other elements left to the judgment of the performer, since they are too subtle to be indicated in the music.

Expressionism A style in twentieth-century music penetrating to the essence of a subject by expressing it abstractly. See discussion in Chapter 13.

False Accent Accent on a normally weak beat in bar.

Fantasy, or Fantasia or Fantasie Instrumental composition free in form and in the way thematic material is presented and developed.

Fermata Symbol indicating holding of note or rest.

Fifth Two notes, the first and fifth, separated by three whole tones and a semitone in a major or minor scale.

Figuration Ornamental passage.

Figured Bass, or Basso Continuo In the seventeenth and eighteenth century a system in which accompaniment was improvised from a given bass line, usually provided with numerals to indicate desired harmonies. It is also sometimes known as Thorough Bass. See discussion in Introduction.

Fingerboard The part of a string instrument between the body and the pegboard over which strings are stretched and are stopped by the fingers of the player.

Fingering Technique of applying fingers to keys, strings, holes, or valves of a musical instrument.

Fioritura An embellishment or ornament to a melody.

Flat Symbol indicating the lowering of a note by half a step.

Flautando, or Flautato Flutelike sounds produced on the violin through harmonics or by bowing over the fingerboard with the tip of the bow.

Form Structure of a musical composition.

Fugato Passage in fugal style.

Fugue A complex contrapuntal form generally for three, four, or five parts called "voices." See discussion in Chapter 1.

G Clef Treble clef.

Galant Style, or Galanter Stil A graceful, elegant style favored in the mid-eighteenth century.

Glissando Technique of sliding from one note of a scale to another on keyboard, bowed instrument, harp, etc., to produce continuous tone.

Ground Bass (also Basso Ostinato) A theme or figure repeated in bass throughout a composition.

Harmonics Flutelike sounds produced on a string instrument by placing fingers lightly on the string instead of pressing down.

Harmony Science of combining notes in chords and chords into progressions.

Harpsichord Keyboard instrument, predecessor of the piano. See discussion in Introduction.

Homophony Style emphasizing single melody and its harmony.

Idyl A composition of pastoral character.

Imitation Polyphonic technique wherein a phrase or theme is repeated by another "voice," usually in a lower or higher pitch, while original "voice" continues with the theme.

Impressionism A style seeking to express the feeling or impression a subject arouses in the composer rather than the subject itself. See discussion in Chapter 12.

Impromptu A composition for piano in extended song form giving the suggestion of improvisation. See discussion in Chapter 6.

Improvisation, or Extemporization A spontaneously conceived performance.

Interlude Short section connecting two movements.

Interval Distance in pitch between two notes.

Intonation Correctness of pitch.

Introduction Preface to a musical composition or to a movement of a sonata, etc.

Kammermusik German term for chamber music.

Key The first, principal, or tonic note of a scale.

Key Signature Written grouping of sharps or flats placed immediately after clef at the beginning of staff to indicate key of section of composition.

Keyboard Black and white keys on piano or organ.

Klavier (or Clavier) German for keyboard instrument, such as harpsichord, clavichord, or piano.

Legato Smooth passage from one note to next without pause.

Legend, or Légende A composition suggesting a story or poem through its narrative character but without a definite program.

Linear Counterpoint Contrapuntal music in which lines move independently of harmonic relationships, a twentieth-century idiom. See discussion in Chapter 13.

Major Scale Scale whose half steps occur between third and fourth and seventh and eighth degrees of the octave.

Malagueña   Spanish dance in triple meter originating in Malaga whose main melody has the character of an improvisation.

Martellato   In string or keyboard music, a hammering style of bowing or playing.

Mazurka   A Polish national dance in triple time and in two or four sections with accent usually on second or third beat. See discussion in Chapter 7.

Measure   *See* Bar.

Melody   Succession of single tones in a logical and pleasing pattern; a tune.

Meter   Recurrent series of emphasis with which music is measured.

Minuet   Graceful dance in moderate tempo and ¾ meter of French origin, popular in eighteenth century. It has three sections, the third repeating the first and the middle one called a "trio." It is sometimes found as a movement in the Baroque suite or in the Classical sonata, quartet, or quintet, etc.

Mode   A type of scale—major or minor. Preceding the time when major-minor tonality was evolved, music was constructed from a medieval system of scales known as church modes.

Monodony   Homophony.

Monothematic   Use of a single theme.

Mordent   An ornament made by a quick alternation of a note with the note below it.

Moto Perpetuo   *See* Perpetual Motion.

Motto Theme   A theme that recurs in several movements of a composition.

Movement   A significant, self-sufficient part of a larger composition such as a sonata.

Mute   Device for muffling sound of an instrument.

Natural   Symbol nullifying sharp or flat.

Nonet   Composition for nine instruments.

Note   Symbol representing a tone.

Octave   Consecutive series of eight diatonic notes, beginning and ending on a note with the same key.

Octet   A musical composition for eight instruments.

Opus   Term meaning "work" used with a number to indicate the order of composition and publication of a composer's work.

Organ Largest and most complex of keyboard instruments. See discussion in Introduction.

Organ Point, or Pedal Point A bass tone sustained below moving voices.

Ornament An embellishment, such as grace note, trill, mordent.

Partita An eighteenth-century term used interchangeably with "suite" for a several-movement composition made up mostly of dance movements.

Passacaglia In seventeenth century, a form of instrumental music that originated as a slow Spanish dance. See discussion in Chapter 1.

Pedal An appliance operated by foot on organ, piano, harp.

Pedal Point *See* Organ Point.

Period A musical sentence usually built from two or more four-measure phrases.

Perpetual Motion, or Moto Perpetuo A brief instrumental work built from short notes of equal time value and played as quickly as possible to give the impression of continual motion.

Phrase Smallest division of a melody.

Phrasing Marking off phrases of a composition, either indicated in the music or as interpreted by the performers.

Piano The musical direction meaning soft; also a modern keyboard instrument developed from the harpsichord and clavichord but whose strings are struck by hammer action. For discussion *see* Introduction.

Piano Quartet, Piano Quintet, Piano Trio *See* Quartet, Quintet, Trio.

Pitch Relation of one tone to another in highness or lowness of sound.

Pizzicato Plucked, instead of bowed, strings.

Polonaise Courtly Polish dance that became popular outside Poland in the eighteenth century. It is marked by syncopations and accents on the half beat. It is sometimes used as a movement in the Baroque suite.

Ponticello The bridge of a string instrument.

Portamento Gliding from one tone to another in continuous sound.

Position In violin playing, the place occupied by fingers of left hand on the fingerboard.

Prelude In keyboard music of the Baroque era, the first movement of a suite; also a preface to another self-sufficient piece of music. With Chopin it became an independent composition for the piano, introducing nothing and of no special form but establishing a mood. See discussion in Chapter 7.

Progression Advance of melody from one tone to another, or of harmony from one chord to another.

Quadruple Time Four beats to a measure.

Quartet A composition for four instruments. The most familiar combinations are: string quartet (two violins, viola, cello); piano quartet (piano, violin, viola, and cello); clarinet quartet (clarinet, violin, viola, and cello); flute quartet (flute, violin, viola, and cello); and oboe quartet (oboe, violin, viola, and cello).

Quintet A composition for five instruments. A string quintet comprises two violins, two violas, and cello or sometimes two cellos, one viola, and two violins. The piano quintet is made up of piano and string quartet. Quintets have also been written for clarinet and string quartet, and for various other combinations of instruments.

Recapitulation The third section of the sonata form, in which the exposition of themes is repeated with modifications.

Recital Concert performance by one or two performers.

Resolution Passing from dissonance to consonance.

Rhapsody In piano music a composition free in form and rhapsodic in character, sometimes utilizing popular melodies. With Brahms the rhapsody assumed epic character.

Rhythm Arrangement of notes in time forming patterns of short and long notes, accented and unaccented notes.

Ricercar In the sixteenth and seventeenth centuries a type of instrumental music derived from the vocal motet which developed some germinal idea fugally. The form has been revived by several composers in the twentieth century.

Rococo Delicate, refined, graceful style favored in the last half of the eighteenth century. For discussion *see* Chapter 4.

Romance An instrumental composition in the style of a romantic song.

Romantic Period Period in music history beginning roughly with late Beethoven and continuing through the nineteenth century. See discussion in Chapter 6.

Rondo Form in which main subject is repeated several times, with new subjects appearing between repetitions. It is sometimes used as the last movement of a sonata.

Saltando A technique for bowing on a string instrument in which bow performs a series of leaps from the string while moving in one direction.

Scale Formal succession of notes into an octave (a group of eight).

Scherzo   Music in quick time and in a light style. The scherzo is usually in ¾ time and in three-part form. It succeeded the minuet as the third movement of compositions, beginning with some of Beethoven's piano sonatas, symphonies, and quartets. It is also an independent composition, principally for the piano.

Scordatura   Unusual tuning of a string instrument to create a special effect.

Septet   Composition for seven instruments.

Sforzando   Sudden emphasis on a note or group of notes.

Sharp   Sign raising a note half a step.

Signature   *See* Key Signature.

Slur   A small curve above or below notes indicating they are to be played in a connected and smooth manner.

Sonata   An extended form most usually for solo piano or solo instrument and piano. For discussion *see* Introduction and Chapters 1, 2, 3, 4, and 5.

Sonata da Camera   "Chamber sonata" popular in the late seventeenth century in instrumental music consisting of a group of dances prefaced by a prelude. See discussion in Introduction and Chapter 1.

Sonata da Chiesa   "Church sonata" popular in the late seventeenth century usually made up of four movements in the slow-fast-slow-fast pattern. See discussion in Introduction and Chapter 1.

Sonata Form   An important form encountered in orchestral and instrumental literature in the concerto, symphony, sonata, and sometimes the concert overture. The sonata form comprises an exposition, a development, and a recapitulation. See discussion in Chapters 3 and 4.

Sonatina   A small sonata, less ambitious in structure and content than the sonata and making less technical demands on the performer. It is usually used for piano instruction. See discussion in Chapter 5.

Song Form   Form made up of two or three parts. When in two parts it consists of subject and countersubject; in three parts, the third repeats the first.

Sonority   Richness of sound.

Sordino   Mute.

Sostenuto   Sustained.

Staccato   A sharp, detached manner of playing.

String Quartet, String Quintet   *See* Quartet, Quintet.

Subject   A musical theme or motive.

Suite   In the seventeenth and eighteenth centuries an extended form comprising several movements mostly in dance forms. See discussion in Introduction and Chapters 1 and 2. In Romantic music, an extended form comprising pieces representing different facets of one subject. See discussion in Chapter 10.

Sul Ponticello   Playing on the bridge of a string instrument.

Suspension   In harmony, producing a discord by retaining one or more notes of a chord while other notes pass on to the next chord.

Tenuto   Held.

Theme   Melodic subject of a section, movement, or a composition.

Theory   Science of composition.

Tie   Curved line between two notes of equal pitch to make them into a single note whose value is the sum of both.

Timbre   Tone color of a particular instrument.

Time   Rate of speed, tempo.

Toccata   A form basically of organ music, though also found in harpsichord and piano literature featuring rapid and elaborate passage work and having the character of an improvisation.

Tonic   Principal note of scale, key, or chord; the tonal center to which other notes are related.

Touch   The weight used in keyboard instrument to bring key into action; a term used for pianists designating quality of tone produced.

Transcription   Adaptation of a musical piece for instrument or instruments different from that or those for which it was originally written.

Treble   A high register.

Tremolo   Quick repetition of a single note on string instrument while pitch remains steady.

Triad   Chord with three notes.

Trill   Rapid alternation of a note with its auxiliary note (major or minor second) to produce quivering effect.

Trio   A composition for three instruments. The usual combination of instruments is violin, piano, and cello.

Triplet   Group of three notes played in the time it would normally take to play two notes of the same value.

Tuning   Adjusting an instrument to correct pitch.

Twelve-Tone System, or Row or Technique   Construction of a composition from an established row of twelve tones of the chromatic scale according to a set plan. For explanation *see* Chapter 13.

Variation Technique of subjecting a given theme to harmonic, rhythmic, and melodic transformations, with the theme usually stated before the variations.

Vibrato A vibrating tremulous tone on a string instrument.

Viol Family of string instruments played with a bow and prominent in sixteenth and seventeenth centuries. See discussion in Introduction.

Viola String instrument of violin family, larger in size than violin but smaller than cello. It is pitched a fifth lower than the violin.

Violin Most important and lyrical of string instruments. It has the highest pitch of bowed string instruments.

Violoncello, or Cello Member of string family, larger in size and an octave lower in tone than the viola.

Virginal A predecessor of the piano; a small, oblong instrument of the harpsichord family popular in the sixteenth and early seventeenth centuries. See discussion in Introduction.

Virtuosity Display of brilliant technique.

Whole-Tone Scale A scale consisting entirely of whole tones. See explanation in Chapter 12.

Index